Siegel's

PROPERTY

Essay and Multiple-Choice Questions and Answers

Fifth Edition

BRIAN N. SIEGEL
J.D., Columbia Law School

LAZAR EMANUEL
J.D., Harvard Law School

Revised by
Rhonda Reaves
Professor of Law
Florida A&M University College of Law

Published by Wolters Kluwer Law & Business in New York.

Wolters Kluwer Law & Business serves customers worldwide with CCH, Aspen Publishers, and Kluwer Law International products. (www.wolterskluwerlb.com)

To contact Customer Service, e-mail customer.service@wolterskluwer.com, call 1-800-234-1660, fax 1-800-901-9075, or mail correspondence to:

Wolters Kluwer Law & Business
Attn: Order Department
PO Box 990
Frederick, MD 21705

Printed in the United States of America.

1 2 3 4 5 6 7 8 9 0

ISBN 978-1-4548-0930-2

About Wolters Kluwer Law & Business

Wolters Kluwer Law & Business is a leading global provider of intelligent information and digital solutions for legal and business professionals in key specialty areas, and respected educational resources for professors and law students. Wolters Kluwer Law & Business connects legal and business professionals as well as those in the education market with timely, specialized authoritative content and information-enabled solutions to support success through productivity, accuracy and mobility.

Serving customers worldwide, Wolters Kluwer Law & Business products include those under the Aspen Publishers, CCH, Kluwer Law International, Loislaw, ftwilliam.com and MediRegs family of products.

CCH products have been a trusted resource since 1913, and are highly regarded resources for legal, securities, antitrust and trade regulation, government contracting, banking, pension, payroll, employment and labor, and healthcare reimbursement and compliance professionals.

Aspen Publishers products provide essential information to attorneys, business professionals and law students. Written by preeminent authorities, the product line offers analytical and practical information in a range of specialty practice areas from securities law and intellectual property to mergers and acquisitions and pension/benefits. Aspen's trusted legal education resources provide professors and students with high-quality, up-to-date and effective resources for successful instruction and study in all areas of the law.

Kluwer Law International products provide the global business community with reliable international legal information in English. Legal practitioners, corporate counsel and business executives around the world rely on Kluwer Law journals, looseleafs, books, and electronic products for comprehensive information in many areas of international legal practice.

Loislaw is a comprehensive online legal research product providing legal content to law firm practitioners of various specializations. Loislaw provides attorneys with the ability to quickly and efficiently find the necessary legal information they need, when and where they need it, by facilitating access to primary law as well as state-specific law, records, forms and treatises.

ftwilliam.com offers employee benefits professionals the highest quality plan documents (retirement, welfare and non-qualified) and government forms (5500/PBGC, 1099 and IRS) software at highly competitive prices.

MediRegs products provide integrated health care compliance content and software solutions for professionals in healthcare, higher education and life sciences, including professionals in accounting, law and consulting.

Wolters Kluwer Law & Business, a division of Wolters Kluwer, is headquartered in New York. Wolters Kluwer is a market-leading global information services company focused on professionals.

Introduction

Although law school grades are a significant factor in obtaining a summer internship or entry position at a law firm, no formalized preparation for finals is offered at most law schools. For the most part, students are expected to fend for themselves in learning how to take a law school exam. Ironically, law school exams may bear little correspondence to the teaching methods used by professors during the school year. At least in the first year, professors require you to spend most of your time briefing cases. This is probably not great preparation for issue-spotting on exams. In briefing cases, you are made to focus on one or two principles of law at a time; thus, you don't get practice in relating one issue to another or in developing a picture of an entire problem or the entire course. When exams finally come, you're forced to make an abrupt 180-degree turn. Suddenly, you are asked to recognize, define, and discuss a variety of issues buried within a single multi-issue fact pattern. Alternatively, you may be asked to select among a number of possible answers, all of which look inviting but only one of which is right.

The comprehensive course outline you've created so diligently, and with such pain, means little if you're unable to apply its contents on your final exams. There is a vast difference between reading opinions in which the legal principles are clearly stated and applying those same principles to hypothetical essay exams and multiple-choice questions.

The purpose of this book is to help you bridge the gap between memorizing a rule of law and ***understanding how to use it*** in an exam. After an initial overview describing the exam-writing process, you see a large number of hypotheticals that test your ability to write analytical essays and to pick the right answers to multiple-choice questions. ***Read them—all of them!*** Then review the suggested answers that follow. You'll find that the key to superior grades lies in applying your knowledge through questions and answers, not through rote memory.

GOOD LUCK!

Table of Contents

Preparing Effectively for Essay Examinations

Essay Questions

Essay Answers

Preparing Effectively for Essay Examinations

To achieve superior scores on essay exams, a law student must (1) learn and understand "blackletter" principles and rules of law for each subject; (2) analyze how those principles of law arise within a test fact pattern; and (3) clearly and succinctly discuss each principle and how it relates to the facts. One of the most common misconceptions about law school is that you must memorize each word on every page of your casebooks or outlines to do well on exams. The reality is that you can commit an entire casebook to memory and still do poorly on an exam. Our review of hundreds of student answers has shown us that most students can recite the rules. The students who do ***best*** on exams are able to analyze how the rules they have memorized relate to the facts in the questions, and they are able to communicate their analysis to the grader. The following pages cover what you need to know to achieve superior scores on your law school essay exams.

The "ERC" Process

To study effectively for law school exams you must be able to "ERC" (***E***lementize, ***R***ecognize, and ***C***onceptualize) each legal principle covered in your casebooks and course outlines. ***Elementizing*** means reducing each legal theory and rule you learn to a concise, straightforward statement of its essential elements. Without knowledge of these elements, it's difficult to see all the issues as they arise.

For example, if you are asked, "What is adverse possession?" it is ***not*** enough to say, "Adverse possession is where someone possesses another's land adversely." A more accurate statement of the adverse possession doctrine would go something like this: "Adverse possession is a doctrine whereby one can gain title to another's land when, without permission, one continuously occupies the land in an open and exclusive manner for a long period of time." This formulation correctly shows that there are separate, distinct elements that must be satisfied before one can gain title of property through adverse possession: (1) the actor must **actually occupy** the land of another; (2) without the permission of the owner; and (3) the occupation must be open, exclusive, and continuous for some period of time.

Recognizing means perceiving or anticipating which words or ideas within a legal principle are likely to be the source of issues and how those issues are likely to arise within a given hypothetical fact pattern. With respect to the adverse possession concept, there are five ***potential*** issues. Did the person actually occupy the land of another? Was the occupation visible and open? Was it without the owner's permission? Did the intruder intend to reside on the land to the exclusion of others? Did the intruder occupy the land for a sufficiently long period to establish a claim of ownership?

Conceptualizing means imagining situations in which each of the elements of a rule of law can give rise to factual issues. ***Unless you can imagine or construct an application of each element of a rule, you don't truly understand the legal principles behind the rule!*** In our opinion, the inability to conjure up hypothetical fact patterns or stories involving particular rules of law foretells a likelihood that you will miss issues involving those rules on an exam. It's ***crucial*** (1) to ***recognize*** that issues result from the interaction of facts with the words defining a rule of law and (2) to develop the ability to ***conceptualize*** or ***imagine*** fact patterns using the words or concepts within the rule.

For example, a set of facts illustrating the "open and notorious" element of the adverse possession rule might be the following:

Illustration 1:

T came across a vacant home. A sign on the front lawn indicated that the bank had foreclosed upon the house. T removed the sign and moved in. T immediately began making the place her own. She put out a welcome mat, painted the exterior of the house her favorite shade of puce, and dug up the yard and planted a rock garden, complete with a cascading waterfall. T introduced herself to all of the neighbors by throwing a grand party to which all the neighbors were invited.

Illustration 2:

T came across a vacant home. A sign on the front lawn indicated that the bank had foreclosed upon the house. T waited until dusk to sneak into the house. She carefully drew the curtains so that no light would escape. Before dawn the next morning, T checked carefully before leaving to make sure no one saw her. She continued this pattern of entering after dark and leaving before sunrise for several years.

The "open and notorious" element requires the adverse possessor to engage in visible acts of ownership sufficient to put a reasonable owner on notice of the ownership claim. In the first illustration, T's occupation is clearly visible to anyone who cared to notice. In the second illustration, however, there would certainly be an issue whether T's occupation was sufficiently visible to put the owner on notice.

A fact pattern illustrating the "continuous" element for adverse possession might be the following:

> When B built his house, the house encroached 10 feet onto his neighbor A's land. B used the house sporadically as a vacation home. Since B worked and had an inconsistent vacation schedule, his visits were infrequent and sometimes as much as 4 to 7 months apart. A discovered the encroachment years after the house was built, when she had a new survey made of her property. She told B to move the house from her land, but B replied, "That house has been there for more than 10 years, and I'm not moving it."

B's possession does not appear to satisfy the element of continuous possession. His visits were sporadic and there were relatively large gaps in time when he was not in possession. Although the facts state that this was a vacation home, B's visits would seem too infrequent to satisfy the test of continuous possession.

"Mental games" such as these must be played with every element of every rule you learn.

Issue-Spotting

One of the keys to doing well on an essay examination is issue-spotting. In fact, issue-spotting is ***the*** most important skill you will learn in law school. If you recognize a legal issue, you can find the applicable rule of law (if there is one) by researching the issue. But if you fail to see the issues, you won't learn the steps that lead to success or failure on exams or, for that matter, in the practice of law. It is important to remember that (1) an issue is a question to be decided by the judge or jury and (2) a question is "in issue" when it can be disputed or argued about at trial. The bottom line is that ***if you don't spot an issue, you can't raise it or discuss it.***

The key to issue-spotting is to learn to approach a problem in the same way an attorney does. Let's assume you've been admitted to practice and a client enters your office with a legal problem involving a dispute. He will recite his facts to you and give you any documents that may be pertinent. He will then want to know if he can sue (or be sued, if your client seeks to avoid liability). To answer your client's questions intelligently, you will have to decide the following: (1) what principles or rules can possibly be asserted by your client; (2) what defense or defenses can possibly be raised to these principles; (3) what issues may arise if these defenses are asserted; (4) what arguments each side can make to persuade the fact finder to resolve the issue in his favor; and (5) finally, what the ***likely*** outcome of each issue will be. ***All the issues that can possibly arise at trial will be relevant to your answers.***

How to Discuss an Issue

Keep in mind that ***rules of law are the guides to issues*** (i.e., an issue arises where there is a question whether the facts do, or do not, satisfy an element of a rule); a rule of law ***cannot dispose of an issue*** unless the rule can reasonably be ***applied to the facts.***

A good way to learn how to discuss an issue is to study the following mini-hypothetical and the two responses that follow it.

Mini-Hypothetical

A bought Blackacre from B. When she bought the property, D, B's cousin, occupied the guesthouse near the southwest border of the estate. D had visited B 12 years ago and decided to stay to work on a novel. B had asked A to let D stay there for a while "since he was finding himself." A said it probably would be "all right if D did not get in her way." D built a separate mailbox outside the guest house and placed a doormat in front of the entrances that read "Welcome to D's." (Assume a 10-year statute of limitations applies to claims of adverse possession). Discuss D's rights against A.

Pertinent Principle of Law:

1. Adverse possession. In order to bring a claim for adverse possession one must actually possess another's property in a manner that is exclusive, open and notorious, continuous, adverse or hostile, for the period of time defined by statute.

First Sample Answer

D claims to own the guesthouse through adverse possession. He must prove actual possession, open and notorious use, exclusive use, hostile or adverse use, and continuous use of the property for a statutory period. Here, D shows that he actually possessed the land in an open and notorious manner by D building a mailbox outside the guest house and placing a doormat in front of the entrance that read, "Welcome to D's." D used the southwest portion of the land without a break, thereby satisfying the continuous element. Since B had asked A if it was all right if D could occupy the land to wit A responded that it probably would be "all right if D did not get in her way" proves that D was given permission to use the southwest portion of the land. Although D has met most of the requirements, he failed to satisfy hostile or adverse possession, which demonstrates that D does not have a claim for adverse possession of the guest house.

Second Sample Answer

D will claim he obtained title through adverse possession. Under the adverse possession doctrine, title transfers by operation of law from the record title holder to the adverse possessor provided the adverse possessor can satisfy each element by clear and convincing evidence. The elements are possession that is (1) actual, (2) open and notorious, (3) adverse or hostile, (4) exclusive, and (5) continuous for the statutory period.

Actual possession requires the possessor to physically occupy the land in some manner. Here, D occupied the guesthouse on the southwest border of the estate. Since there are no facts to suggest D's occupation went beyond the guesthouse, if D is successful, he will gain title only to the land he actually occupied, that is, the guesthouse, but not the entire estate.

D must also show that his possession was open and notorious. D may have trouble establishing this element. Open and notorious possession is possession that is sufficiently visible to put the true owner on notice. Here, D built a separate mailbox outside and placed a doormat in front of the entrance. A would argue that these acts are not sufficient to put her on notice that D was making an ownership claim. A would argue that D's actions were consistent with those of a long-term guest or tenant. D would argue that the phrase, "Welcome to D's" on the mat undercuts A's argument that D was not staking an ownership claim. Since D's initial entry was with B's permission and A was aware of D's occupation, a court would likely find that D's actions, while visible, were not sufficient to put the owner on notice that D was staking an ownership claim.

D must also establish that his possession was adverse and hostile, meaning without the true owner's permission. D may have trouble proving this element. Here, D's initial entry was permissive. B let him stay for a while to "find himself." Generally, where the initial entry was permissive, the adverse possessor must communicate clearly when making an ownership claim. D would argue that his possession was adverse to A because his right to stay on the land based on B's permission expired when B sold the land to A. His argument will likely fail, however, as the facts suggest that A allowed his possession to continue. A told B that it probably would be "all right if D did not get in her way." On the other hand, D could argue that (1) he was unaware of A's statement (the facts do not state whether either B or A told D of their conversation); and (2) even if he was aware, A's equivocal statement (that it probably be all right as long as D was not in the way) was not a clear grant of permission. A court would likely find that A has the stronger argument.

As for the remaining elements, the facts appear to support D's claim. Exclusive possession means that the adverse possessor has not shared possession with the owner or the public. There are no facts to suggest that D shared his possession with anyone. The continuous element is satisfied where the possession continues uninterrupted for the statutory period. Here, there are no facts to suggest any interruption in D's possession. Finally, the possession must satisfy the applicable statute of limitations. Here, a 10-year statute of limitations applies. Since D has been living on the property for 12 years, this element is met.

Critique

Let's start by examining the First Sample Answer. There are several ways to improve Answer A. First, while the writer states the general requirements to establish adverse possession, the writer fails to state the legal standard for each of the elements. For example, to establish "open and notorious" possession the occupier must engage in acts that are sufficiently open and visible to put others on notice of the claim. Here, the writer identifies "open and notorious" as an element that must be satisfied and describes the facts relevant to that determination but fails to demonstrate to the grader that she knows the legal standard that must be satisfied in order to make a showing of "open and notorious" possession.

Second, the writer has failed to address one of the elements necessary to establish adverse possession, that the use must be exclusive. A more thorough answer would address the exclusive element by stating the applicable legal standard (possession was not shared with the true owner or the public) and applying the relevant facts, if any. While there are no facts to suggest D shared his possession, acknowledging the absence of facts on this issue demonstrates to the grader she knows the law as it relates to this element.

The writer, perhaps in an attempt to save time, conflates the discussion of the element of actual possession with her discussion of the open and notorious element. A grader can only guess why the writer thinks the facts set forth in the sentence meet either element.

The Second Answer is stronger than the first. By laying out the elements at the beginning of the essay and separately addressing each element in the subsequent paragraphs, the writer provides an easy to follow organization. This writer goes beyond a superficial treatment of the facts and examines the facts from both sides. The writer also follows the IRAC formula for each of the elements, thus demonstrating to the grader that the writer understands that each element has a separate legal requirement.

Structuring Your Answer

Graders will give high marks to a clearly written, well-structured answer. Each issue you discuss should follow a specific and consistent structure that a grader can easily follow.

One format for analyzing each issue is the ***I-R-A-A-O format.*** In this format, the ***I*** stands for ***Issue***; the **R** for ***Rule of law***; the first **A** for ***one side's Argument***; the second **A** for ***the other party's rebuttal Argument***; and the **O** for your ***Opinion as to how the issue would be resolved.*** The ***I-R-A-A-O*** format emphasizes the importance of (1) discussing ***both*** sides of an issue and (2) communicating to the grader that, where an issue arises, an attorney can only advise his or her client as to the ***probable*** decision on that issue.

A somewhat different format for analyzing each issue is the ***I-R-A-C format.*** Here, the ***I*** stands for ***Issue***; the **R** for ***Rule of law***; the **A** for ***Application of the facts to the rule of law***; and the **C** for ***Conclusion. I-R-A-C*** is a legitimate approach to the discussion of a particular issue, within the time constraints imposed by the question. The ***I-R-A-C format*** must be applied to each issue in the question; it is not the solution to the entire answer. If there are six issues in a question, for example, you should offer six separate, independent ***I-R-A-C*** analyses.

We believe that the ***I-R-A-C*** approach is preferable to the ***I-R-A-A-O*** formula. However, either can be used to analyze and organize essay exam answers. Whatever format you choose, however, you should be consistent throughout the exam and remember the following rules:

First, ***analyze all of the relevant facts.*** Facts have significance in a particular case ***only as they come under the applicable rules of law.*** The facts presented must be analyzed and examined to see if they do or do not satisfy one element or another of the applicable rules, and the essential facts and rules must be stated and argued in your analysis.

Second, you must communicate to the grader the ***precise rule of law*** controlling the facts. In their eagerness to commence their arguments, students sometimes fail to state the applicable rule of law first. Remember, the ***R*** in either format stands for ***Rule of law.*** Defining the rule of law ***before*** an analysis of the facts is essential in order to allow the grader to follow your reasoning.

Third, it is important to treat ***each side of an issue with equal detail.*** If someone were to lose land that had been in their family for generations, your sympathies might understandably fall on the side of the landowner. The grader will nevertheless expect you to see and make every possible argument for the other side. Don't permit your personal viewpoint to affect your answer! A good lawyer never does! When discussing an issue, always state the arguments for each side.

Finally, don't forget to ***state your opinion or conclusion*** on each issue. Keep in mind, however, that your opinion or conclusion is probably the ***least*** important part of an exam answer. Why? Because your professor knows that no attorney can tell his or her client exactly how a judge or jury will decide a particular issue. By definition, an issue is a legal dispute that can go either way. An attorney, therefore, can offer the client only his or her best opinion about the likelihood of victory or defeat on an issue. Because the decision on any issue lies with the judge or jury, no attorney can ever be absolutely certain of the resolution.

Discuss All Possible Issues

As we've noted, a student should draw ***some*** type of conclusion or opinion for each issue raised. Whatever your conclusion on a particular issue, it is essential to anticipate and discuss ***all of the issues*** that would arise if the question were actually tried in court.

In an adverse possession hypothetical, for the adverse possessor to prevail he must prevail on each of the issues. If the adverse possessor fails on any one element, the claim is lost. Nevertheless, even if you feel strongly that the adverse possessor clearly established one or more of the elements, you ***should*** go on to discuss all of the other potential issues as well. If you were to terminate your answer after a discussion of one element only, you'd likely receive an inferior grade.

Why should you have to discuss every possible issue if you are relatively certain that the outcome of a particular issue would be dispositive of the entire case? Because at the commencement of litigation, neither party can be ***absolutely positive*** about which issues he or she will prevail upon at trial. We can state with confidence that every attorney with some degree of experience has won issues he or she thought he or she would lose, and has lost issues on which victory seemed assured. Because one can never be absolutely certain how a factual issue will be resolved by the fact finder, a good attorney (and exam writer) will consider ***all*** possible issues.

To understand the importance of discussing all of the potential issues, you should reflect on what you will do in the actual practice of law. If you represent the defendant, for example, it is your job to raise every possible defense. If there are five potential defenses, and your pleadings rely on only three of them (because you're sure you will win on all three), and the plaintiff is somehow successful on all three issues, your client may well sue you for malpractice. Your client's contention would be that you should be liable because if you had only raised the two additional issues, you might have prevailed on at least one of them, and therefore liability would have been avoided. It is an attorney's duty to raise ***all*** legitimate issues. A similar philosophy should be followed when taking essay exams.

What exactly do you say when you've resolved the initial issue in favor of the defendant, and discussion of any additional issues would seem to be moot? The answer is simple. You begin the discussion of the next issue with something like, "Assuming, however, the plaintiff prevailed on the foregoing issue, the next issue would be . . . ." The grader will understand and appreciate what you have done.

The corollary to the importance of raising all potential issues is that you should avoid discussion of obvious nonissues. Raising nonissues is detrimental in three ways: First, you waste a lot of precious time; second, you usually receive absolutely no points for discussing an issue that the grader deems extraneous; and third, it suggests to the grader that you lack the ability to distinguish the significant from the irrelevant. The best guideline for avoiding the discussion of a nonissue is to ask yourself, "Would I, as an attorney, feel comfortable about raising that particular issue or objection in front of a judge?"

Delineate the Transition from One Issue to the Next

It's a good idea to make it easy for the grader to see the issues you've found. One way to accomplish this is to cover no more than one issue per paragraph. Another way is to underline each issue statement. Provided that time permits, we recommend that you use both techniques. The essay answers in this book contain numerous illustrations of these suggestions.

One frequent student error is to write two separate paragraphs in which all of the arguments for one side are made in the initial paragraph, and all of the rebuttal arguments by the other side are made in the next paragraph. This organization is ***a bad idea.*** It obliges the grader to reconstruct the exam answer in his or her mind several times to determine whether all possible issues have been discussed by both sides. It will also cause you to state the same rule of law more than once. A better-organized answer presents a given argument by one side and follows that immediately in the same paragraph with the other side's rebuttal to that argument.

Understanding the "Call" of a Question

The statement ***at the end*** of an essay question or of the fact pattern in a multiple-choice question is sometimes referred to as the "call" of the question. It usually asks you to do something specific such as "discuss," "discuss the rights of the parties," "list X's rights," "advise X," "give the best grounds on which to find the statute unconstitutional," "state what D can be convicted of," "recommend how the estate should be distributed," and so forth. The call of the question should be read carefully because it tells you exactly what you're expected to do. If a question asks, "what are X's rights against Y?" or "what is X liable to Y for?" you don't have to spend a lot of time on Y's rights against Z. You will usually receive absolutely no credit for discussing issues or facts that are not required by the call. On the other hand, if the call of an essay question is simply "discuss" or "discuss the rights of the parties," then ***all*** foreseeable issues must be covered by your answer.

Students are often led astray by an essay question's call. For example, if you are asked for "X's rights against Y" or to "advise X," you may think you may limit yourself to X's viewpoint with respect to the issues. This is ***not correct***! You cannot resolve one party's rights against another party without considering the issues that would arise (and the arguments the other side would assert) if litigation occurred. In short, although the call of the question may appear to focus on the rights of one of the parties to the litigation, a superior answer will cover all the issues and arguments that person might ***encounter*** (not just the arguments he or she would ***make***) in attempting to pursue his or her rights against the other side.

The Importance of Analyzing the Question Carefully Before Writing

The overriding ***time pressure*** of an essay exam is probably a major reason why many students fail to analyze a question carefully before writing. Five minutes into the allocated time for a particular question, you may notice that the person next to you is writing furiously. This thought then flashes through your mind: "Oh my goodness, he's putting down more words on the paper than I am, and therefore he's bound to get a better grade." It can be stated ***unequivocally*** that there is no necessary correlation between the number of words on your exam paper and the grade you'll receive. Students who begin their answer after only five minutes of analysis have probably seen only the most obvious issues and missed many, if not most, of the subtle ones. They are also likely to be less well organized.

Opinions differ as to how much time you should spend analyzing and outlining a question before you actually write the answer. We believe that you should spend at least 12 to 18 minutes analyzing, organizing, and outlining a one-hour question before writing your answer. This will usually provide sufficient time to analyze and organize the question thoroughly ***and*** enough time to write a relatively complete answer. Remember that each word of the question must be scrutinized to determine if it (1) suggests an issue under the operative rules of law or (2) can be used in making an argument for the resolution of an issue. Because you can't receive points for an issue you don't spot, it is usually wise to read a question ***twice*** before starting your outline.

When to Make an Assumption

The instructions for a question may tell you to ***assume*** facts that are necessary to the answer. Even when these instructions are ***not*** given, you may be obliged to make certain assumptions about missing facts in order to write a thorough answer. Assumptions should be made only when you are told or when you, as the attorney for one of the parties described in the question, would be obliged to solicit additional information from your client. On the other hand, assumptions should ***never be used to change or alter the question.*** Don't ever write something like "if the facts in the question were . . . , instead of . . . , then . . . would result." If you do this, you are wasting time on facts that are extraneous to the problem before you. Professors want you to deal with ***their*** fact patterns, not your own.

Students sometimes try to "write around" information they think is missing. They assume that their professor has failed to include every piece of data necessary for a thorough answer. This is generally ***wrong***. The professor may have omitted some facts deliberately to see if the student ***can figure out what to do*** under the circumstances. However, in some instances, the professor may have omitted them inadvertently (even law professors are sometimes human).

The way to deal with the omission of essential information is to describe (1) what fact (or facts) appears to be missing and (2) why that information is important. For example, suppose the facts do not state the statutory period that applies to establish adverse possession in this jurisdiction This facts are important because the statutory period for which the adverse possessor must maintain possession varies greatly from state to state.

Assumptions should be made in a manner that keeps the other issues open (i.e., they lead to a discussion of all other possible issues). Don't assume facts that would virtually dispose of the entire hypothetical in a few sentences.

Case Names

A law student is ordinarily ***not*** expected to recall case names on an exam. The professor knows that you have read several hundred cases for each course and that you would have to be a memory expert to have all of the names at your fingertips. If you confront a fact pattern that seems similar to a case you have reviewed (but you cannot recall its name), just write something like, "One case we've read held that . . ." or "It has been held that. . . ." In this manner, you have informed the grader that you are relying on a case that contained a fact pattern similar to the question at issue.

The only exception to this rule is in the case of a landmark decision (e.g., *Roe v. Wade*). Landmark opinions are usually those that change or alter established law.[1] These cases are usually easy to identify, because you will probably have spent an entire class period discussing each of them. *Palsgraf v. Long Island Rail Road* is a prime example of a landmark case in Torts; in Property, *Kelo v. City of New London* is worth remembering. In these special cases, you may be expected to recall the case by name, as well as the proposition of law it stands for. However, this represents a very limited

1. In Constitutional Law and Criminal Procedure, many cases will qualify as "landmark" cases. Students studying these subjects should try to associate case names with the corresponding holdings and reproduce both in their exam answers.

exception to the general rule that counsels against wasting precious time trying to memorize and reproduce case names.

How to Handle Time Pressures

What do you do when there are five minutes left in the exam and you have only written down two-thirds of your answer? One thing ***not*** to do is write something like, "No time left!" or "Not enough time!" This gets you nothing but the satisfaction of knowing you have communicated your personal frustrations to the grader. Another thing ***not*** to do is insert in the exam booklet the outline you may have made on a piece of scrap paper. Professors will rarely look at these.

First of all, it is not necessarily a bad thing to be pressed for time. The person who finishes five minutes early has very possibly missed some important issues. The more proficient you become in knowing what is expected of you on an exam, the greater the difficulty you may experience in staying within the time limits. Second, remember that (at least to some extent) you're graded against your classmates' answers and they're under exactly the same time pressure as you. In short, don't panic if you can't write the "perfect" answer in the allotted time. Nobody does!

The best hedge against misuse of time is to ***review as many old exams as possible.*** These exercises will give you a familiarity with the process of organizing and writing an exam answer, which, in turn, should result in an enhanced ability to stay within the time boundaries. If you nevertheless find that you have about 15 minutes of writing to do and 5 minutes to do it in, write a paragraph that summarizes the remaining issues or arguments you would discuss if time permitted. As long as you've indicated that you're aware of the remaining legal issues, you'll probably receive some credit for them. Your analytical and argumentative skills will already be apparent to the grader by virtue of the issues that you have previously discussed.

Formatting Your Answer

Make sure that the way you write or type your answer presents your analysis in the best possible light. In other words, if you write, do so legibly. If you type, remember to use many paragraphs instead of just creating a document in which all of your ideas are merged into a single lengthy block of print. Remember, your professor may have a hundred or more exams to grade. If your answer is difficult to read, you will rarely be given the benefit of the doubt. On the other hand, a paper that is easy to read creates a very positive mental impact upon the professor.

The Importance of Reviewing Prior Exams

As we've mentioned, it is ***extremely important to review old exams.*** The transition from blackletter law to essay exam can be a difficult experience if the process has not been practiced. Although this book provides a large number of essay and multiple-choice questions, ***don't stop here***! Most law schools have recent tests online or on file in the library, by course. If they are available only in the library, we strongly suggest that you make a copy of every old exam you can obtain (especially those given by your professors) at the beginning of each semester. The demand for these documents usually increases dramatically as "finals time" draws closer.

The exams for each course should be scrutinized ***throughout the semester.*** They should be reviewed as you complete each chapter in your casebook. Sometimes the order of exam questions follows the sequence of the materials in your casebook. Thus, the first question on a law school test may involve the initial three chapters of the casebook; the second question may pertain to the fourth and fifth chapters; and so forth. In any event, ***don't wait*** until the semester is nearly over to begin reviewing old exams.

Keep in mind that no one is born with the ability to analyze questions and write superior answers to law school exams. Like any other skill, it is developed and perfected only through application. If you don't take the time to analyze numerous examinations from prior years, this evolutionary process just won't occur. Don't just ***think about*** the answers to past exam questions; take the time to ***write the answers down.*** It's also wise to look back at an answer a day or two after you've written it. You will invariably see (1) ways to improve your organizational skills and (2) arguments you missed.

As you practice spotting issues on past exams, you will see how rules of law become the sources of issues on finals. As we've already noted, if you don't ***understand*** how rules of law translate into issues, you won't be able to achieve superior grades on your exams. Reviewing exams from prior years should also reveal that certain issues tend to be lumped together in the same question. For instance, when the plaintiff seeks to prevent the defendant from doing something on defendant's own land, potential issues includes whether defendant's activities constitute a nuisance and whether defendant's land is burdened by a negative servitude.

Finally, one of the best means of evaluating if you understand a subject (or a particular area within a subject) is to attempt to create a hypothetical exam for that subject. Your exam should contain as many issues as possible.

If you can write an issue-packed exam, you probably know that subject well. If you can't, then you probably haven't yet acquired an adequate understanding of how the principles of law in that subject can spawn issues.

As Always, a Caveat

The suggestions and advice offered in this book represent the product of many years of experience in the field of legal education. We are confident that the techniques and concepts described in these pages will help you prepare for, and succeed at, your exams. Nevertheless, particular professors sometimes have a preference for exam-writing techniques that are not stressed in this book. Some instructors expect at least a nominal reference to the ***prima facie*** elements of all pertinent legal theories (even though one or more of those principles are ***not*** placed into issue). Other professors want their students to emphasize public policy considerations in the arguments they make on a particular issue. Because this book is intended for nationwide consumption, these individualized preferences have ***not*** been stressed. The best way to find out whether your professor has a penchant for a particular writing approach is to ask him or her to provide you with a model answer to a previous exam. If a model answer is not available, speak to second- or third-year students who received a superior grade in that professor's class.

One final point. Although the rules of law stated in the answers to the questions in this book have been drawn from commonly used sources (casebooks, hornbooks, etc.), it is still conceivable that they may be slightly at odds with those taught by your professor. In the area of property law, there are differences from jurisdiction to jurisdiction, and your professor may advise you to follow the Restatement of Property or the laws of the state in which you are located. In instances in which a conflict exists between our formulation of a legal principle and the one taught by your professor, ***follow the latter***! Because your grades are determined by your professors, their views should always supersede the views contained in this book.

Essay Questions

Question 1

Oscar was the owner of Sandyacres, a seafront property that lies between a highway and a public beach. Thirty-three years ago, he sold Alan an option to purchase the southeast quarter of Sandyacres for $2,500. The option agreement provides that the option can be exercised "by Alan or by his widow at any time while either shall live." Alan promptly recorded the agreement. Alan and his wife are alive.

Thirty years ago, Oscar constructed a tunnel through a sand dune on Sandyacres to provide access to the beach. He also conveyed to Nabor, an adjoining owner, a right-of-way easement across Sandyacres and through the tunnel to the beach for Nabor and his motel guests to use. This deed of conveyance was acknowledged before a notary public whose commission had expired. Nabor promptly recorded the deed. Three years ago, the tunnel collapsed. It has not been reconstructed.

Twenty years ago, Oscar granted Sandyacres for value to Edward "in fee simple so long as he never marries." Edward, who had no actual knowledge of Oscar's transactions with Alan and Nabor, promptly recorded his deed. Edward is alive and has never married.

Client is now negotiating to buy Sandyacres from Edward. Client plans to build a resort hotel, a portion of which will sit directly above the collapsed tunnel.

A title insurance company has agreed to insure Client's title to Sandyacres subject to exceptions that might arise out of each of the following matters:

1. Alan's option agreement
2. The conveyance to Nabor
3. The conveyance to Edward

Discuss how you would advise Client regarding the extent, if any, to which each of the matters referred to in the title insurance exceptions may affect her rights in Sandyacres if she purchases that property.

Question 2

Owen owned Blackacre, which consisted of a house on a lot. He conveyed Blackacre to his two children, Sam and Doris, by a deed that read as follows: "Owen hereby grants Blackacre to Sam and Doris, to be held by them jointly." The deed was duly recorded.

Thereafter, Sam borrowed money from Bank and gave Bank a mortgage on Blackacre to secure repayment of the loan. In the mortgage document, Sam covenanted for himself, his successors and assigns, that Blackacre would not be used for any purpose other than as a single-family residence. Bank recorded the mortgage in due course.

Sam died before the loan became due. His will left all his property to his friend Tom. As applicable law permits, Bank elected not to file a claim against Sam's estate or to call the loan, but rather to rely on whatever rights it had under the mortgage.

Shortly after Sam's death, the area in which Blackacre is located was rezoned to permit multiple-family dwellings. Tom decided to convert the house on Blackacre into a three-unit apartment building.

Bank, upon learning of Tom's plans, sought an injunction against Tom to prohibit the conversion.

Doris brought an action against Bank and Tom to quiet title to Blackacre in herself.

Discuss the result in each case.

Question 3

Ten years ago, O, the owner of Blackacre, executed a conveyance "to A and B, exclusively, as joint tenants, with right of survivorship, to be used as a parking lot, but if said premises should ever be used for a different purpose, then this conveyance shall immediately become void." At the time of this transfer, A and B each had an independent retail establishment located across the street from Blackacre. A and B immediately began using Blackacre as a parking area for the convenience of their customers. Four years later, B sold her store and her interest in Blackacre to C.

One year after the sale to C, C decided to enlarge his store. He asked A if A would have any objection to C building a storage facility on Blackacre that would encompass approximately 20 percent of that parcel. C told A that without such increased storage area, it was not economically feasible for C to enlarge his retail establishment. A told C that he had no objections. To save time and money, C installed a prefabricated aluminum structure on Blackacre using metal bolts that were permanently attached to a suitable concrete foundation. C then expanded his retail store by adding a second floor to it. C and A continued to invite their customers to park on the rest of Blackacre. O made five or six trips to A's store during the time that the storage facility was being erected, parking in the Blackacre lot in three instances.

One year after the storage facility had been erected, O executed a conveyance of all his "right, title and interest in and to Blackacre" to M. O died shortly thereafter, leaving all of his property to H (his only heir at law). It is now four months after O's death, and H has demanded possession of Blackacre from A and C. In addition, M has advised A and C that he owns Blackacre.

Discuss the respective rights of M, A, C, and H.

Question 4

Three years and four months ago, two brothers, Bill and Murray, bought 20 acres of land as joint tenants on the outskirts of the city of Myth. Originally, they each intended to build their family homes on the land and farm the remainder for extra income. However, Murray ran into some financial difficulties and was unable to build a house.

Bill constructed two single-family dwellings on the premises. He and his family occupied one of the dwellings and rented the other dwelling to Henrietta and her family for $500 per month. In addition, Bill paid the taxes on the land each year and also paid the fire insurance premiums on the two houses. Four months ago, Henrietta and Bill verbally entered into a one-year lease.

Bill cleared the remaining acreage of its timber. He sold the timber and kept the money for himself. He then cultivated the land and planted half of it as a fruit orchard and the other half as seasonal crops. Each year, he harvested the fruit and the seasonal crops and sold them. He kept all of the income for himself.

Six months ago, Murray had paid off all of his debts and was ready to build his house. Bill told him, "Listen, buddy boy, I'm the one who has taken care of this land all these years. You're not going to just come in here now and take out fruit trees or growing crops to build your stupid house." Murray, greatly upset, has sued Bill for possession of the premises, half the rentals paid by Henrietta over the years, half the value of the timber sold by Bill when he cleared the land, half the value of the crops harvested by Bill, and half the reasonable rental value of the property occupied by Bill. When Bill was served with the summons, he became so angry that he countersued for partition of the land in kind.

Discuss

1. The merits of Murray's suit against Bill. Include in your discussion any counterclaims that Bill might have against Murray.
2. Whether Henrietta is obliged to vacate the land.
3. The affect on Murray's claim if Bill dies before the suit is tried and is survived by his wife Wilma, to whom he leaves all his property.

Question 5

L rented (by a signed written lease) a furnished apartment in his building to T, a law student, for two years, beginning June 1. When T arrived at the apartment on June 1, R (the prior tenant) was still there. T complained to L, and L evicted R on June 15. T came into possession of the apartment on June 16. In early July, some children playing baseball broke a windowpane in T's apartment. T demanded that L replace the windowpane, but L refused. Rain coming through the broken pane caused damage to the living room floor, which began to warp.

The apartment above T's was occupied by C, a member of the famous rock group, the Pebbles. The Pebbles rehearsed daily (typically 2:00-6:00 P.M.), which interfered with T's law studies so much that she complained repeatedly to L. On July 15, three of C's friends (the other members of the Pebbles) were arrested at C's apartment and charged with possession of narcotics. The noise stopped immediately thereafter.

On August 30, T discovered that the stove in her apartment was no longer functioning. On August 31, T, disgusted with all these events, knocked on L's door, tendered the key to L, and said, "This place is a zoo; I wouldn't live here if you paid me!" L took the key without saying a word. L now comes to you wanting to sue T for both the accrued and prospective rent (T has yet to pay any rent).

Discuss what you would advise L.

Question 6

On February 1, 2010, O leased space in an office building to T, effective as of that date "for an aggregate rent of $48,000, payable at $2,000 on the first day of each month." The properly executed written agreement also provided, *inter alia*:

1. Lessee shall not assign or sublet the leased premises without the written consent of Lessor, which shall not be unreasonably withheld;
2. Lessee shall install all fixtures required for operation of a retail clothing store at the premises, which fixtures shall belong to Lessor at the conclusion of the lease term;
3. Lessee shall keep such fixtures fully insured for Lessor's benefit; and
4. Lessee shall not hold Lessor liable for the negligent acts of Lessor's employees or agents.

T installed the necessary fixtures and commenced operation of the store. In early April 2011, T decided to retire and introduced S to O as a possible successor. O, shortly thereafter, delivered the following written statement to T: "Without prejudice to my rights, I consent to adding S to the lease provided that all terms between O and T apply to S, too." That same day, T assigned the lease to S but reserved the right to reenter the premises if S failed to pay rent due to O.

In May 2011, S installed dry cleaning and pressing equipment valued at $4,500.

S made all his rent payments on time and removed his inventory prior to February 1, 2012. However, because the new premises that S was to occupy had been damaged by a fire, S was unable to remove the dry cleaning and pressing equipment by that date. On February 10, 2012, S received a note from O that stated: "Rent will be due for one more year since you're still occupying my property." A copy of this note was mailed to T at his old address, but T had moved in the interim and the letter was not forwarded to T's new address. On February 15, 2012, S introduced Z to O as a possible successor, but O refused to accept Z because of Z's ethnic origin.

On April 1, 2012, O's night security guard accidentally dropped a lighted cigarette into a can of dry cleaning fluid that S had left at the premises. The ensuing explosion and fire gutted the premises and destroyed the fixtures and equipment, valued at $2,500 and $4,500, respectively, at the time of the accident. S had allowed the insurance to lapse on February 1, 2012. On April 10, 2012, S notified O that he no longer considered himself to be liable for rent.

Discuss O's rights against T and S.

Question 7

Omar owns a gasoline station. Tom is the lessee and operator of the gas station under a three-year written lease running from January 1, 2009, through December 31, 2011. The monthly rental is $1,000 payable on the first business day of each month. Tom remained in possession beyond the expiration date and continued to pay the rent as before.

On January 31, 2012, Tom offered to purchase the premises from Omar for $80,000, with title to pass in 90 days. Omar verbally accepted the offer, and the parties agreed that no additional lease payments would be required of Tom. With Omar's knowledge, Tom then installed new gas pumps, lube racks, and wheel alignment equipment at an aggregate cost to him of $18,000.

On March 5, a portion of the building was damaged by a mudslide caused by a severe rainstorm. Tom asked Omar either to repair the damage caused by the mudslide (cost approximately $1,600) or to reduce the purchase price by a corresponding amount. Omar refused. On March 15, Tom informed Omar that, under the circumstances, he was moving out and had no more interest in purchasing the property. On March 17, Tom vacated the premises.

Two weeks later, Tom received a letter from Omar telling him that the property had been relet to Jill for $800 a month, effective April 1, 2012. Omar also stated that he held Tom responsible for both the rent for the months of February and March and the $200 per month difference in the rent that would accrue through the end of the year. Omar further informed Tom that he had signed a contract to sell the premises to Samuel, with title to pass on January 1, 2010. It is now April 5, 2012. Tom has decided that he still wants to purchase the gasoline station on the original terms to which Omar had agreed.

Discuss the probable outcome of the following actions:

1. An action brought by Tom against Omar to enforce specific performance of the agreement of sale
2. An action by Omar against Tom for rent from February through December 2012

Question 8

Owen owned a city block consisting of eight lots, each of which he had purchased from a different owner. In 2008, he conveyed by deed Lots 1 and 2 to Xavier Corporation, which built a department store thereon. The deed, which had been recorded promptly, contained covenants by Owen for himself, his heirs, successors and assigns (1) to provide, maintain, repair, and keep available a parking area for at least 500 automobiles on the remainder of the block for the nonexclusive use of department store customers; and (2) to refrain from selling tires or petroleum products on any of the remaining lots.

Owen then developed a shopping center with a 550-car parking lot on Lots 3 through 8. In 2010, he sold the shopping center to Annie, who knew about the covenant restricting the sale of tires and petroleum products but was unaware of the covenant about the parking lot.

A municipal zoning ordinance encompassing the area in which the shopping center is located prohibits freestanding signs more than 15 feet high.

Annie now proposes to build a service station on the shopping center parking lot, which will eliminate 100 parking spaces. A marketing survey reveals that unless the station has a 50-foot-high freestanding sign to attract customers from a nearby freeway, the service station will be unprofitable. A 15-foot sign will be barely visible from the adjoining streets.

1. Discuss whether Xavier can prevent Annie from building the service station.
2. Assuming that Xavier cannot prevent Annie from building the service station, discuss whether the municipality can prevent Annie from erecting a 50-foot sign in the parking area.

Question 9

Alicia has just shown you a deed that was recorded 40 years ago. This document reads as follows:

> In consideration of love and affection, I hereby grant Sweetholm to my friend Josiah and the heirs of his body, this conveyance to take effect ten years from the date hereof, provided that if Josiah dies without issue the estate is to go to my brother Ludwig and his heirs, and further provided that if animals, birds, or children are ever kept on the property, the estate is to cease and determine.
>
> Signed, Vladimir

You ascertain from Alicia that her house, with its surrounding grounds of about 10 acres, is known as Sweetholm. Alicia tells you that she bought Sweetholm from Josiah's niece, Jennifer, 11 years ago. The deed transferred to Alicia "all my right, title, and interest in Sweetholm." Alicia also tells you that, when she bought the property, the guest house near the southwest boundary of the estate was occupied by Danny, Jennifer's cousin. Danny had visited Jennifer 12 years ago and decided to stay to work on a novel. Jennifer had asked Alicia to let Danny stay there for a while "since he was finding himself." Alicia said it probably would be "all right, if Danny did not get in her way." Alicia thought it might be a good idea to have another person on the property to frighten away prospective thieves. Soon after Jennifer vacated Sweetholm, Danny built a separate mailbox outside the guest house and placed a doormat in front of the entrance that read "Welcome to Danny's."

It appears that the estate bordering Sweetholm on the west, Laurel Hill, was purchased 14 years ago by Wilson, a scientist doing research on the territorial habits of wild dogs, coyotes, and wolves. Wilson had captured several wolves and brought them to Laurel Hill. When Alicia took over the property from Jennifer, Wilson talked to her about the wolves. Alicia promised him, in a valid writing, that she would allow the wolves to wander freely over Sweetholm. The wolves soon manifested their territorial behavior and took up residence on the southwest corner of Sweetholm.

Unfortunately, when Danny saw one of the animals wandering around near the guest house about two months ago, he suddenly took it into his head that it would make a nice pet. Danny enticed the wolf into his enclosed patio and kept it there, even after it resisted his first efforts to make friends and bit his hand when he tried to feed it.

About a week ago, Alicia received an unpleasant visit from Trivers, another scientist with whom Wilson is working, who had purchased Laurel Hill from Wilson last summer. Trivers threatened to sue Alicia because Danny had tampered with a subject involved in his experiment. Alicia became upset with the whole situation, evicted both Danny and the wolves from Sweetholm that very evening, and hastily constructed a chicken-wire fence on the western boundary of Sweetholm so that the wolves could not get back in. Last night, (1) Danny called and claimed that he owned the guest house, and (2) Trivers called and threatened to obtain an injunction requiring Alicia to remove the chicken-wire fence.

Alicia asks you whether Trivers and Danny really have any viable claims against her. She also wants to know whether there are any other people who might show up to claim an interest in Sweetholm.

In response to your initial questions, Alicia tells you that Vladimir is dead and Gustaf is his sole heir; that Ludwig is dead and Richard is his sole heir; and that Josiah is also dead, but Jennifer, his niece and only heir, is still alive. You have also learned that the statute of limitations for actions to recover real property is ten years. Please evaluate the possible claims of Danny, Trivers, and any other person(s) you think might have a plausible claim to some interest in Sweetholm.

Question 10

Twenty years ago, Owen subdivided his family estate into several hundred building lots, which he sold in subsequent years. Most, but not all, of the deeds contained restrictions that required setbacks of at least 50 feet from the street, single-story, ranch-style houses, all garages to be located on the rear quarter of the lots, and white split-rail fences.

Alex purchased Lot 15 from Owen 10 years ago. There was no restrictive covenant in her deed, but she built a ranch-style house 65 feet from the street with a garage on the rear quarter of the lot.

The deeds to Lots 14 and 16, which adjoin Lot 15 on either side, did contain the above restrictions. Although Lots 14 and 16 had been sold and passed through several owners, they were among the few lots that were unimproved when Alex bought Lot 15.

Baker bought Lot 14 last year and later built an expensive home that complied with the restrictions in the original deed from Owen. He started building an elaborate swimming pool but lost his job before the pool was completed. He then quitclaimed his interest in Lot 14 to Commercial Bank in lieu of foreclosure. Two months after the Bank took title, Alex's prize flower bed slid into the excavation Baker had dug for his pool.

Dave now owns Lot 16 and plans to build a two-story brick house, with an attached garage, set back 15 feet from the street. Alex asked Dave to comply with the deed restrictions. When Dave refused, Alex erected a brick wall 20 feet high on her lot, adjacent to and paralleling the entire boundary with Dave's Lot 16. Alex painted the side of the wall facing Dave's lot black and coated it with creosote, a foul-smelling preservative. This wall would darken Dave's planned house and make use of his patio unpleasant.

All deeds were recorded. Owen no longer owns any of the lots but lives in an exclusive hotel that overlooks the subdivision.

1. Discuss whether Alex can prevent Dave from building as planned.
2. Discuss whether Owen can prevent Dave from building as planned.
3. Discuss whether Dave has any rights against Alex.
4. Discuss whether Alex can recover from Commercial Bank.

Question 11

Albright owned adjoining lots in a city, Lots 1 and 2, each improved with a single-family residence. The lots are located in a district where business buildings were rapidly replacing houses. Albright sold Lot 1 to Bayard, who planned to erect a large commercial structure that would require a deep foundation. The parties agreed orally that Bayard should be permitted to excavate without providing support for the house on Albright's remaining lot since Albright intended to replace it with a similar commercial structure.

A period of depression for business followed the sale, and Bayard postponed his plans to build while Albright abandoned his plans and sold Lot 2 to Cullom, who repaired and occupied it as her home.

Economic conditions improved, and Bayard razed the house on his lot. While this was being done, Bayard discovered that the pipe connecting Cullom's house with the public sewer ran across the Bayard lot. The pipe was beneath the surface of the land outside where the house had been, but it was above the surface in a "crawl space" beneath the floor of the razed house where the basement was not fully excavated. The right to maintain such a line was not reserved in Albright's deed to Bayard and was not disclosed in any recorded document.

Bayard demanded that Cullom remove the sewer line and also notified her to protect her house against possible subsidence during the excavation for the new building Bayard was about to build. Cullom consulted qualified engineers, who advised her that the cost of strengthening her foundation and the cost of securing a new outlet for the sewer would be prohibitive.

Discuss the respective rights of Bayard and Cullom.

Question 12

Fifteen years ago, Vera inherited a tract of land, consisting of Lots 1-12. Ten years ago, she sold Lots 1-4 and 7-10. The deeds to these lots imposed an easement over the northerly 15 feet of Lots 1-5 for the use and benefit of Lots 2-6. This easement presently provides the only access to Lots 2-6. The deeds to Lots 1-5 and 7-10 also contained the following restriction: "To preserve high quality within this development, this lot is conveyed on condition it be used solely for residential purposes, and any other use may be enjoined and shall be cause for forfeiture." Immediately, residences were built on Lots 1-4 and 7-10. Lot 5 remained vacant. Vera sold Lot 6 five years ago to Barb, without including any restrictions in the deed.

Three years ago, Barb, a rock music promoter, began operating a nightclub on Lot 6. One year ago, Phil purchased Lot 5. The deed he received from Vera was identical to that received by Lot owners 1-4. Phil built a family home, but has frequently complained to Barb about the noise level emanating from Barb's club, especially on weekends.

All of the deeds were recorded.

Occasionally, inebriated patrons of Barb's club throw empty bottles on the lawns of Lots 1-5.

Fifteen months ago, a zoning ordinance was enacted and Lots 1-12 were zoned "Single Family Residential." Barb ignored this zoning change.

Barb's club has prospered. Three months ago, by quitclaim deed, Barb acquired a one-acre parcel adjoining Lot 6 on the west from Farmer to use as a parking lot and cemetery. Farmer owns another 59 acres of rural land surrounding Vera's tract on the north, west, and south. Barb now plans to use a few rooms in the building on Lot 6 for a mortuary featuring recently deceased rock stars. The dead stars would then be buried in the cemetery.

Yesterday, despite Phil's appearance and objections, the County Commissioners rezoned Lot 6 and the parking lot to "Commercial," stating that Farmer's adjacent land was a likely site for a shopping center. This rezoning permits Lot 6 and the parking lot to be used for mortuaries and nightclubs. As Phil left the meeting, he told Barb that he intended to retain an attorney and use every means legally available to close or hinder Barb's nightclub and mortuary operations.

Barb consults you before investing any more money in Lot 6 or paving the parking lot. She wants to know what legal action Phil and the owners of the other lots might take, what defenses she might reasonably assert, and what the likelihood is that she will be successful. Discuss.

Question 13

For many years, Olga operated a tavern on property owned by her at 2 Harvard Place in the town of Waterbury. On June 13, 2008, she broke her leg and closed the tavern, but did not remove any of the merchandise or fixtures. She reopened the tavern on September 19, 2008.

On July 1, 2008, Waterbury adopted a zoning ordinance (effective immediately) restricting use of property on Harvard Place to single-family dwellings, but providing for continuation of any existing nonconforming uses by the owner or successors in title, subject to the following provision: "No nonconforming use, once abandoned, shall be reinstated. For the purpose of this section, 'abandoned' is defined as cessation of the nonconforming use for six or more consecutive months."

On March 15, 2010, Olga executed and delivered a grant deed to 2 Harvard Place to Dr. Baker to pay a past-due bill for personal medical services. Baker allowed Olga to continue to operate the tavern and did not record her deed immediately.

On September 5, 2010, Olga, for valuable consideration, executed and delivered a conveyance of "all my right, title and interest in 2 Harvard Place" to Charles, who had no knowledge of Baker's deed. Dr. Baker recorded her deed on October 1, 2010, and Charles recorded his deed two days later.

Charles operated the tavern continuously from September 15, 2010, to January 19, 2012, when he closed the tavern because his liquor license was suspended for nine months by the State Board of Liquor Control.

1. Discuss who should prevail in a quiet title action between Baker and Charles.
2. If Charles prevails, discuss whether he will be legally entitled to reopen the premises as a tavern when the suspension of his liquor license terminates.

Question 14

Twelve years ago, Able purchased a 400-acre tract of land in the state of Myth. The north end of this tract is bounded by a flowing river. Two years later, Able died. He was survived by one daughter, who didn't know until 2 months ago that her father had bought the tract of land. Eleven years ago, Baker built a fence around the 400-acre tract and began growing crops on it. Baker has paid taxes for all but 4 of the years he has occupied the land.

Four years ago, Carla asked permission to drill some test wells on the tract occupied by Baker to determine whether there were oil deposits beneath the land. After determining that there appeared to be substantial oil deposits, Carla asked Baker to lease the land to her for oil and gas production. Baker told Carla that he was not the true owner, and so he could not give Carla permission to drill. Carla then bought an adjacent tract of land and drilled wells to produce oil from the reservoir underneath both Baker's and Carla's tract. Baker, realizing that Carla probably would deplete the oil supply, drilled wells on the tract he occupied and pumped oil into storage tanks, waiting for the price of oil to go up. Carla has been selling her oil as it is produced, rather than storing it.

Eight years ago, Baker had begun appropriating 100,000 cubic feet of water per day from the river to irrigate his crops. When there was a drought two years later, Baker built an earthen dam to create a pool from which to irrigate the tract. This dam reduced the flow of water to downstream owners, most of whom relied on it for manufacturing purposes. Baker also entered into a contract with City, a small town two miles away. Baker agreed to drill several water wells and to sell the water produced to City. The result was to reduce the general water table in the area.

Baker has just discovered that one of Carla's wells was not drilled properly and encroached upon the substrata of Baker's tract.

Assuming Myth requires possession for ten years in order to gain title by adverse possession, discuss the following:

1. What rights does Baker have in and to the 400-acre tract?
2. What rights, if any, does Carla have against Baker involving the oil?
3. What rights do the downstream owners have as to the water in the river?
4. What rights does Baker have against Carla regarding the oil produced from the slant-hole well?

Question 15

A was the owner of Blackacre, a vacant tract of land. A conveyed Blackacre to B by warranty deed on July 1, 2011, and B recorded the deed on December 1 of that same year. A then conveyed Blackacre to C by warranty deed on September 1, 2011. C conveyed Blackacre to D by quitclaim deed on November 1, 2011, and D recorded the deed the next day. D later discovered that C's deed was unrecorded. She obtained C's deed from him and recorded it on February 1, 2012. The land was still vacant at the time of the conveyance to D, but D immediately went into possession. Neither C nor D had actual notice of the prior conveyance by A to B at the time each received their respective deeds. C paid a fair price for Blackacre in cash; D took the quitclaim deed from C in full satisfaction of an antecedent debt. When B learned that D was in possession of Blackacre, he brought an action to recover possession from D. B notified A of the lawsuit, but A was not a party and did not participate in the action.

The applicable recording statute provides: "Every conveyance of real property is void as against any subsequent purchaser of the same property in good faith and for a valuable consideration, whose conveyance is first duly recorded." Discuss the following questions.

1. What result in B's action?
2. What result if the last six words were omitted from the recording statute?
3. If judgment is for D, what is B's recourse against A?

Question 16

On Daughter's twenty-first birthday, her father, Vendor, gave her a house and lot to which Vendor had a good record title. The gift was made orally, and Vendor gave Daughter the keys to the house. Daughter promptly took possession and occupied the premises for the next six years. During this time, she made substantial improvements to the house at considerable expense. At the end of the six years, Daughter's business required her to move to another city, and she listed the property with a local real estate agent for sale or to rent.

After Daughter vacated the premises, Vendor, without Daughter's knowledge, entered into a written contract to sell the house and lot to Purchaser, with transfer of title and possession to take place in 60 days. Purchaser paid Vendor one-half of the purchase price when they signed the contract. When Vendor and Purchaser were negotiating the sale, Purchaser told Vendor that he intended to raze the building and erect a commercial structure on the land, and the intended improvement would not be in conflict with the local zoning ordinance. Purchaser inspected the premises at the time of the contract, but Daughter was not in possession; there were no "For Sale" signs nor were there any other indications of Daughter's interest. A preliminary title insurance report obtained by Purchaser disclosed no such interest.

Two days before the scheduled transfer, fire destroyed the house, but through no fault of Vendor. In the meantime, Purchaser learned that Daughter claimed title to the premises, and he found another lot better suited to his purposes. He then notified Vendor that he considered the contract terminated and demanded the return of his payment.

Discuss the rights and obligations of Vendor, Daughter, and Purchaser, and to what relief, if any, each is entitled.

Question 17

Twenty-two years ago, Owens purported to sell Greenacre to Able for $1,000 cash. Greenacre is a parcel of unimproved mountain land that is inaccessible by road during six months of each year due to snow. Owens gave Able a deed that granted Greenacre to Able in fee simple and contained all warranties of title. Able did not have a title examination made. Able immediately recorded his deed and obtained an unsecured loan from Bank. He used the funds to build a vacation cabin on the land. Unknown to Able, Owens's grandmother was the true and sole owner of Greenacre.

Since the time of the purported transfer, Able has paid taxes on Greenacre and lived in the cabin for one month each summer. The cabin and land have otherwise been unoccupied. Bank placed a metallic sign on the land at the time the cabin was built that read: "Built by Able with financing from Bank." The sign has remained in place ever since.

Five years ago, Owens borrowed $5,000 from Charlie. Three years ago, Owens's grandmother died, leaving Greenacre to Owens by will. Recently, Charlie induced Owens to deed Greenacre to him in full satisfaction of the $5,000 debt, which was then three-and-a-half years past due. Charlie had no actual knowledge of Able's claim to Greenacre. Owens's grandmother had no knowledge of the purported transfer to Able or of Able's activities on Greenacre.

Title searches in the state are customarily made in the grantor/grantee indexes of the official records. The recording statute reads "Any unrecorded conveyance is deemed void as against a subsequent taker for value and without notice."

Discuss the rights of all the parties to Greenacre.

Question 18

Henry was the owner of Greenacre, a vacant parcel of land in the state of Utopia. Twelve years ago, Henry handed his friend JoAnn a warranty deed granting "all my land in the state of Utopia to my niece and nephew Paula and Mark as joint owners." Henry orally advised JoAnn that he wanted his niece and nephew to have Greenacre since they were the only ones who loved him, but that he wanted to live there until he died. The deed was not recorded.

Paula died eight years ago. Soon afterwards, Henry, who had become angry at Mark's lack of devotion toward him, conveyed Greenacre by a quitclaim deed for $5,000 to Ruth. Ruth was aware of the deed from Henry to Paula and Mark, but she thought that because the deed to Paula and Mark had not been recorded, she would have priority to Greenacre. Ruth promptly recorded her deed. Ruth then built a two-bedroom house upon Greenacre, immediately made it her home, and has lived there ever since.

Three months ago, Henry died. Mark thereafter learned for the first time of Henry's deed to him and Paula. Mark consults you about his rights and informs you that (1) he recorded his deed (which JoAnn delivered to him when Henry died), and (2) Henry owned no land in Utopia except Greenacre.

Advise Mark as to his rights in Greenacre and against Ruth.

Question 19

Ollie owned Goldacre, an oil-rich ranch in the state of Lotus. Five years ago, Ollie summoned her foreman, Art, into her office and handed Art a deed transferring Goldacre to Art, and said, "I want you to have Goldacre if I die before you."

Four years ago, Ollie's accountant, Cap, discovered that Art had been embezzling. Ollie immediately discharged Art. With Cap as a witness, Ollie called in her bookkeeper, Bill, showed Bill a deed conveying Goldacre to Bill and said, "I am now giving Goldacre to you. You have the combination to my safe. When I die, get this deed out of my safe and record it."

A month later, Ollie discharged Bill for incompetence. Before leaving, Bill, without Ollie's knowledge, took the deed to Goldacre from the safe.

One year later, Ollie told Cap she had revoked both of the deeds to Art and Bill and that she wanted to retire. Nine months ago, Ollie conveyed Goldacre to Cap for a valuable consideration. Cap recorded the deed immediately. Ollie died two months later. Art recorded his deed one day after Ollie died, and Bill recorded his deed one day later. At Ollie's funeral, Bill and Art informed Cap of their respective recordations.

Cap then mortgaged Goldacre to Elk Mortgage Co., which recorded it the same day.

Elk Mortgage Co. has now brought an action for declaratory relief to determine the rights of Art, Bill, Cap, and Elk Mortgage Co. in Goldacre. Assume all deeds were properly completed.

Discuss the parties' respective rights.

Question 20

Art was the record owner of Greenacre, a vacant tract of land. Art and Barb discussed the sale of this land to Barb, and they orally agreed on a purchase price of $5,000 in cash. Art then typed up a statement setting forth all the terms that had been agreed upon. This included the fact that Art would deliver to Carl, a real estate broker, a warranty deed conveying Greenacre to Barb and that Carl would hand deliver the deed to Barb if Barb paid Carl the purchase price within one month.

Art placed one copy of this statement—unsigned, unwitnessed, and undated—in an envelope and mailed it to Barb. When Barb received it, she telephoned Art and told him that the statement accurately reflected their understanding and that she would deliver $5,000 in cash to Carl within the month in accordance with their agreement.

Art then executed the warranty deed, complete in all respects, and gave it to Carl with a copy of his statement.

One week later, Art learned that a highway was to be built near Greenacre, greatly increasing its value. Art immediately wrote to Carl, telling Carl he had changed his mind and wanted the deed returned to him.

One day later and before Carl had received Art's last letter, Barb called Carl and said she had to show the deed to her bank to obtain a loan for the $5,000. Carl sent the deed to Barb, who promptly recorded it and immediately executed and delivered a warranty deed for Greenacre to Dale.

Barb disappeared and has not paid the $5,000 to Art or Carl.

1. In an action to quiet title between Art and Dale, discuss who will prevail.
2. Discuss what rights, if any, Art and Dale have against Carl.

Question 21

Owen is the record owner of Flatacre, a one-acre vacant tract of land. Ten years ago, Alex paid for, and received a deed to, Flatacre from Swindler, who, unbeknownst to her, did not own Flatacre.

Alex immediately moved onto Flatacre, built a home, and resided there openly for the next three years. Alex then entered into a written lease of Flatacre with Bill. Under the terms of the lease Bill agreed to a two-year tenancy at an agreed rental of $2,000 per month, beginning January 1 of that year. The agreement also gave Bill the option to purchase Flatacre during Alex's life at a price to be set following an appraisal by a mutually selected appraiser. Bill took possession of Flatacre and faithfully paid rent to Alex for 19 months. Bill then sent Alex timely notice of his desire to purchase Flatacre. However, unbeknownst to Bill, Alex had recently embarked upon a trip around the world and had left instructions with her neighbor, Norma, to receive and deposit rent checks for Alex. Norma received Bill's letter but misplaced it.

Six months later, having patiently awaited a response from Alex, Bill, who had paid no rent since sending the letter to Alex, became disgusted and vacated Flatacre, taking his belongings with him. When Alex returned one year later (six months after Bill left) and observed that Flatacre was vacant, she moved back in and has resided there to date.

Owen, the true owner of Flatacre, has just learned of both Swindler's conveyance to Alex and that Alex and Bill had occupied Flatacre. He now seeks to recover possession of Flatacre. The applicable statute of limitations is five years, and there is no requirement concerning the payment of property taxes.

What are the rights of the parties?

Question 22

Five years ago, Olivia purchased from Builder a single-family home in Tranquilacres. At the time of her purchase, Tranquilacres was a brand-new development. Within days of taking possession of her new home, Olivia noticed an unpleasant sulfur-based odor in the house. Olivia planned to hire an inspector to investigate the cause of the odor but never had enough money at any one time to pay an inspector. Olivia financed the purchase by taking out a conventional 30-year mortgage from Lender. For the first three years of the loan, Olivia made her mortgage payments on time but fell behind on the payments after she lost her job. When Olivia was approximately $24,000 behind in her mortgage payments, Lender instituted foreclosure proceedings.

A few weeks before the foreclosure sale, Olivia was approached by Second Chances. According to its sales literature, Second Chances is devoted to assisting delinquent borrowers so that they don't lose their homes to foreclosure. Second Chances offered to pay the delinquent amounts owed to Lender in return for a deed to the property. Second Chances also agreed to give Olivia a 3-year lease for $1,500 per month, with an option to repurchase her home for a price of $125,000 during the term of the lease. During the term of the lease, Second Chances was to pay the mortgage payments. The lease provided that the rental payments would be used to pay the existing mortgage on behalf of Olivia, including taxes, insurance, principal, and interest, and that any additional funds "will be deemed to cover administrative and overhead costs and time and efforts expended (by Second Chances)." Under the lease, Olivia undertook all responsibility for maintaining and repairing the property, even structural repairs. Second Chances did not record the deed or notify the lender of the transfer. Olivia continued to reside on the property.

Six months ago, Olivia received notice from Lender that the mortgage was again delinquent. Olivia immediately stopped making payments to Second Chances and arranged with Lender to sell the house at a short sale to Petra. Petra agreed to take the property "as is." Petra made a cursory inspection of the property but was unwilling to spend the money to hire an inspector. Petra noticed an unpleasant odor but was too polite to mention the odor to Olivia. Petra diligently researched the title but found nothing other than Lender's mortgage. (Second Chances never filed its deed.) Petra did not ask, and Olivia did not mention, the unpleasant sulfur odor. At closing, Petra received a quitclaim deed. Shortly after she moved in, Petra noticed cracks beginning to form in the walls. An inspection later revealed that the drywall Builder used to create the interior walls was emitting sulfur-based gases that are corroding the air conditioning coils and computer wiring. It will cost several thousand dollars to repair.

The recording act in this jurisdiction protects bona fide purchasers for value who take without notice. Discuss any rights and duties of the parties.

1. Does Petra have any rights against any party with respect to the drywall problem?
2. Is Petra's deed subject to any interest of Second Chances?
3. Does Olivia have any claims against Second Chances?

Question 23

City approved a development plan to revitalize one of its economically distressed areas. The development plan encompassed six one-acre parcels. According to the plan, Parcel 1 was designated for new housing, including low-cost housing. Parcels 2 and 3 were designated for office and commercial development. Parcels 3 and 4 were designated for restaurants and shopping. Parcels 5 and 6 were designated for parks and other open spaces.

City was able to purchase all the parcels of land it needed except one. Holdout, the owner of a small, well-kept home in the area designated for retail development, refused to sell. City used its power of eminent domain to condemn Holdout's parcel. City paid Holdout $50,000 for her property, the market value of her parcel at the time. Holdout is challenging City's right to condemn her property.

City conveyed a largely abandoned one-square-block tract of land within Parcel 1 to NonProfit, a nonprofit entity dedicated to providing affordable housing for low- and moderate-income households. The tract included a combination of abandoned buildings and debris-strewn lots. NonProfit employed teams of volunteers to clear vacant lots of debris in preparation for the new construction. While taking a break from his lot-clearing project, Victor, one of the volunteers, wandered into an abandoned apartment building next door. Victor noticed a loose ceiling tile in one of the units. Victor removed the tile and found a cardboard box concealed in the ceiling. The box, which was covered with dust, contained $43,000 in old currency. When NonProfit learned of Victor's find, it demanded that Victor turn the money over to NonProfit. Victor is suing to have the court declare that the money is his.

NonProfit, after clearing the vacant lots and razing the existing buildings, constructed a new high-rise condominium unit and placed the new units up for sale. NonProfit sold the units to qualifying low-income homeowners for the cost of construction—a discount of approximately 30 to 40 percent below the cost of comparable dwellings on the open market. To ensure the continued availability of affordable homes, NonProfit included the following restriction in each deed:

> Resale Provisions: Each homeowner agrees to sell his/her home only to other low- or moderate-income persons at the price he/she paid.

NonProfit has recently learned that Owner, an owner of one of the affordable housing units, plans to sell her unit to Speculator for $25,000 more than Owner paid for the unit. NonProfit is suing to prevent the sale.

Discuss the probable outcome of

1. The action between Holdout and City
2. The action between Victor and NonProfit
3. The action between NonProfit and Owner

Question 24

Arthur and Betty are neighbors. Their backyards are separated by an old fence made with wire. They had always had a friendly relationship until five years ago when Betty's nephew, Ned, moved in with Betty. According to Arthur, Ned brought home "junk" automobiles that he would work on in Betty's backyard. Because he didn't like looking at the "junkyard" Betty's yard had become, Arthur decided to build a fence to block his view of Betty's backyard. Believing that the old fence was built on his property, Arthur tore it down and built a new wooden privacy fence. Betty was aware of Arthur's activities but made no comment.

Last year, Betty mentioned to Arthur in passing that she was considering adding a pool and a two-car garage to her home. Arthur complained that Betty was turning her house into a "tacky, mini-mansion." From there, the relationship between the neighbors deteriorated. Issues arose over Arthur's pecan tree. The tree grew on Arthur's property, but some branches hung over the fence and caused pecans to fall into Betty's yard and onto the roof of her house, filling her gutters and causing water to back up onto her roof. Betty sought Arthur's permission to trim the branches; Arthur declined. Concerned that Betty might try to trim the tree anyway, Arthur installed a security camera to monitor access to his yard. Arthur's security camera caught images of a chainsaw-wielding Betty trimming back the branches of Arthur's pecan tree. Betty, irritated by the use of the camera, eventually built, on her own property, a higher privacy fence to block the camera's view of her yard. The height of Betty's fence prevents sunlight from reaching Arthur's prized tulips, causing them to wither and die.

Betty has sued Arthur demanding that Arthur remove his wooden fence, which is on Betty's property, and that Arthur compensate her for the damage to her roof caused by the falling pecans. In a properly pleaded cross-action, Arthur has countersued to force Betty to remove her fence.

Discuss the probable outcome of

1. Betty's action against Arthur
2. Arthur's action against Betty

Question 25

Westley and Esther are adjoining landowners in a rural area of County. Their properties were once part of a single large tract of land owned by Orson, which Orson later divided into two parcels: Westacre and Eastacre. Five years ago Westley purchased Westacre, and the small cabin located thereon, from Orson. Esther purchased Eastacre a year later. Eastacre did not contain a house or any other structure. Neither party resides full time on his/her respective property.

Prior to purchasing his property, Westley visited the property on "two or three" occasions with Orson, and during each of these visits, he utilized the old logging road ("Old Logging Road"), which runs for "about a mile," across Eastacre as a means of reaching Westacre. Although Old Logging Road is a curvy dirt and gravel road, Westley easily traversed it in his car. At the time he purchased his property, Westley was not aware of any other road leading to his property. Prior to purchasing her property, Esther also visited the property. On one occasion when she was driving around with Orson, she encountered Westley using Old Logging Road to bring building materials to his property to enlarge his cabin. She was introduced to Westley at that time. Orson informed Esther that he believed Westley would like to continue using Old Logging Road if she purchased the property, and Esther indicated to Orson that she would ***not*** be amenable to that.

Two years ago, Esther sold her land to Buyer. A few months after the purchase, Buyer encountered Westley utilizing Old Logging Road. Buyer informed Westley he was going to place a locked cable across the road but gave Westley a key to the lock. Westley had Buyer's permission to use Old Logging Road with the exception he did not want him using it during deer hunting season.

Last year Buyer placed a gate at the entrance to Old Logging Road to bar Westley from using the roadway because, according to Buyer, Westley had used Old Logging Road during deer season and had guests who frequently utilized the road and often left the cable down and unlocked. Since that time, Westley has not used Old Logging Road and has had to find alternative means of accessing his property. He was granted permission from several neighboring property owners to cross their land via a gravel road ("Schoolhouse Road") to enter his land. This route takes him up and down several difficult-to-traverse hills and across a creek. According to Westley, periodically, the Schoolhouse Road is impassable. Westley has sued Buyer demanding access to Old Logging Road.

Discuss the parties' rights.

Question 26

Jack, the owner of several acres of land, used his land as a white tiger sanctuary. Jack allowed members of the public to visit the sanctuary and observe the tigers in a more natural habitat. His land was located two miles on the outskirts of the nearest city, and there was no regulation barring such activity. After several years of raising white tigers safely and to accommodate increasing demand, Jack expanded the sanctuary to include many other endangered species, hired several employees, and began operating public tours and charging admission fees. Business is booming. Jack's sanctuary took in more than $1 million in revenue last year. Jack projects he will take in at least that amount this year.

Meanwhile, partially in response to Jack's booming business, the population of the nearby city continues to grow. City residents have increasingly expressed their fears about living so close to to Jack's sanctuary and have vocally demanded that the city council take immediate steps to address the danger posed by the sanctuary. Recently, Murray, a billionaire real estate mogul and owner of a professional baseball team, has expressed an interest in building a training facility near town. Jack's land is the ideal location. Murray agrees to devote 10 percent of the land as a park and open a picnic area for visitors to the ballpark.

A few weeks ago, as the residents always feared, a tiger escaped from the compound and killed three people. Wary of the negative publicity and fearful of another accident, the town decided to exercise its powers of eminent domain to take Jack's land and transfer it to Murray for development of a sports training facility.

The town has offered Jack $5,000 for the land. Jack says his business currently brings in $1 million per year. The current property market value is $10,000. Jack comes to your office and demands the town give his land back or compensate him in the amount of $1 million. Under the theory of eminent domain what result?

Question 27

Tom owned 100 acres of undeveloped land. A public road ("Eastern Road") bordered his land to the east. On 10 acres in the center of the lot, Tom built a home and used the remaining land as farmland. Tom created a paved road from his house to Eastern Road and used the road to access his house.

Tom was a lifelong advocate for the fair treatment of racehorses. When news broke that a former Kentucky Derby Winner—Luck Stripes—had perished in a slaughterhouse, Tom decided to divide his land into two parcels and to donate a large portion of his land (approximately 90 acres) (Parcel A) to Out to Pasteur (OTP), a charitable organization for the care of retired racehorses and to keep the remaining 10 acres (Parcel B) for himself. In his will, Tom devised Parcel A as follows: "*To Out to Pasteur, but if it should cease to exist, to Thoroughbred Racing Society of America (TRSA).*" Tom devised Parcel B to his college fraternity. Tom devised: "*to Phi Epsilon Pi, but if any hazing takes place, to Thoroughbred Racing Society of America (TRSA).*"

Tom died in 2000 while attending a horse race when a bleacher collapsed on top of him. Upon receiving notification of Tom's gift by the executors of Tom's will, the OTP gratefully accepted Tom's gift, immediately took possession of the land, and created a state-of-art facility for the care of retired race horses. Similarly, the fraternity immediately took possession of Tom's house and the surrounding acres. The fraternity members drove their sporty cars across the paved road to access the house.

Since the economic downturn began in 2007, donations to OTP have fallen off, and the charity has been slow or delinquent in paying for the upkeep of the horses. OTP has decided they can no longer operate the facility. Its board has decided to dissolve the foundation and sell the land to a developer who intends to build a residential subdivision.

Upon learning of the proposed sale, TRSA has sued to stop the sale and has demanded possession of the land. Meanwhile the local newspaper reported a tragic hazing-related death at the fraternity. TRSA immediately placed a barricade across the road leading to the frat house and is suing the fraternity for possession of the house and surrounding acreage. The fraternity has countersued to quiet title and to remove the barricade.

Discuss the parties' respective rights.

Question 28

As a result of the foreclosure crisis, many homes in Jack's subdivision are empty. Jack, a member of the neighborhood watch, often patrols the neighborhood at night, shining his flashlight into the windows of the empty homes. Last night, during his nightly patrol, Jack shined his flashlight into the front window of a vacant home and noticed a brightly colored box on the mantel. Jack entered through an open door and reached for the box. Jack inspected the box carefully but could not see a way to open it. When he held it up to his ear and shook it, he heard something rattle inside. Planning to inspect it more closely later, Jack removed the box from the mantel, placed it in his knapsack, and exited the house, carefully closing the door behind him and continued on his patrol. Once he arrived home, Jack retrieved the box from his knapsack and placed it under his bed. (Jack still lives at his mother's house and shares a bedroom with his younger brother, Adam.) Before Jack could open the box to see what was inside, he received an urgent phone call from Fran that she needed help hanging some pictures. While walking to Fran's house, Jack noticed a gold watch lying on the walk leading to Fran's house. Jack picked up the watch and showed it to Fran as he entered her home. Fran responded, "Thank you, I'll take that," and she slipped the watch into the front pocket of her apron.

While Jack was helping Fran at her house, his younger brother, Adam, walked into Jack's room and noticed the box under Jack's bed. Adam quickly determined the box was a puzzle box. After several twists and turns, Adam quickly located the hidden mechanism and opened the box, which contained a diamond engagement ring. Adam removed the ring from the box and placed the empty box back under Jack's bed. Adam then called Pat, his companion of five years, and told Pat to meet him at central park. When Adam got down on one knee and asked for Pat's hand in marriage, Pat declined, telling Adam to keep the ring because Pat wanted to date other people. A downcast Adam put the ring back in his pocket. Upon arriving home, Adam placed the ring from the box under his (Adam's) bed. When Jack returned home, he saw the open box under Adam's bed and discovered the ring inside. Just as Jack took the ring from the box to inspect it, Adam walked in and plucked the ring from Jack's fingers, declaring, "Hey, that's mine."

Discuss the parties' respective rights to:

1. The diamond engagement ring
2. The gold watch

Question 29

Places for People to Stay (PPS) is a non-profit entity dedicated to providing affordable housing for low- and moderate-income households. PPS purchased a largely abandoned 6-square-block tract of land in a depressed inner city neighborhood in San Angeles. PPS employed teams of volunteers to raze the existing structures and construct new homes. The newly constructed neighborhood was named Hope Village. PPS sold the new dwellings for the cost of construction, which is 40 to 50 percent below the cost of comparable dwellings on the open market.

In order to achieve its goal of establishing and maintaining quality affordable housing, PPS included the following language in the deed to each of the homes:

> 1. Resale Provisions: Homeowner agrees to sell his/her home to only other low or moderate-income persons at the price the Homeowner paid when s/he acquired the property. Except, upon a Homeowner's death, the interest may pass through will or intestacy to the Homeowner's spouse, children, or member(s) of the household who resided with the Homeowner for at least one year prior to the Homeowner's death.

Five years ago, Mrs. Misty Smith, a 67-year-old woman, purchased a home in Hope Village at cost, in this case for $100,000. At the closing Smith received a quitclaim deed that said: "To Smith in fee simple." The deed, which contained the above restrictions, was duly recorded.

Years later, Herb Wesson, a successful, well-to-do corporate lawyer, offered to buy Smith's home for $200,000. Smith accepted the deal, planning to buy a place in a senior living facility and use the rest of the money to play bingo. At the close of the sale, Smith conveyed a quitclaim deed to Wesson. The deed did not contain the resale restriction. Wesson immediately recorded the deed.

While packing up her belongings in preparation for her move, Mrs. Smith suffered a heart attack and died. Upon being notified of Mrs. Smith's death, Chanel, Mrs. Smith's granddaughter and only living relative, arrived from out of state to settle her grandmother's estate. While going through her grandmother's possessions, Chanel located an unlocked box under her grandmother's bed. Chanel remembered her grandmother showing her the box years ago, before Chanel moved away. (Right after Mrs. Smith purchased the property, she (Mrs. Smith) showed Chanel the box and told Chanel if anything ever happened to her (Mrs. Smith), Chanel should open the box). Inside the box, Chanel found a copy of the original deed from PPS to Misty Smith and a second deed, dated one month after the purchase, from Misty Smith to "my granddaughter, Chanel, but if the property is ever used for commercial purposes, to It Takes A Whole Village." (It Takes A Whole Village is an international humanitarian organization.) Chanel immediately recorded the deed and placed the property up for sale.

Chanel has entered into a contract to sell the property to Stop-Shop-N-Go, a chain of neighborhood convenience stores, for $250,000. Wesson has sued to prevent the proposed sale and to be declared the owner of the premises. PPS has notified Wesson and Chanel Smith that the organization is exercising its right to purchase the property for $100,000.

San Angeles is a race-notice jurisdiction for recording act purposes. San Angeles courts apply the rule against perpetuities in its traditional form.

Discuss:

1. The state of the title to the property
2. Whether PPS can re-purchase the home for $100,000

Essay Answers

Answer to Question 1

> *Important aspects:*
>
> At the start of each answer to each essay question is a listing of the main ideas you should have in mind after you've read the question and begun to think about it. Please go back and read the question another time if there are big differences between these "important aspects" and your own initial reactions to the question.

Important aspects:

The rule against perpetuities, option agreements, lives in being, bona fide purchasers, recording defects, notice.

Summary:

Alan's option agreement. The option agreement is unlikely to affect Client's rights in Sandyacre as the option agreement is likely invalid because it violates the Rule Against Perpetuities.

The conveyance to Nabor. The conveyance to Nabor is unlikely to affect Client's rights in Sandyacre as the easement likely terminated when the tunnel collapsed.

The conveyance to Edward. The conditional conveyance to Edward is unlikely to affect Client's rights in Sandyacre as the condition ("so long as Edward never marries") is likely void on public policy grounds so Edward holds the property in fee simple absolute.

Answer:

(1) Alan's (A) option agreement:

Is the option to purchase Sandyacres (S/A) valid?

The option is likely invalid, so the existence of the option is unlikely to affect C's rights in S/A. An option to purchase is a right to buy property for a stated price at some point in the future. It is akin to an executory interest and therefore is ordinarily subject to the RAP.Under the Rule Against Perpetuities (RAP), executory interests are void unless they must vest, if at all, within 21 years after an ascertainable life in being at the time the interest was created. The Third Restatement, however, recommends changing the rules so that options are not subject to the RAP. (*See* Rest. 3d Prop. (Servitudes), §3.3.) Here, assuming this jurisdiction applies the RAP to options to purchase, A's option agreement violates the RAP because of the possibility that (1) A's present wife might die, (2) A might then remarry a woman who is younger than 33 years old (i.e., ***not*** a life in being at the time the interest was created), and (3) the second wife might then outlive A and attempt to exercise the option more than 21 years after A's death. (This is an application of the unborn widow's rule).

A might contend in rebuttal, however, that the words "by his widow" in the option agreement should be read as including only A's present wife since this was probably the only person A and Oscar (O) had in mind when they made the agreement. Under this interpretation, the option does ***not*** violate the RAP because the option would vest or fail at the later of the death of A or A's then wife. Moreover, some states have passed statutes whereby the reference to a "spouse" of a living person is conclusively presumed to be that person's then extant husband or wife.

Thus, unless this jurisdiction has enacted a statute as described above or recognizes the presumption contained therein, the validity of A's option is doubtful.

(2) The conveyance to Nabor (N):

Is the easement granted in favor of N valid against Edward (E) (and thereby against Client (C))?

The validity of N's easement depends upon whether the deed provided notice to E and whether the tunnel collapse terminated the easement. An easement is a privilege to use the land of another. It is commonly created in a writing that complies with the Statute of Frauds. Here, O conveyed to N a right-of-way easement in a deed. Whether the easement granted in favor of N is valid against E (and thereby against C) turns upon whether the burden of the easement runs with the land. Generally, when the servient estate is transferred, the new owner takes it subject to the burden of the easement unless she is a bona fide purchaser for value with no notice of the easement.

(a) Is E a bona fide purchaser for value without notice of N's easement?

In states with a recording system, an unrecorded express easement is extinguished when a bona fide purchaser acquires title to the servient estate without notice of the easement. (In a race-notice jurisdiction, the bona fide purchaser must take without notice and record first). Here, since O granted S/A to E for value (i.e., E appears to be a purchaser for value), the issue is whether E had notice of the prior interest.

Courts generally recognize three types of notice: actual (subsequent owner in fact knows of the easement), inquiry (visible signs on the property would lead a reasonable buyer to inquire further), or constructive (easement is recorded within the chain of title). In this case, the facts state that E had no actual knowledge. Further, E would argue that he had no inquiry notice because the tunnel collapsed. It is unclear from the facts, however, whether evidence of the collapsed tunnel remains. If the debris remains, N could argue that E should have inquired. Although the deed in this case was recorded, it was acknowledged before a notary public whose commission had expired. In some states, a notary must certify that the person whose signature appears on the document appeared in person before the notary and executed the instrument. In some states, a defective recording (including one involving a faulty acknowledgment) does ***not*** provide constructive notice to a subsequent purchaser (E). In such a state, E would ***not*** be subject to N's express easement because N's interest terminated automatically when the land was subsequently purchased for valuable consideration by E, a party who had no notice of the earlier transfer (in a race-notice jurisdiction, E would also have to record first).

In most jurisdictions, however, where the defect is latent (i.e., does appear upon the face of the document), a subsequent grantee (in this case, E) is deemed to be on constructive notice of the earlier interest; further, many jurisdictions have curative statutes, whereby a defect in a document is deemed to be remedied when no dispute arises with respect to it for a specified period of years (usually 10 to 15 years). Here, 30 years passed without any dispute. Finally, a few states permit a defective document to afford at least inquiry notice to a subsequent grantee (and in such an instance, E would have learned of N's easement had he asked O or N about it). Thus, the validity of N's easement vis-à-vis C depends upon the applicable rule in this jurisdiction.

(b) Did the destruction of the tunnel terminate N's easement?

The majority view is that when an easement is destroyed through no fault of the servient tenement owner, the easement terminates and the servient tenement owner has no obligation to reconstruct it. Since the tunnel simply collapsed, it probably would be held that N's easement terminated. It seems that N has, in a manner, acquiesced in this result by (apparently) not making any demand upon O to reconstruct the tunnel.

Thus, assuming the tunnel was the only access to the beach (the facts are unclear on this point), N's easement probably has ceased to exist even if E had notice of it.

(3) The conveyance to E:

Is the condition ("so long as E does not marry") on the conveyance to E valid?

The interest conveyed to E by O appears to be a fee simple determinable. The words "so long as" indicate an intent by the grantor to create a fee simple determinable, an estate that terminates upon the occurrence of the stated event (i.e., when E marries), at which time the land automatically returns to the grantor (O). E would argue, however, that the condition of E remaining unmarried is void on public policy grounds since most states seek to encourage, ***not*** discourage, the institution of marriage. In such event, the anti-marriage clause would be deemed deleted from O's grant of S/A to E, which would result in E having been granted a fee simple absolute (the most unrestricted estate and that of the longest duration). C should therefore be advised that if this jurisdiction has an obvious pro- marriage public policy, it is possible that S/A would ***not*** revert back to O even if E eventually married.

Thus, C should be advised that it appears the conveyance to E is good and that E would be able to pass good title to C.

Suggested Reading

Rule against perpetuities; ELO ch.5-IX(C)(5); IX(E)(2) Easement:

- Creation of; ELO ch.9-I(A); II(B)
- Transfer of; ELO ch. 9-I(B); IV(A)
- Notice of; ELO ch.12-II(E); II(I)-II(L)
- Termination of; ELO ch.9-V(D)

Estate classification; or ELO ch.4-II(B)

Answer to Question 2

Important aspects:

Interpreting ambiguous conveyances, severance of joint tenancy, changed conditions.

Summary:

Bank v. Tom. Despite Owen's awkward language, a court could find a joint tenancy was created by Owen's grant to Sam and Doris. If Sam and Doris held Blackacre as joint tenants and these events occurred in a "lien theory" state, Bank's interest in Blackacre was probably extinguished by Sam's death. If Sam and Doris held Blackacre as tenants in common or if they held Blackacre as joint tenants in a "title theory" state, Bank may have grounds to stop Tom.

Doris v. Tom and Bank: Doris could quiet title in herself if (1) Blackacre was granted to Sam and Doris as joint tenants, and (2) no severance occurred when Sam mortgaged his interest in Blackacre to Bankk. Otherwise, D's action would ***not*** be successful.

Answer:

(1) Bank (Bk) v. Tom (T):

Whether Bk can obtain an injunction against T will depend upon the type of interest Owen created in the conveyance to Sam and Doris, the effect of S's mortgage on the state of the title, and whether the covenant is enforceable against T.

(a) Did Owen (O) create a joint tenancy or tenancy in common when he transferred Blackacre (B/A) to Sam (S) and Doris (D)?

In a joint tenancy, two or more people own a single, unified, interest in property. By contrast, in a tenancy in common, each tenant has a separate, undivided interest in the property. The most important distinction between the two is that a joint tenancy carries with it a right of survivorship, whereas the tenancy in common does not.

Whether an estate is held in joint tenancy or as a tenancy in common depends on both the grantor's intent as shown in the granting language and the surrounding circumstances. Here, O's language "to Sam and Doris, to be held by them jointly" is ambiguous as to O's intent. Bk will argue that the language should be interpreted to create a tenancy in common because joint tenancies are normally disfavored and that they should ***not*** be found to exist without specific granting language (e.g., "to S and D as joint tenants with right of survivorship"). In response, T would contend that since S and D were related, O probably intended to keep B/A in the family. T's argument is buttressed by the fact that there was only a single residence upon B/A. O probably would ***not*** have created a situation where either sibling could devise his or her interest, thereby forcing the other sibling to share B/A with a stranger. A court could find that despite O's awkward language, a joint tenancy was created by O's grant to S and D.

(b) What is the effect of S's mortgage?

If S and D held B/A as joint tenants and these events occurred in a "lien theory" state (addressed below), Bk's interest in B/A might be completely extinguished by S's death. If S and D held B/A as tenants in common or if they held B/A as joint tenants and this is a "title theory" state (addressed below), Bk may have grounds to stop T.

Generally, a co-tenant's interest is freely alienable, meaning a co-tenant can sell, transfer, or mortgage his interest without the consent of his co-tenants. Here, S borrowed money from Bk and gave Bk a mortgage on B/A to secure repayment of the loan but died before the loan came due. If a tenant in common encumbers his interest (for example, by taking out a mortgage) and then fails to repay the obligor, the creditor will succeed to the tenant in common's interest. Thus, if O's grant were determined to create a tenancy in common, the effect of S's mortgage and subsequent death would be that Bk would succeed to S's interest and Bk and D would share B/A as tenants in common.

However, if B/A has been granted in joint tenancy, the effect of S's mortgage may depend upon whether the jurisdiction is a "title theory" or a "lien theory" state; that is, whether the state treats the mortgage as a transfer of title or as a lien to secure repayment. In "title theory" states, the mortgage of a joint tenant results in a severance of the joint tenancy (and it turns the estate into a tenancy in common), and so Bk would succeed to S's interest if its loan were ***not*** repaid. If this is a "lien theory" state, however, there is a split in authority. In some jurisdictions, Bk's interest would be extinguished by S's death, meaning D would own B/A free of Bk's mortgage. In other jurisdictions, the lien would simply attach to the survivor's interest in the mortgaged portion of the property, and Bk's interest would, in essence, be the same as in a "title theory" state.

(c) Assuming this is a "title theory" state and Bk retained an interest in B/A after S's death (or even assuming this is a "lien theory" state that treats Bk's interest in the same fashion as a "title theory" state), can Bk enforce the covenant in the mortgage document against T?

Since Bk is seeking an injunction (rather than monetary damages), the covenant would be analyzed as an equitable servitude (ES). For the burden of an ES to run with the land, (1) the original parties must have intended it to run; (2) the burden must touch and concern the allegedly burdened land (although the Third Restatement abandons the "touch and concern" requirement); and (3) the party against whom enforcement is sought must have either actual, inquiry, or constructive notice of the ES. The intent requirement is satisfied by an express statement of intention, such as here where the mortgage document specifically states that it is to be binding upon S's successors and assigns. The touch and concern requirement is generally satisfied by any restrictions that limit the promissor's use of his land. Here, that element also appears to be satisfied because the use of the land is limited to use as a single-family residence. Finally, the notice requirement appears to be met as the mortgage was recorded and T likely would be charged with constructive notice of the restriction (a buyer is generally on constructive notice of any instrument recorded within the buyer's chain of title). Thus, the covenant should be good against T.

(d) Assuming the ES runs with the land, should a court enforce it against T?

T would argue that since the area has been rezoned (albeit after S's death), a change in the entire neighborhood is likely to occur soon, thereby making enforcement of the restriction against him inequitable. T's argument likely would fail because a change in zoning alone is ***not*** sufficient evidence of changed conditions to warrant lifting a residential restriction. T probably would also argue that allowing him to convert the house to a three-unit apartment building would increase the value of Bk's interest in the land. Bk would argue, however, that its original reasons for wanting S to covenant not to use B/A for any purpose other than as a single-family dwelling have not changed, and that both its original intent and agreement should be respected and upheld. Bk would argue further that the question of whether a potential increase in the value of Bk's interest will change Bk's decision should remain within Bk's discretion. Given the fact that the ES runs with the land, a court should enforce it against T. Thus Bk would be able to prevent the conversion.

(2) D v. T and Bk:

D's success depends on what interest, if any, D retains in the property as a result of O's conveyance and S's mortgage. D could quiet title in herself if (1) B/A had been granted to S and D in joint tenancy, and (2) no severance occurred when S mortgaged his interest in B/A to Bk. (See discussion, above) If B/A had been conveyed as a tenancy in common, ***or*** if this jurisdiction is a "title theory" state (or a "lien theory" state that treats the Bk's interest in the same fashion as a "title theory" state), D's action would ***not*** be successful. (See discussion, above.)

Suggested Reading

Concurrent interests

- Distinction; ELO ch.7-I(A); ELO ch.7- II(A)
- Interpretation of; ELO ch.7-I(C)(3)
- Severance of; (*See* ELO ch.7-I(E)(2)

Equitable servitude

- Transfer of; ELO Ch.9-IX(F), (H)-(J)
- Termination of; ELO ch.9-IX(O)(4)

Answer to Question 3

Important aspects:

Interpreting ambiguous conveyances, severance of joint tenancy, alienability, conditions requiring forfeiture; fixtures.

Summary:

H's rights. H likely has no right to possession of Blackacre because it appears, at his death, O had no property for H to inherit. Most courts would likely conclude that O transferred any future interest O retained in Blackacre to M before O's death. Even if H succeeded to O's future interest, H still does not likely have the right to immediate possession of the property as the placement of the storage facility probably did not result in a forfeiture.

M's rights. M has a stronger claim than H to succeed to O's retained rights. But, like H, M likely received no right to possession because the property remains in the possession of the present interest holders.

A's rights. A has the right to continue in possession as co-owner with C as the placement of the storage facility likely did not result in a forfeiture of the co-owner's interest.

C's rights. C succeeds to B's interest. Although A and B held the property as joint tenants, B's conveyance to C likely severed the joint tenancy and created a tenancy in common between C and A. As a co-owner with A, C has equal right of possession. If the placement of the storage facility resulted in a forfeiture of possession, C probably could not remove the storage facility as it likely constitutes a fixture.

Answer:

H's Rights:

H's claim rests upon what, if any, interest O retained in B/A at O's death. Whether O had any remaining interest in B/A depends upon what type of future interest O retained in B/A as a result of O's conveyance to A and B, whether O effectively transferred that future interest to M. Even if O retained an interest, the building of the storage facility may have resulted in a forfeiture of B/A.

Interpreting the O to A and B conveyance:

H would contend that the estate originally given to A and B was a fee simple subject to a condition subsequent, followed by a right of entry for condition broken ("right of entry") (also known as power of termination) in O. M, on the other hand, would contend that the estate was a fee simple determinable and O retained a possibility of reverter. If O retained a right of entry, O's attempted conveyance of that future interest to M may have been ineffective. On the other hand, if O retained a possibility of reverter, then O's conveyance of that future interest to M was likely effective. If the conveyance to M was effective, then O had no property left to convey to H and H has no right to possess B/A.

A fee simple determinable is an estate that terminates automatically upon the happening of a particular event. A fee simple subject to condition subsequent, on the other hand, does ***not*** end automatically when the event occurs. Instead, the grantor must exercise his right to take back the property. Here, the granting language ("to A and B, exclusively, as joint tenants, with right of survivorship, to be used as a parking lot, but if said premises should ever be used for a different purpose, then this conveyance shall immediately become void") is ambiguous. The words "but if" are usually associated with a condition subsequent that is subject to a grantor's right of entry. The words "immediately" and "void," on the other hand, suggest an intent to create a fee simple determinable that automatically reverts to the grantor upon the happening of the event.

Effect of O to M conveyance:

If construed as a fee simple subject to condition subsequent, followed by a right of entry in the grantor (O), H would argue that O's subsequent attempt to convey the right of entry to M was void, and therefore, H inherited O's interest upon O's death. In some jurisdictions, a right of entry cannot be conveyed by an *inter vivos* transfer to a third party. The modern and majority rule, however, is that the right of entry is transferable *inter vivos.* If this is a jurisdiction in which a right of entry cannot be conveyed *inter vivos*, O's attempt to give M an interest in Blackacre (B/A) was ineffective. Thus, O's interest would have passed to H at O's death. Or, in a small minority of jurisdictions where an attempt to make an *inter vivos* transfer of a right of entry results in the right of entry being extinguished completely, O's right of entry was extinguished altogether, and O had no property interest to convey to H or M.

If the language is construed as conveying a fee simple determinable, then O would have retained a possibility of reverter. Although a few states continue to follow the common law rule that the possibility of reverter is ***not*** transferable *inter vivos*, a large majority of jurisdictions allow it. Assuming this jurisdiction has adopted the majority view (that a possibility of reverter can be transferred intervivos), and assuming that it does ***not*** matter whether O's conveyance to M was a sale or a gift (the facts are not clear on this point), M would argue O validly conveyed his interest to M and, therefore, O retained no interest in B/A that could pass by inheritance to H.

Since courts dislike forfeitures, when confronted with vague granting language, courts tend to construe such language as creating a fee simple subject to a condition subsequent followed by a right of entry rather than a fee simple determinable followed by a possibility of reverter. However, here O's insertion of the words "shall" and "void," which seems to intend an automatic forfeiture, weighs in favor of a court interpreting the conveyance as creating a fee simple determinable followed by a possibility of reverter, which O conveyed to M, leaving nothing for H to inherit at O's death. H likely has no right to possession of B/A.

Effect of Placing Storage Facility on B/A:

H would contend that the condition in the O to A and B conveyance that B/A be used as a parking lot was violated when C placed a storage facility on B/A. H's argument raises three issues: whether the condition was indeed violated when C placed a storage facility on part of B/A; if the condition was violated, whether B/A automatically forfeit to O (the future interest holder); and whether O waived or acquiesced in the violation

H would contend that the storage facility violated the condition of the grant ("to be used as a parking lot, but if said premises should ever be used for a different purpose, then this conveyance shall immediately become void"). H, of course, would contend that the word "different" should be interpreted literally (i.e., if B/A is used for ***any*** purpose other than exclusively as a parking lot). A and C, on the other hand, would claim that the triggering event has ***not*** occurred since the granting language should be read as allowing for the termination of their fee interest only if the land is used ***exclusively*** or ***primarily*** for another purpose. Because the majority of B/A still serves as a parking lot, they would argue that it is ***not*** being used "for a different purpose." While this is a close question, given the judicial reluctance to disturb established property interests, it is likely that A and C would prevail on this issue.

Even if placement of the storage facility on B/A violated the condition, H might nevertheless have to show that H moved promptly to regain possession of the property. Many states have passed statutes requiring the holder of a possibility of reverter or right of entry to exercise the right within a specified period of time, or the right is deemed to be extinguished. Here, O was aware of the storage facility for at least year, but did not take any action to regain possession of B/A. The facts indicate that O visited the store five or six times, parking in the lot on three of those occasions, while the storage facility was being erected, and thus he must have known about it.

If no such legislation exists or it does not apply (because the specific period within which such right must be exercised has *not* expired), A and C might still contend that O (and through him, H or M) waived or should be estopped from enforcing the provision in question. After all, O failed to object to the storage facility on B/A after knowing that it was being built. In addition, since O did ***not*** object and instead appeared to acquiesce, C incurred substantial expense in enlarging his store. While H could contend in rebuttal that it is unclear whether O was actually aware that C was building a permanent storage facility on B/A (rather than, for example, a multilevel parking facility), it is likely that A and C would prevail.

M's Rights:

As between H and M, M's claim to B/A would be stronger. As discussed above, a court would likely interpret the conveyance from O to A and B as creating a fee simple determinable in A and B, followed by a possibility of reverter in O, which O conveyed to M. Since the conveyance from O to M was likely valid (see discussion, above), O had no property to devise to H at O's death.

With respect to M's rights vis-à-vis A and C, M would raise the same arguments as B (placement of the storage facility on B/A violated the conveyance and the property should forfeit to the future interest holder) and that M moved promptly to assert his rights in B/A

A's Rights:

As discussed above, A would argue that placement of the storage facility on B/A did not violate the conveyance. If that argument is unsuccessful, A might contend that only C's interest in B/A should be forfeit.

O conveyed B/A to A and B as "joint tenants, with right of survivorship," meaning A and B owned a single, unified interest in B/A. However, a conveyance by one joint tenant generally severs the joint tenancy (by destroying the unity of interest), converting the property to a tenancy in common. A might contend that B's transfer to C of B's joint tenancy interest severed the joint tenancy and resulted in B/A converting to a tenancy in common (i.e., each tenant has a separate, undivided interest rather than equal interest in the whole). While H or M would contend in rebuttal that O's grant encompassed all of B/A and clearly designated A and B as joint tenants.

C's Rights:

With respect to C's rights vis-à-vis H or M, C would raise the same argument that A raised (that placement of the storage facility on B/A did not violate the condition).

Even if C loses title to B/A, C could nevertheless argue that he should be able to remove the storage facility. At common law, a chattel (an item of personal property) annexed to the soil or attached to an existing structure became a permanent part of the land, a "fixture." Here, if the prefabricated storage facility constitutes a "fixture," C would ***not*** be entitled to remove it (unless it could be classified as a trade fixture). In determining if chattel has become a fixture (and therefore a part of the land), the courts ordinarily focus upon the intention of the party who annexed the item to the realty. This intention is usually determined from an analysis of several factors: (1) the permanence with which the item has been affixed to the land, (2) the extent of damage that will occur to the land if the fixture is removed, and (3) the usefulness of the land without the personalty at issue. H and M might contend that C intended the prefabricated storage facility to be permanently affixed to B/A, as evidenced by the facts that (1) C presumably intended to operate the retail store indefinitely, and (2) metal bolts were attached to a concrete foundation. C could argue in rebuttal, however, that (1) a prefabricated structure by its very nature is usually detachable from its cement foundation with relatively minor damage to the land, and (2) where an item is used in the land occupier's business, there is ordinarily a presumption that he intended to take it with him if the commercial operation ceased to exist. C is likely to prevail, and therefore C could remove the storage facility.

Suggested Reading

Freehold estates

- Fee simple defeasible; ELO ch.4-II(B)

Future interest

- The possibility of reverter; ELO ch.5-II(B)
- The right of entry; ELO ch.5-II(C)

Fixtures. ELO ch.8-VI(C)

Joint tenancy, severance of; ELO ch.7-I(E)

Answer to Question 4

Important aspects:

Right of co-owners to rents and profits, waste, ouster, severance of joint tenancy, oral leases, partition actions.

Summary:

Murray v. Bill. As common owners, both Murray and Bill have an equal right of possession. If Bill refuses to permit Murray's occupancy (it is not clear from the facts whether Bill has actually refused to allow Murray to join in possession), Murray will have a claim for ouster and can claim one-half rental value for the time he was ousted. Bill is probably liable to Murray for half of the profits from the timber sale and half of the rent payment received from Henrietta, but Bill may be entitled to an offset for some of the amounts he spent constructing the rental unit.

Henrietta's lease. Henrietta may be obliged to vacate the land. While Henrietta's oral lease is likely enforceable since the lease was only for a year, the lease may not survive Bill's death and probably will not survive the partition action.

Bill's death. Bill's death probably will not affect Murray's claim. The lease likely did not sever the joint tenancy; therefore, at his death, Bill's interest would go to Murray.

Answer:

(1) Murray (M) v. Bill (B):

Possession of the premises: is M entitled to possession?

M and B hold the property as joint tenants. In a joint tenancy, two or more people own a single, unified, interest in real or personal property. Each joint tenant has an equal right of possession and use of the entire concurrently owned property, subject only to the same right of occupancy by the other tenants. Here, although B currently occupies the land, M has an equal right to occupy the land. If B refuses to permit M's occupancy, M will have a claim for ouster (see below).

Lease to Henrietta (H): must B share rents collected from H?

A joint tenant may ordinarily lease all or a portion of the land to a third party, subject to the right of other co-tenants to use the entire property. The majority view is that rents received by one co-tenant from leasing a portion of the concurrently owned property must be shared with the other co-tenant(s). Thus, B probably would be liable to M for one-half of the rent payments received from H. In many states, however, B would be entitled to deduct monies he expended for improvements that enhanced the rental value of the property. Thus, if the second house B built enabled B to charge H $500 rent, but without the structure the land would have rented for only $100 per month, B would be entitled to offset $400 each month against the rentals received from H, up to the total amount he spent, before dividing the rental income with M.

Sale of timber: is B liable for waste?

A co-tenant who derives net income as a consequence of an activity that depletes the land is usually accountable to other co-tenants for their *pro rata* share of the profits. While the concept of waste is most often applied to life tenants and tenants for years, in a few jurisdictions, a co-tenant has been found liable for waste when she diminished the value of the concurrently owned land. M could therefore contend that B is liable for one-half of the net income derived from B's sale of timber. B could conceivably argue that since trees can be replanted and regrown over time, the land has ***not*** been permanently depleted. However, M probably could successfully respond that because growing trees to the timber stage ordinarily takes a very long time, B's actions should be viewed as permanent in nature. Thus, B probably would be liable to M for one-half of the profits from the timber.

On the other hand, B could argue that clearing the standing timber may actually have increased the overall value of the land. If so, B could argue that his acts ameliorated the situation and that therefore M should ***not*** recover any damages. B could also argue that his actions were motivated by a desire to make a more profitable use of the land (i.e., to cultivate fruit and crops) rather than by a desire to cause injury to it.

Profits from fruit and crops:

A co-tenant need not ordinarily account to other co-tenants for profits derived from the land that do not deplete the property. In some jurisdictions, however, B would be liable to M for one-half of the profits derived from the fruit and crops ***after*** M was refused entrance onto the land. The rationale is that B's ouster prevented M from helping B cultivate the orchard and crops.

Rental obligation of B: Does B owe rent for the value of his occupation?

While there is a minority view to the contrary, normally, unless there has been an ouster, sole exclusive possession does ***not*** interfere with the rights of the tenant out of possession, therefore the occupying co-tenant has no duty to account for the value of his exclusive possession. An ouster occurs when the tenant who is ***not*** in possession attempts to physically occupy the premises and the occupying tenant refuses to allow access. If an ouster does occur, the ousted joint tenant is entitled to recover his pro rata share of the reasonable fair rental value of the premises from the other. M might contend that an ouster occurred three years and four months ago because B occupied the land, leased one-half of the real property to H, and paid taxes on it. However, it is unlikely that M's argument would prevail because the conduct described above is consistent with the rights of a co-tenant. Nevertheless, B's refusal to permit M to enter the land six months ago ("Listen, buddy boy . . .") probably would constitute an ouster, assuming M physically tried to occupy the land (the facts indicate only that M was "ready to build his house"). If there was an ouster, B would be liable to M for one-half the reasonable rental value of the land for the six-month period preceding the partition action, unless a partition of the land had occurred prior to that time, as discussed below.

B's partition action:

B will succeed on his counterclaim for partition. A joint tenant ordinarily has an absolute right to bring an action for partition at any time. Where possible, the courts prefer to divide the land into equal shares. "Equal shares" in this context does not necessarily mean that each co-tenant receives exactly the same amount of land. Rather, it means that B and M will each receive land equal in value. The facts are silent about the value of the two houses, the fruit orchard, and the crop field. If the land cannot be divided equally, a court may require the co-tenant who would receive land of greater value to make up the difference through a cash payment to the other co-tenant (sometimes referred to as owelty).

B likely can also recover for expenses he incurred in maintaining the property. Before the proceeds from a partition are distributed, a tenant who has paid more than his share for repairs, mortgages, taxes, or improvements will be repaid from the proceeds. Thus, in B's countersuit for partition he would be able to deduct the taxes and insurance payments he made.

Moreover, while ordinarily a co-tenant is ***not*** entitled to immediate reimbursement for improvements made upon the land that other co-tenants have not agreed to, in the event of partition (to the extent that such improvements have enhanced the value of the land), the improving co-tenant usually receives a *pro rata* credit. Thus, to the extent not previously deducted from rental payments received from H, B would be entitled to recover one-half of the costs incurred in (1) creating the fruit orchard and crop field and (2) building the two houses upon the land.

(2) Rights of H:

Whether H must vacate the land will likely depend upon the validity of the verbal lease, whether the lease to H severed the joint tenancy, whether the lease survives the death of B, and whether the lease survives the partition action. H and B verbally entered into a one-year lease. While B and M might argue H's oral lease is unenforceable under the Statute of Frauds, this argument will likely fail. The general rule is that only leases for more than one year must be in writing.

The next issue is whether the lease severed the joint tenancy. Theoretically, when one joint tenant leases her interest in jointly held property, the lease destroys the unity of interest and thereby should effect a severance (which is the view taken by some states). But other states hold that the joint tenancy is ***not*** destroyed but is merely temporarily suspended (for the length of the lease). There is a split among states following the latter view (temporary severance) on what happens if the lessor/joint tenant dies before the end of the lease. Some courts hold that since the lessor's own right to possession would cease on her death, so must the right of any lessee. Others hold that the lease operates as a temporary severance and the remaining joint tenant's survivorship rights are therefore postponed until the end of the lease.

If the lease permanently severed the joint tenancy, H and B become tenants in common. H's interest would attach to B's (or in this case, since B is dead, to W's) interest. If the lease only temporarily suspended the joint tenancy, upon B's death, H's interest would be extinguished in some jurisdictions. On the other hand, if this jurisdiction follows the view that a lease operates as temporary severance and the death of the lessor/joint tenant does ***not*** extinguish the lease, then H's lease would continue.

Even if the lease did not sever the joint tenancy, the lease may not survive B's partition action. In many jurisdictions, in a partition action, the sale of premises ordinarily is made free of an existing lease; although the rule in some jurisdictions is that a sale will not affect the lessee's estate and right to possession. In the event of a physical partition, the parcel set off to the lessor/co-tenant remains subject to the lease. Thus, while H may have a cause of action against B for damages resulting from her eviction as a consequence of the partition action, H probably would ***not*** be able to successfully resist the eviction itself. If, however, the land upon which H lives is distributed to B in the partition action, H probably could prevent B from dispossessing her until the conclusion of the lease term. Since the lease term did not exceed one year, there would be no necessity for a writing signed by B for the contract to be enforceable.

(3) B's death before trial:

When one joint tenant dies, his interest automatically passes to the surviving joint tenant. M would therefore contend that he became the sole owner of the property upon B's death. Wilma could contend in rebuttal that a severance of the joint tenancy occurred before B died due to (1) B's prior lease of a portion of the land to H or (2) B's commencement of the action for partition. Wilma likely will not succeed on her first contention. While courts are in dispute about whether a lease by one joint tenant severs the joint tenancy, most courts probably hold that such a lease is not a severance. Nor would Wilma's second contention be convincing. While there is a minority view that supports it, the prevailing view is that the mere filing of a partition action does ***not*** automatically result in a severance of the joint tenancy; there is always the possibility that the parties may reconcile their differences or that the suit may be dismissed prior to a court decree dividing the property. Consequently, if B dies before the trial, it is likely that Wilma's interest dies too, so B's death will ***not*** likely affect M's claim.

Suggested Reading

Joint tenancy, severance of; ELO ch.7-I(E);

Relations between co-tenants

- Possession by one tenant; ELO ch.7-IV(B)
- Premises rented to third party; ELO ch.7-IV(C)
- Payments made by one tenant; ELO ch.7-IV(D)
- Partition; ELO ch.7-IV(E)

Future interests

- Waste; ELO ch.5-VIII(B), (D)

Statute of Frauds; ELO ch.8-II(A)(1)

Answer to Question 5

Important aspects:

Duty to deliver possession, constructive eviction, breach of the implied warranty of habitability, lease surrender.

Summary:

L's rights and remedies. L is likely liable for damages for the time R held over, but L unlikely liable for the noise disturbance, depending on the applicable housing codes (which vary by jurisdiction), may be responsible for the broken window and perhaps the broken stove.

Answer:

To advise L of his rights against T, it is necessary to first determine if T can successfully assert any defenses against L. Since there was a signed lease, there is no Statute of Frauds problem even though the period of the lease exceeded one year.

Duty to deliver possession:

Under the English rule, a landlord has the obligation to assure the incoming tenant that no other party will be in possession of the premises when the lease term commences. T might assert that L breached his duty since R was still in the apartment when T's lease term began. However, even assuming this jurisdiction adheres to the rule that the landlord has an obligation to evict holdover tenants, T probably has waived L's breach of this obligation by taking possession of the premises after R moved out. Still, T can refuse to pay any rent attributable to the period R remained in the apartment — from June 1 through June 15, and can seek to recover any damages T suffered during this period. If the American rule is followed in this jurisdiction, L has a duty only to deliver ***legal*** possession, not actual possession. Here, T obtained legal possession on June 1 when the lease began, so R would be T's problem.

Constructive eviction (CE):

A constructive eviction occurs if there is a substantial interference with a tenant's right of use and enjoyment, due to a cause for which the landlord is responsible, and the tenant vacates the premises within a reasonable time thereafter. T might argue that a CE occurred by reason of (1) the noise caused by the Pebbles, (2) the broken windowpane and warped floor, and (3) the stove's malfunction.

In response, however, L could assert the following arguments. First, with respect to the noise caused by the Pebbles, L would claim not to be responsible for the activities of other tenants. In some states, where the lease contains a provision permitting the landlord to evict lessees who are disturbing other tenants, the landlord is given responsibility for noisy tenants. However, there is nothing in the facts provided that indicates such a clause exists here. Second, even assuming the Pebbles' noise persisted from June 16 through July 15 (the date three band members were arrested), L would argue that this did ***not*** constitute a substantial deprivation of T's right to the beneficial enjoyment of the premises. The noise occurred during daylight hours, not in the evening when other tenants would be home or trying to sleep. Finally, L could argue that T waived the right to assert a CE by waiting 45 days after the noise had ceased before vacating the premises.

As to the broken windowpane and warped floor, T can maintain that the landlord's failure to maintain the property in habitable condition is sometimes considered a violation of the right of quiet enjoyment. L could argue that, at common law, it is T's duty to make repairs; thus T cannot complain about being deprived of the beneficial enjoyment of the premises when the condition that made the premises unsuitable was not L's fault. But most jurisdictions impose a continuing duty on the landlord to maintain the premises in habitable condition. L could argue that T waived the right to assert a CE by waiting two months after the window was broken before vacating the premises.

With respect to the broken stove, L could argue again that this was T's responsibility and that T apparently never even advised L about this problem, thus depriving L of the opportunity to remedy that particular problem.

The implied warranty of habitability:

Many states recognize an implied warranty of habitability that leased premises will not become uninhabitable by reason of the landlord's failure to make repairs attributable to the natural deterioration of the premises. (A few jurisdictions limit this doctrine to situations involving housing code violations.) T might argue that defects vital to the use of the premises existed in the form of the broken windowpane and subsequent warped floor and the broken stove.

Since the warping was the result of the failure to repair the broken window, whoever was responsible for repairing the window would be liable for the warped floor. L could argue that the window should have been repaired by T since (1) the pane was broken by a third party (e.g., children playing ball), as opposed to the natural deterioration of the premises; and (2) a broken window is not a defect that causes premises to become uninhabitable. With respect to the nonfunctioning stove, L could argue that the stove would not cause the premises to fall below minimal living requirements and that L was never told about the broken stove, if such is the case.

In response, T would argue that a broken window should fall within the phrase "natural deterioration" since it is to be expected that a window might break at some time through no fault of the tenant's, particularly if one lives in a neighborhood with children, and that a broken window would cause the premises to become unsafe and thus uninhabitable. In addition, T would argue that a broken stove impinges upon a very basic living requirement — the ability to cook one's own food in one's own kitchen — and thus T would contend that the premises did fall below minimal living requirements. T should contend, though, that she did not inform L about the stove because she was at wit's end. Despite T's contentions, it is likely that L would prevail against T on this issue, too.

Surrender:

T probably will also argue that L's acceptance of the keys to the apartment constituted a surrender, and therefore T is not liable for any rent accruing after August 31. However, the mere fact that L accepted the keys, without more, probably does not demonstrate a willingness to allow T to avoid her prospective obligations under the lease.

Advice on the extent of L's recovery:

(Assume that rent was payable monthly and that the lease did ***not*** have an accelerated rent or liquidated damages clause.)

L should be able to recover both T's unpaid rent for the June 16 through August 31 period and for the future months' rent payments as they become due. However, L should be advised to actively seek a new tenant for the premises; many states require a landlord to mitigate a tenant's liability, and it may be difficult for L to recover any judgment against T (even if one were obtained). Finally, L should be advised to notify T that if a sublet occurs, it is being done for T's account. This would preclude T from successfully contending that subletting the apartment constituted a surrender of the premises.

Suggested Reading

Landlord's duty to deliver possession; ELO ch.8-III(A), (B)

Landlord's remedies where tenant abandons; ELO ch.8-VII(E)

Tenant's right of quiet enjoyment; ELO ch.8-III(B), (D)

Answer to Question 6

Important aspects:

Tenancy for term of years, holdover tenants, renewal of tenancy, lease assignment, subleases, consent clauses, third party beneficiary, constructive eviction.

Summary:

O v. T. O will likely prevail on the issue of the lease renewal. O gave sufficient notice of intent to renew. Even though O breached the agreement by unreasonably withholding consent to the assignment, S waived the breach by failing immediately to remove the equipment. T (jointly with S) would be liable for rent from February to April. T's obligation to pay rent ended when fire gutted the premises, but O can recover for the value of the fixtures destroyed in the fire.

O v. S. Even though no privity of estate existed between O and S, O could nevertheless enforce the lease against S under third-party beneficiary theory. S (jointly with T) is liable to O for rent from February through April (when the constructive eviction occurred), as well as for the value of the fixtures.

Answer:

O v. T (rent):

O's ability to collect rent from T will depend upon the length of the lease between O and T, whether T remained liable on the lease after T's conveyance to S, whether S improperly held over at the end of the lease.

Tenancy for Term of Years:

O would contend that the original lease with T was for a fixed term of two years, from February 1, 2010, to January 31, 2012. T could contend that the original lease arrangement was merely a periodic tenancy (rather than one for a fixed term) because the precise date upon which the term would conclude was apparently not stated in the written lease. The termination of a periodic tenancy takes effect at the conclusion of the term following the one in which notice is given. T would assert that the applicable term in this instance is month-to-month since the rental payments were made monthly and O was notified on April 10, 2012, that S "no longer considered himself to be liable for rent," therefore any liability to O under the lease ended as of May 31. O could argue in rebuttal that the lease was for a fixed term since the concluding date of the lease was easily calculable (i.e., January 31,

2012) in that the lease referred to both an aggregate rental amount and a constant monthly amount. Indeed, a court probably would conclude that the original lease was for a fixed term of two years.

Holdover Tenancy:

O likely would prevail on his argument that the lease renewed for one year when S failed to remove his dry cleaning equipment within a reasonable time upon expiration of the lease term. When a tenant holds over after his lease has ended, the landlord has the right to choose to bind the holdover tenant to a new term. In some jurisdictions, the new term is limited by statute to one year, regardless of whether the original lease was for a longer period of time.

T, however, could make several arguments in rebuttal to O's assertion. First, T would argue that S, not T was in possession at the end of the fixed term as T assigned his interest to S and had no further liability upon expiration of the lease. But given that T had reserved the right to reenter the premises if S failed to pay the rent, T's argument will likely fail. Moreover, O would contend that T was nevertheless liable because S and T were tenants in common. When T introduced S as a possible successor tenant, O consented only to "add" S to the lease, without prejudice to O's rights against T.

Second, even if S and T were tenants in common, T might contend that leaving the equipment in the building did not constitute sufficient "possession" of the premises to justify applying the holdover tenancy doctrine. However, since dry cleaning equipment is probably large enough to have prevented O from reletting the premises, O should prevail on this issue.

Notice of Renewal:

Third, T would contend that he was not properly notified that O intended to renew the term. Generally, a holdover tenant must be notified that the landlord is renewing the lease. Here, while S received notice of O's intent to renew, the copy mailed to T at his old address was not forwarded to T's new address. Thus, T might next contend that he never received actual notice of O's election to renew the original tenancy. O might also argue that notifying one co-tenant constitutes constructive notice to all co-tenants. Alternatively, O could argue that T was properly notified. The success of this argument would depend upon whether notice in this jurisdiction is satisfied by mailing a properly stamped, addressed, and deposited envelope or by actual receipt by the addressee. The facts are silent about T moving to a new address or why the note was not forwarded.

Consent to Assignment:

T could next contend that even if the lease was renewed, O materially breached the contract on February 15, 2012, by not permitting S to sublet the premises to Z based on Z's ethnicity. (The contract specifically stated that the lessor's consent to an assignment or sublease shall not be "unreasonably withheld.") Some courts require that the landlord offer a commercially reasonable reason for objecting to the assignment. Such reasons generally cannot rest on illegal grounds or grounds that violate public policy. Here, a desire to discriminate based on ethnicity may be illegal (while the fair housing act is limited to residential dwellings, some state civil rights statutes prohibit commercial landlords from discriminating on various basis, including race and national origin). Even if not explicitly illegal, discrimination on the basis of ethnicity likely violates public policy. Thus, T would assert that he is not liable for rent accruing after that time. However, O could probably successfully argue in rebuttal that even if her conduct (unreasonably withholding consent) constituted a material breach, this breach was waived by S's failure to remove his equipment immediately thereafter.

Constructive Eviction:

T could argue that a constructive eviction (CE) occurred on April 1. A CE occurs where a tenant is deprived of the beneficial enjoyment of the leased premises because of some occurrence or condition for which the landlord is responsible. T could contend that a CE occurred when O's security guard negligently caused the fire that gutted the premises. O would attempt to counter this assertion by claiming that, in the lease agreement, the Lessee waived any acts of negligence by O or her employees. However, T could probably successfully argue in rebuttal that (1) the provision exculpates only acts of negligence, not gross negligence (smoking near highly flammable cleaning fluid would constitute gross negligence); and (2) the clause in question pertains only to lawsuits for negligence asserted by the Lessee, not to the assertion of a CE as a defense to the payment of rent by the Lessee. T should prevail and therefore probably would ***not*** be liable to O for rent accruing after April 1, 2012, but would remain liable for the rent during February and March.

O v. T (fixtures):

O could contend that as a result of S's failure to comply with the lease provision to maintain insurance, O sustained a loss in the amount of $7,000, the value of the destroyed fixtures and equipment. However, T could argue in rebuttal that (1) the Lessee was obligated to keep only the fixtures insured (not the equipment) and only the fixtures belonged to the Lessor at the end of the lease, so he is not liable for the equipment; and (2) the phrase "fixtures required for operation of a retail clothing store" is too vague to be enforceable (since one could presumably operate a retail clothing store without any fixtures, those installed by T were not so "required").

While the first argument probably would succeed, the second one would not. A court probably would rule that the fixtures T installed were "required" regardless of whether one could hypothetically operate a retail clothing store without them; therefore, T would be liable to O for the value of the fixtures destroyed in the April 2012 fire.

O v. S (rent and fixtures):

S could contend that he has no liability to O since (1) he never expressly agreed to be liable under the lease (O merely agreed with T that S could be added to the lease); and (2) there was no privity of estate with O since S was merely a sublessee (rather than an outright grantee of T's leasehold interest), as evidenced by the fact that T reserved the right to reenter the premises if S defaulted. However, O could argue in rebuttal that (1) S, in effect, agreed to be liable under the lease since the latter was presumably aware of O's written statement to T; and (2) because T transferred his rights under the lease to S, S should also be deemed to have assumed T's duties thereunder. Thus, O would be a third-party beneficiary between T and S, and it is likely that O would prevail on each of the foregoing contentions. Even though no privity of estate existed, S probably would be liable to O for any obligations arising under the lease.

If S had assumed T's obligations under the lease, he would assert the defenses described above under ***O v. T*** (except for the notification issue).

Summary:

S and T are liable to O for rent from February 1, 2012, through April 1, 2012 (when the CE occurred), as well as for the $2,500 value of the fixtures.

Suggested Reading

Types of tenancies; ELO ch.8-II

Tort liability of landlord and tenant; ELO ch.8-V(C)

Assignment and subletting; ELO ch.8-VII

Answer to Question 7

Important aspects:

The Statute of Frauds, part performance, anticipatory repudiation, surrender, conditions of lease premises.

Summary:

Tom v. Omar. Tom's action for specific performance will likely fail. Tom probably can overcome Omar's anticipated Statute of Frauds defense and show an enforceable contract based on Tom's actions in part performance. But, Tom's action would ultimately fail because of Tom's repudiation of the contract when he advised Omar he was moving out and was no longer interested in purchasing the land.

Omar v. Tom. Tom is liable for rent for February and March but not responsible for rent after O re-let to Jill because Omar failed to take the steps necessary to hold Tom to a new term and accepted Tom's surrender when Omar re-let to Jill

Answer:

(1) Tom (T) v. Omar (O) in Specific performance action:

If T sues O for specific performance, O probably would raise the defenses of Statute of Frauds (SOF) and anticipatory repudiation (AR).

According to the SOF, contracts for the sale of land must be embodied in a writing that contains the essential terms and is signed by the party against whom enforcement is sought. Even assuming the verbal understanding between O and T was sufficiently definite as to its material terms, O could contend that since his agreement with T to sell the land was not in writing, it is unenforceable. T could argue in rebuttal that, under the part performance doctrine, where a grantee has done acts that "unequivocally refer" to the existence of the alleged oral contract, the SOF is overcome. In a number of states, this standard is satisfied when the grantee has entered upon the grantor's land and made valuable improvements thereto. Although T was already on O's land as the operator of the gas station, he could argue that absent a contract to purchase the land, he would not have expended $18,000 on improvements ***after*** his lease term had expired, and the fact that O did not demand rent in February and March indicated that their relationship was changing. The facts are silent about whether the new equipment could be removed by T without incurring great expense and creating substantial damage to the premises. The more difficult and expensive it would be to remove the equipment, the greater is the likelihood that

T would be successful on this issue. While O could contend that making the improvements described above could be explained by T's ***expectation*** that a contract for sale would be arranged subsequently (rather than by the existence of an actual agreement), T should prevail on this issue.

Even assuming that T prevailed on the SOF issue, O could contend that T made an AR of the contract when he advised O that he was moving out and was no longer interested in purchasing the land. (An AR occurs when one party unequivocally advises the other that she will ***not*** perform her prospective contractual obligation.) Retraction of an AR is ***not*** possible once the innocent party has relied upon it to his detriment. Since, in the interim, O entered into a nine-month lease with Jill and a contract to sell the land to Samuel (and therefore would be liable to S for damages if he were to complete the transaction with T), it is unlikely that T would be permitted to retract his repudiation at this point. Thus, T's action for specific performance should fail.

(2) O v. T for rent:

O could initially contend that T was a holdover tenant, thereby entitling O to renew the lease for a period of time equal to the original lease term or, presumably, for any shorter period of time. (Many states have enacted legislation that limits this renewal period to one year.) However, T could probably successfully contend in rebuttal that a landlord is required to notify the tenant of such an election, and since O failed to notify T of the renewal before March 15 (the date T advised O that he would be moving out), O's attempted renewal of the first term was no longer possible. T's arrangement with O probably would be characterized as a month-to-month tenancy since, under the lease, T paid rent on a monthly basis.

Assuming a month-to-month tenancy existed, T's notice of termination must be given prior to the month at the conclusion of which the lease is to be terminated. Consequently, O could argue that the March 15 notification would not take effect until May 1, and T would be liable for rent for February and March, as well as for the $200 difference in April.

T, however, could make several counterarguments. First, T could contend that O had agreed that no further rent would be required of him, and thus T had been released from any further obligation to make rental payments. However, O could probably successfully contend in rebuttal that (1) since this understanding was an integral part of their land sales contract, evidence of it is inadmissible under the SOF (discussed above); and (2) this understanding (even if admissible) was impliedly conditional upon T purchasing the land within 90 days. O should be successful with respect to the second argument, and therefore T would ***not*** be released from paying rent.

T could next contend that he was relieved of his rent obligation under the lease by reason of O's failure to repair the premises after the March 5 mudslide. However, since a landlord of commercial premises ordinarily has no obligation to make repairs unless she was somehow responsible for the condition or occurrence that caused the damages, this argument will also probably fail. Even in the few jurisdictions that do recognize a landlord's obligation to maintain leased commercial premises, this duty is ordinarily ***not*** extended to repairs required by acts of providence. Finally, T could probably successfully contend that a surrender by operation of law occurred when O relet the premises to Jill. While a surrender will ***not*** be presumed where the landlord notifies the prior tenant that the reletting has been done for the latter's benefit, no such statement was made by O in this instance. O merely informed T that T would be held responsible for rent in February and March, as well as for the rent differential through December 31.

In summary, O probably can recover rent only for February and March (an aggregate amount of $2,000).

Suggested Reading

Statute of Frauds, part performance doctrine; ELO ch.11-I(B)(3)

Types of tenancies; ELO ch.8-II(E)

Condition of leased premises; ELO ch.8-IV(G)

Landlord's remedies, T abandons; ELO ch.8-VII(E)

Answer to Question 8

Important aspects:

Servitudes, notice, zoning, inverse condemnation.

Summary:

Xavier v. Annie. The proposed station would mean the elimination of 100 parking spaces and likely violates the covenant between Owen and Xavier. Although Annie was not a direct party to the covenant, Annie, who had notice of the covenant, is likely bound by the promise Owen made to Xavier.

City v. Annie. Even in the unlikely event the ordinance constituted an inverse condemnation, City could still prevent Annie from erecting the sign. Annie would only have the right to compensation equal to the diminished value of the land.

Answer:

(1) Can Xavier (X) prevent Annie (A) from building the service station?

The issues are (1) whether the burden of the covenants that Owen (O) made to X runs with the land (i.e., binds A) and (2) whether X can enforce the benefit of the promise that O made to him against A.

Does the burden of the covenant run with the land?

Since X is seeking an injunction (i.e., equitable relief rather than monetary damage), under traditional analysis O's promise to X should be analyzed as an equitable servitude (ES). Traditionally, for the burden of an ES to run with the land, (1) the promise must be enforceable between the original parties, (2) original parties must have intended it to run, (3) it must touch and concern the burdened land (the Third Restatement abandons the "touch and concern" requirement), and (4) the burdened parcel owner must have been on notice of the promise. (See Rest. 3d Prop. (Servitudes), §3.2.)

Since the deed between O and X stated that O had covenanted for his "heirs, successors and assigns," there seems to be little doubt that the covenant was intended to run with the land. Also, the promise touches and concerns the burdened land (Lots 3-8), since A's use of her land is restricted by the requirement that at least 500 parking spaces will be available.

In a minority of courts, for the burden to run, both the benefit and burden of the covenant must meet the "touch and concern" test. The Third

Restatement rejects this view. Indeed, the Third Restatement advocates eliminating the "touch and concern" element altogether. (*See* Rest. 3d Prop. (Servitudes), §3.2.) However, if this is a jurisdiction that requires that the restriction "touch and concern" the benefited parcel, X will contend that the covenant touches and concerns his land, too, since the unavailability of the parking area will render X's planned use of Lots 1 and 2 virtually ineffective. X will also contend that such unavailability would arguably diminish the value of the land since prospective department store customers would simply choose to shop at a more convenient establishment. A would argue in rebuttal that (1) the covenant does not affect X's use of its land since X is not required or restricted from doing anything with respect to it, and (2) X's fear that the value of the land will be diminished because potential shoppers will be discouraged is only speculation. X likely will prevail because the value of his land probably would be affected by the significantly reduced amount of available parking.

X will next contend that A was either on constructive or inquiry notice of the parking area covenant. In some jurisdictions, a subsequent grantee is deemed to be on constructive notice of ***all*** prior recorded conveyances within the county made by her grantor (even if they were not directly within the grantee's chain of title). This is because a prospective grantee, in searching the typical grantor/grantee index, would ascertain the point at which the grantor obtained the land being conveyed. The grantee would then inspect all subsequent grants made by the grantor. In such jurisdictions, A presumably would have discovered the deed that O had delivered to X and therefore would have notice of O's promises in that deed. However, some jurisdictions consider a grantee to be on notice only of promises made by the grantor that are contained in the grantee's direct chain of title. Since A, searching through the grantor/grantee index for information about Lots 3-8, would not discover the promises that O made to X involving Lots 1 and 2, A would ***not*** be on constructive notice of O's promise. This is a close question since courts are about evenly split on the issue.

Even if A is not on constructive notice, X might be able to contend that A was on inquiry notice. Inquiry notice exists where there are facts or circumstances that would lead a prospective grantee to believe that the land that she is acquiring may be subject to some unrecorded interest or claim. The prospective grantee is charged with whatever notice a reasonable inquiry would have revealed. Here, the facts are silent as to how A became aware of O's covenant to X concerning the sale of tires and petroleum products. X might contend, however, that since A was aware that O had promised X no tires or petroleum products would be sold on Lots 3-8, A should have asked X whether O had made any other promises involving the same lots. X should prevail on this argument, and therefore A probably would be deemed to be on notice of O's promise to X concerning the parking area.

Should the court enforce the ES?

Since equitable relief is always discretionary, even if the burden of an ES does run with the land, the court may elect to deny X's request for an injunction.

A could contend that upon a balancing-of-hardships analysis, the construction of the service station should not be prevented since (1) A is leaving 90 percent of the stipulated, nonexclusive parking spaces that were to be available to X (O had promised X there would be at least 500 parking spaces, and here 450 spaces would remain); (2) any lost profits to X from the decreased parking are purely speculative; and (3) the inconvenience to X is outweighed by the definite financial loss that A believes she will incur by her inability to build a service station (this assumes that the service station will be profitable, which is also speculative). However, X probably could argue in rebuttal that (1) the inability to prove damages is precisely why an injunction should be permitted (money damages will not suffice since X could never show with reasonable certainty the number of potential department store customers who went elsewhere because of insufficient parking); and (2) since the construction of the service station would violate a covenant of which A clearly had notice (i.e., that no tires or petroleum products may be sold on the premises), A does not have "clean hands." Again, X should prevail unless there is evidence of an abundance of parking spaces in the surrounding area, with little likelihood of growth there. Consequently, A probably will not be able to build her service station.

(2) Assuming that A was permitted to build the service station, can the municipality enforce the zoning ordinance?

A might contend that the zoning ordinance is invalid because it represents an improper use of the police power (i.e., the statute in question appears to be concerned exclusively with aesthetics). However, the municipality can probably successfully argue in rebuttal that the ordinance is a safety measure and thus is reasonably related to the health and welfare of its citizenry. It presumably would enhance driver visibility and thereby reduce the possibility of vehicular accidents. Assuming the ordinance was passed ***after*** A acquired her interest in Lots 3-8, A might contend that the imposition of the ordinance results in a deprivation of property (i.e., A's right to make the most profitable use possible from her land) without due process of law. However, to constitute a "taking" for Fifth Amendment purposes (applicable to the states via the Fourteenth Amendment), the restriction on the owner's use of her land must be substantial and result in a significant diminution of the owner's economic expectations with respect to that land. Since the curtailment on A's use of Lots 3-8 is relatively minor (the shopping center can still be maintained, and that asset presumably represents the bulk of A's economic return from the land), the municipality should prevail. In addition, even if an inverse condemnation was found to have occurred, the statute probably would not be deemed to be null and void. Instead, A probably would have only the right to compensation equal to the diminished value of her land.

Of course, if the ordinance had been passed before A acquired Lots 3-8, then she would have virtually no possibility of success. In such a case, she would be held to have recognized that the land must be used in a manner consistent with the ordinance.

Suggested Reading

Equitable servitudes; ELO ch.9-IX(H)

Notice; ELO ch.12-II(I)-(L)

Zoning; ELO ch.10-II(B)

Takings; ELO ch.10-I(C)

Answer to Question 9

Important aspects:

Adverse possession, color of title, licenses, easements in gross, interpreting ambiguous conveyances, fee tail.

Summary:

Danny's claims. Danny cannot claim ownership of Sweetholm because his possession likely does not satisfy the "hostility" element for an adverse possession claim. In the unlikely event Danny successfully claims title through adverse possession, Danny could sue Alicia for wrongful eviction and recover the reasonable rental value of the land during his eviction.

Triver's claims. Trivers probably cannot force Alicia to remove the fence. Trivers's purchase of Laurel Hill likely did not include a right to access Alicia's land. While Alicia promised Wilson in writing she would allow the wolves to roam freely over Sweetholm, the writing likely created a license (or perhaps an easement in gross) in Wilson but did not appear to the promise was intended to run with the land.

Other claims. At common law Vladimir's conveyance to "Josiah and the heirs of his body" would have created a fee tail, and, upon Josiah's death without issue, Sweetholm became the property of Richard (Ludwig's sole heir). Most jurisdictions, however, have abolished the fee tail and would view Vladimir's conveyance as creating a fee simple absolute in Josiah. (In that case, title of Sweetholm would pass to Jennifer, Josiah's heir.) On the other hand, a court could find that the presence of the wolves on Sweetholm violated the condition in Vladimir's conveyance and title reverted back to Vladimir's estate (i.e., Gustaf, Vladimir's sole heir). Whether Richard, Gustaf, or Jennifer was successfully declared the owner of record, Alicia's claim to title based on adverse possession likely trumps that of the record owner.

Answer:

Danny's claim to Sweetholm: adverse possession (AP):

Danny (D) will claim that he obtained title to Sweetholm through adverse possession. The elements for AP are satisfied where the adverse possessor enters upon and continuously and exclusively occupies another's land in an open, notorious, visible, and hostile manner throughout the requisite statutory period. In many jurisdictions, the AP must also show that his possession is pursuant to a claim of right. But most courts hold that the claim of right requirement is synonymous with the hostility requirement.

D could claim that by remaining at Sweetholm after the sale to Alicia (A) without A's explicit permission, the "hostile" element is satisfied. In addition, D would argue, having a separate mailbox and putting out a welcome sign that bore his name would meet the "open" and "notorious" requisites. Finally, D would argue that his occupation of the guest house continued for a period of time in excess of the ten-year statute of limitations. Thus, D could claim ownership to the guest house (along with an easement to get to it) under AP, but his claim may not be persuasive.

A could contend in rebuttal that D failed to satisfy the "claim of right" requirement. A minority of courts hold that the claim of right requirement is not satisfied unless the adverse claimant went upon the land with the belief that he was entitled to possess it. If this were such a jurisdiction, D's claim of AP would fail. In most states, however, the claim of right element is satisfied merely by the adverse possessor being in possession of land without the owner's permission. Alternatively A could claim that D's occupation of the guest house was ***not*** "hostile." While this element is usually satisfied by the claimant's use of the land in an "open and notorious" manner, an exception exists where the rightful owner would not necessarily recognize that the adverse possessor's occupation of the land is hostile to her ownership interest, even though she is aware of it. In such situations, the adverse claimant must communicate (via clear words or actions) that the land is being held in derogation of the legal owner's rights. For example, holdover tenants are usually deemed to be occupying the premises with the landlord's implicit permission. Here, A knew when she bought the property that D was already living in the guest house and communicated to J that it probably would be "all right if Danny did not get in her way." The facts are silent as to whether A's statement to J was communicated to D.

A could contend that D should be viewed as having been either her guest (i.e., a continuation of the relationship that D enjoyed with J) or a tenant at sufferance. In either event, D would have been obliged to (1) inform A that his occupation of the guest house was hostile to A's claim of ownership or (2) act in a manner that clearly communicated this view (e.g., by preventing A from entering the structure such as by building a fence around it). The mailbox would not suffice since A could have presumed that while D had felt comfortable in permitting J (D's cousin) to receive his mail, he would not have the same trust in a stranger. Finally, A would assert that the doormat was not adequate to inform her that D was claiming superior title to the guest house.

A probably would prevail upon the "hostile" issue, and therefore it is unlikely that D would prevail upon his claim of AP.

If, however, D's claim of AP were successful, he would have a right of action against A for evicting him. D probably would be entitled to recover the reasonable rental value of the land during his eviction, as well as any other costs and expenses that resulted from the interference with his right to possession.

Trivers' (T) claim to Sweetholm:

Trivers will claim he succeeds to the benefit of an easement created in favor of Wilson (W).

Easement:

The issue here is what type of interest W received from A — an easement or a license — and whether T succeeds to benefit of that interest. T might first contend that A had granted an express easement to Wilson (W) permitting animals involved in the experiment to roam throughout Sweetholm. T will further contend that the easement was appurtenant to W's land and the benefit of the easement automatically passed to T when T purchased the benefited land. A would respond that the right given to W was a license, not an easement, and such interests are (1) ordinarily not assignable and (2) revocable at any time by the licensor (subject to the licensee's right to recover for monetary damages resulting from the revocation). An easement usually is a permanent right to use the land of another. A license, on the other hand, is a revocable privilege to use the licensor's land. A could assert that she did not grant W a permanent right to ***use*** her land. Rather, A would contend that she merely gave W permission to let the wolves wander freely over Sweetholm. Thus, A would contend that the grant made to W was a license. T, however, could argue in rebuttal that being engaged in an experiment whereby the wolves wandered onto A's land, W (and now T) was actually ***using*** the land for a particular purpose (i.e., to record the results of an experiment). A court likely would conclude that W had a mere license.

Even if the grant to W was an easement, A could contend that it was an easement in gross (rather than an appurtenant easement). An easement in gross is one whose benefit is not tied to a particular parcel of land. While most modern courts hold that easements in gross are assignable, some courts maintain that personal easements are not assignable. The grant in question appears to have been made for the purpose of facilitating W's experiment (rather than enhancing the use or accessibility of Laurel Hill).

While T could argue that the use of Laurel Hill is enhanced by having the right to permit animals involved in the experiment to cross onto adjoining land, this probably would not be persuasive, and A's grant probably would be characterized as an easement in gross.

T might contend, however, even if the grant to W was an easement in gross, that it should be viewed as being "commercial" in nature. Such interests have been deemed to be irrevocable where, for example, a severe disruption to a utility (e.g., telephone or sewer lines) would occur. Although T could contend that maintenance of the fence by A would disrupt an experiment that has been carried on for a 14-year period, it is unlikely that T's easement in gross would be considered "commercial." Thus, A probably would prevail on this question.

Covenant:

Finally, T might argue that A's written statement to W, whereby A had agreed that she would take no action to prevent W's animals from coming onto Sweetholm, constituted a covenant that ran with the benefited land. Since T is seeking an injunction, the covenant must be analyzed as an equitable servitude (ES). Traditionally, for the benefit of an ES to run against the covenantor: (1) the promise must be enforceable between the original parties, (2) the original parties must have intended it to run, and (3) in some jurisdictions it must touch and concern the benefited parcel). The Third Restatement advocates eliminating the touch and concern requirement. (*See* Rest. 3d Prop. (Servitudes), §3.2.) Although there was no "successors, heirs and assigns" language, some courts take the view that where the promise touches and concerns the burdened parcel, the original parties probably intended for the covenantor's promise to run with the benefited land. The value and use of Sweetholm is arguably diminished by the fact that wild animals could roam free on a portion of the land. However, A could probably successfully contend in rebuttal that there was no intent that the promise run with the land since the promise was given specifically to ***W*** for the purpose of permitting him to complete ***his*** experiment.

Thus, T probably ***cannot*** obtain an injunction against A.

Other Claims to Sweetholm:

Fee tail:

Richard (Ludwig's sole heir) could contend that the conveyance by Vladimir to Josiah was a fee tail since the grant was followed by the words "and the heirs of his body." Therefore, when Josiah died without issue (Jennifer (J) was merely his niece, rather than a lineal descendant), Sweetholm became the property of Ludwig and his heirs.

A could argue in rebuttal that in many states the fee tail has been abolished entirely and in the majority of states it is viewed as a fee simple absolute. Thus, if viewed as a fee simple absolute, Josiah would have been entitled to transfer the property to Jennifer. In some jurisdictions, however, the failure to have issue results in the estate terminating upon the death of the originally designated party. Under the latter view, Ludwig's heirs (Richard) would obtain title to Sweetholm upon Josiah's death.

Defeasible fee:

Gustaf (G) could contend that the grant from Vladimir was a fee simple determinable or fee simple subject to a condition subsequent with respect to the deed provision pertaining to animals ("If animals, birds or children are ever kept on the property, the estate is to cease and determine."). G would argue that the triggering event occurred when D retained one of the animals for a two-week period. However, A could contend in rebuttal that any future interest held by G is unenforceable because implicit in the grant was that the ***grantee*** (rather than some other person who undertook such conduct without the owner's knowledge or consent) would not "keep" animals on Sweetholm. A should prevail on this argument, and therefore it is unlikely that G could presently claim paramount title to Sweetholm.

Adverse possession under color of title:

Even if Ludwig's heir (Richard) or Vladimir's heir (Gustaf) is deemed to be owner of record of Sweetholm, A could probably claim superior title to Sweetholm through AP. While it is not clear when Josiah died and Jennifer succeeded to possession of Sweetholm, the facts do indicate that A has apparently occupied the realty for 11 years and paid taxes on it. Having purchased the land from Jennifer, A presumably went into possession of Sweetholm under color of title. It therefore appears that A could defeat any claim of Richard to the property.

Suggested Reading

Adverse possession; ELO ch.3-II-IV, VI

Easements; ELO ch.9-I(B). II(B), IV(B)

Fee tail estates; ELO ch.4-III(C)

Answer to Question 10

Important aspects:

Covenant held in gross; implied reciprocal negative servitude; third party beneficiary, spite fences, lateral support.

Summary:

The main issue in this question is whether owners within a subdivision can enforce restrictions against their neighbors where some, but not all, of the lots contain express restrictions. Here, while deeds to Lots 14 and 16 contain restrictions, Lot 16 was sold without a restriction.

Alex v. Dave. While there is no direct promise between Alex and Dave, Alex can nevertheless prevent Dave from violating the restrictions because the benefit of the promise made by the original owner of Lot 16 to Owen runs to Alex, and the burden of the promise runs to Dave.

O v. D. Owen, however, probably cannot prevent Dave from violating the restrictions as Owen no longer owns any land in the subdivision.

Dave v. Alex. Dave may have rights against Alex under a nuisance theory since the fence was erected for the purpose of making Dave uncomfortable.

Alex v. Bank. Even though the excavation was conducted by Baker, Alex can recover against Bank for damages caused by its failure to provide lateral support during the two month period Bank was the legal owner of Lot 14.

Answer:

The language in the deeds appears to be a covenant (as opposed to an easement).

(1) Alex (A) v. Dave (D): can A prevent D from building as planned on Lot 16?

(a) A appears to be a property party to enforce the promise relating to Lot 16.

The covenant A seeks to enforce was made to Owen (O) by the original grantee of D's lot (Lot 16). Since A was not the original grantor of Lot 16, the first inquiry is did the benefit of the covenant made to O by the original grantee of Lot 16 run with the land? Traditionally, for the benefit of an equitable servitude to run with the land, (1) the promise must be enforceable between the original parties, (2) the original parties must have intended the benefit of the covenant to run with the land, and (3) in some jurisdictions, the benefit of the covenant must touch and concern the land. Moreover, the Third Restatement advocates eliminating with the touch and concern requirement. (*See* Rest. 3d Prop. (Servitudes), §5.2.)

While the exact language of the deed is not provided, if the original Lot 16 deed expressly stated that it was binding upon the successors and assigns, then the intent element is met. Even if the original Lot 16 deed did ***not*** expressly state that it was binding upon the successors and assigns of each party; most courts will conclude that restrictions of this type were intended to run with the benefited land. This is so because it is presumed that the developer/covenantee will ultimately sell all of the lots, and therefore the restrictions that she required could be enforced only by her subsequent grantees. Since the covenants in question restrict the use by D of his land, there is little doubt that the "touch and concern" condition is satisfied with respect to the burdened parcel.

D might contend that the covenant does not touch and concern A's (the benefited) land, since the construction of a two-story home might actually enhance the value of adjacent land (presumably, subdivisions within which two-story houses can be built are more valuable than those within which only one-story homes are permitted). However, A could probably successfully argue in rebuttal that permitting deviations from a uniform development plan within a subdivision could ultimately lead to no restrictions at all, which in turn would diminish the value of each landowner's parcel. Thus, the "touch and concern" requirement with respect to the benefited parcel is probably also satisfied.

(b) D is likely burdened by the promise relating to Lot 16.

Since D was not the original grantee of Lot 16, the next inquiry is *did the burden of the covenant run with the land?* Traditionally, for the burden of an ES to run with the land, (1) the promise must be enforceable between the original parties, (2) the original parties must have intended it to run with the land, (3) the burden of the ES must touch and concern the burdened parcel, and (4) subsequent grantees of the land must have been on notice of the covenant. The discussion above with respect to the first three conditions would apply equally here. Since the facts state that all deeds were recorded, D would be on constructive notice of the restrictions agreed to by the initial grantee of Lot 16. Thus, the burden of the ES would also run with the land.

Based upon the foregoing, both the benefit and the burden of the ES ran with their respective parcels of land. Therefore, A has a right to enforce against D.

(c) A can likely enjoin D from building on Lot 16.

D could contend that equitable relief should not be granted in this instance because (1) A has not come into court with "clean hands" (i.e., she never agreed to the covenant that she is attempting to enforce, and she has violated the restrictions by erecting the 20-foot wall); and (2) using a balancing-the-hardships analysis, any diminution in value to A's land would be outweighed by (a) D's inability to construct what he considers to be a comfortable home on his land and (b) the decreased value of D's land (a two-story home is presumably worth more than a single-story residence). In rebuttal, however, A could argue that (1) she built the 20-foot wall only to dissuade D from breaching the restrictions, and she would remove it if D is enjoined from deviating from the restrictive covenants; (2) she has observed, in fact, all the restrictions (except for the 20-foot wall, which she is willing to remove when D agrees to comply with the restrictions); (3) D should not be allowed to repudiate a promise of which he had knowledge; and (4) it is entirely possible that A's land would be significantly devalued if D is permitted to ignore the restrictions since a potential buyer of A's land would be uncertain about whether the covenants pertaining to the subdivision were enforceable.

A should prevail, and therefore a court probably would require D to build in accordance with the restrictions, conditioned upon A removing the creosote wall (which probably constitutes a nuisance — discussed below).

(2) O v. D: O probably cannot enforce the promise relating to Lot 16 against D.

A covenant is enforceable only by persons who own land that was intended to benefit by the promise. Here, the original grantee of Lot 16 made a promise to O in his capacity as owner of the remaining unsold parcels. There was no indication that the original parties intended any land outside of O's subdivision to be benefited by the covenant. It is therefore unlikely that O, who no longer owns any benefited property, could prevent D from building as planned (even though O presently resides immediately adjacent to the subdivision).

(3) D v. A: D probably can require A to remove the wall under nuisance theory, but not under a third party beneficiary theory or theory of implied reciprocal servitudes.

(a) Implied reciprocal negative servitude:

Even if O did not expressly covenant to D that all parcels in the subdivision would contain similar restrictions to those contained in D's deed (the facts are unclear on this point), D can attempt to enforce the restriction under a third-party beneficiary theory or as an implied reciprocal servitude. To imply reciprocal covenants by the developer/grantor into earlier deeds within a subdivision, there ordinarily must have been some justification for the earlier covenantees to have expected subsequent deeds in the subdivision to be bound by similar restrictions (i.e., a plat map evidencing a common scheme or plan, verbal representations by the developer, statements in advertising literature, etc.). The facts do not indicate that O advised any of the original grantees that subsequently sold parcels would be similarly burdened. Thus, there does not appear to have been a plan or scheme of development at the time the original grantee of Lot 16 acquired the land.

In addition, even if a covenant by the developer/grantor were implied into earlier deeds within the subdivision, A, the owner of Lot 16, would not be burdened by the promise unless A was at least on inquiry notice that such a reciprocal covenant might be implied into the original deed given by O. In this case, there would be no reason for A to be on notice of it (Lots 14 and 16 were undeveloped at the times he purchased Lot 15). Thus, there is little likelihood that D would have the right to assert an implied reciprocal covenant against A.

(b) Third-party beneficiary:

Alternatively, D could argue that A is bound to follow the restriction based on a third-party beneficiary theory. Courts recognize that promises between the original covenanting parties may create benefits in third parties. Generally, the parties should make their intent clear in writing, but courts also will infer the intent to benefit third parties from the circumstances. (*See* Rest. 3d Prop. (Servitudes), §2.6.)

(c) Nuisance:

D, however, probably could require A to remove the wall under a nuisance theory. A nuisance occurs when the defendant has, in a nontrespassory manner, caused a substantial and unreasonable interference with the plaintiff's use or enjoyment of the latter's land. Since the motivation for the fence was unreasonable (i.e., it was erected exclusively for the purpose of making D uncomfortable), and darkened surroundings and odor emanating from the wall would constitute more than minor inconveniences to D, a nuisance would be found. Therefore, a court probably would require A to remove the creosote wall.

(4) A v. Commercial Bank (Bank): lateral support:

Every landowner has a right to have her land in its natural state physically supported by the adjacent soil. The landowner has a right to recover from an adjoining landowner where the failure by the adjoining landowner to laterally support her land caused the former's land in an unimproved condition to slide. While the excavating that caused A's prize flower bed to slide onto Lot 14 was done by Baker, Bank (as the legal owner of Lot 14) nevertheless had a two-month period to provide lateral support vis-à-vis Lot 15. Thus, Bank is probably liable for the actual damages suffered by A and will be required to artificially support A's land.

Suggested Reading

Equitable servitudes; ELO ch.9-IX(D), (F), (G), and (K)

Covenants; ELO ch.9-VIII(C)

Nuisance; ELO ch.13-I

Lateral support; ELO ch.13-II(A)

Answer to Question 11

Important aspects:

Lateral support, Statute of Frauds, covenant enforcement, easements by necessity and implication.

Summary:

Bayard v. Cullom. Albrights's oral promise notwithstanding, Cullom, as Albright's successor had right to lateral support from neighbor Bayard and can sue Bayard for the damages that flow from Bayard's excavation. Further, Cullom may keep the sewer pipe and enjoy a permanent easement across Bayar's property as an easement in favor of Cullom was created by implication or by necessity.

Answer:

(1) Cullom (C) v. Bayard (B): excavation:

(a) Lateral support:

A landowner ordinarily must provide whatever lateral support is required to prevent an adjacent neighbor's unimproved land from sliding as a consequence of excavation undertaken by the former. Here, B's proposed excavation will likely cause Albright (A's) land to subside. B, of course, will contend that this obligation has been waived by reason of the oral agreement to this effect between B and A. However, C could assert several theories as to why A's promise to B is unenforceable.

(b) Waiver:

C will contend that since A's promise to B was not contained in A's deed to B, it cannot be enforced by B. Promises that pertain to an interest in real property must satisfy the Statute of Frauds (SOF) (i.e., must be embodied in a writing that describes the interest involved and is signed by the party against whom enforcement is sought). However, B could contend in rebuttal that (1) A's promise was merely collateral to the sale of an interest in land and so was not subject to the SOF, (2) C (as A's assignee) should be promissorily estopped from asserting the SOF since B detrimentally relied upon A's promise in deciding to purchase his lot, and (3) there has been substantial performance of the original contract by B's accepting A's deed and going into possession of the land. B's contentions would be persuasive, and thus, the promise by A to B, though verbal, should be enforceable.

(c) Breach:

Assuming the SOF is avoided, C could next contend that implicit in A's promise to B was that B would begin and conclude his construction of the commercial building within a reasonable period of time. Since a reasonable period of time appears to have passed and A no longer owns the adjoining parcel, the period of time envisioned by A and B during which the promise would be effective has expired.

B, of course, would contend that no time limitation was placed on the original promise. C should prevail on this issue.

(d) Equitable servitude:

Assuming that B is able to enforce the oral promise, the next inquiry is whether B can enforce the promise against C. Since C would be attempting to enjoin B from beginning the excavation without providing lateral support (rather than seeking monetary damages), A's promise must be analyzed as an equitable servitude (ES). Traditionally, for the burden of an ES to run with the land, (1) the promise must be enforceable between the original parties, (2) the original parties must have intended it to so run, (3) the promise must touch and concern the burdened parcel, and (4) the subsequent grantee of the burdened parcel must have had (actual, inquiry, or constructive) notice of the promise.

As discussed above, it is unlikely that the oral promise is enforceable. Even if it were enforceable, there is no indication that A and B intended A's promise to be binding upon subsequent transferees of the land (there was apparently no "successors and assigns" language). B could contend that many courts take the view that any promise that touches and concerns the burdened land must have been intended to run with the property. However, C could probably successfully contend in rebuttal that A's promise to B was predicated upon B's intention to build a commercial structure upon Lot 1 in the ***immediate*** future. It is therefore unlikely that the parties intended the promise to burden subsequent purchasers of Lot 2.

Traditionally, the "touch and concern" requirement usually was deemed to be satisfied where the promise affected the use or value of the burdened land, although there was a minority view that found this element satisfied only where the use of land was affected. The Third Restatement abandons the touch and concern requirement. (*See* Rest. 3d Prop. (Servitudes), §3.2.) B could probably successfully contend that the promise touches and concerns the land because Lot 2 is rendered less valuable if the lateral support requirement normally imposed upon Lot 1 is no longer extant (in fact, Lot 2 might almost be worthless until B's construction is completed). Therefore, B should prevail on the "touch and concern" issue.

The facts do not indicate whether C had notice of A's original promise to B. The promise was not contained in A's deed to B; nor would there be inquiry notice since viewing Lot 1 would ***not*** have suggested to C that A had agreed to waive the lateral support requirement.

Thus, since the "intent to run" and "notice" requirements are absent, A's covenant to B would ***not*** be enforceable vis-à-vis C, even though the "touch and concern" requirement has been met.

(2) C v. B: Removing the sewer line:

C could contend that the sewer line constitutes an easement across B's property and is therefore not removable by B. C would argue that this easement arose by implication or, alternatively, by necessity.

(a) Easement by implication:

An easement by implication arises where (1) the land was previously held by a common grantor, (2) the servient tenement was used for the purpose for which the easement is now being claimed before the severance of the dominant and servient parcels, (3) such use was reasonably apparent and continuous at the time of the severance, and (4) the easement is reasonably necessary to the enjoyment of the dominant tenement. (*See* ELO ch.9-II(C).) Here, Albert owned Lots 1 and 2 and later sold Lot 1 to B and Lot 2 to C. B will contend that the "reasonably apparent" element is absent since the sewer line was not discovered until he had razed the house on his lot. However, C could probably successfully contend in rebuttal that most jurisdictions find the "reasonably apparent" element satisfied if the easement would have been discovered upon a reasonable inspection of the lot. Because a reasonable inspection of a home would include the crawl space beneath the floor, the element should be deemed satisfied. In addition, since the cost of an alternative sewer line would be prohibitive, the "reasonably necessary" element is also met.

Although some jurisdictions are reluctant to find an easement by implication where the alleged easement was retained by the party who transferred the servient tenement (the rationale being that the grantor could have explicitly reserved an easement over the grantee's land if he desired to do so), it is not an absolute bar to recovery.

(b) Easement by necessity:

C would also argue easement by necessity. An easement by necessity arises if the necessity for the easement existed at the time the dominant and servient tenements were severed and the easement is strictly necessary. B might argue that since it was at least possible for C to run the sewer lines across other land, there is no strict necessity and therefore this theory should fail. However, C could probably successfully contend in rebuttal that since the cost of a new outlet for the sewer would be prohibitive, the "high degree" of necessity required in most states is satisfied. Moreover, the Third Restatement proposes relaxing the strict necessity standard to one of reasonable enjoyment standard, unless the language or circumstances of the conveyance indicate a contrary intent. (*See* Rest. 3d Prop. (Servitudes), §2.15.) If the jurisdiction follows the restatement view, C could show that the easement was reasonably necessary even though C might have been able to run the sewer line over other property. Therefore, under either theory (by implication or necessity), an easement in favor of C probably exists. C may keep the sewer pipe and enjoy a permanent easement across B's property.

Suggested Reading

See ELO ch.13-II(B)

See ELO ch.11-I(B)

See ELO ch.9-IX(F)

See ELO ch.9-II(C)(4)

Answer to Question 12

Important aspects:

Implied reciprocal negative servitudes, common plan, nuisance, scope of easement, spot zoning, and trespass.

Summary:

Phil and the Other Lot Owners are likely to sue Barb for breach of covenant, nuisance, trespass, and for exceeding the scope of the easement. Barb is likely not bound by the restrictions on the other lots. Barb purchased lot 6 without a restriction. It is unlikely that P and OLO can make a claim for an implied reciprocal covenant on such weak evidence of a common scheme or plan. Whether P and OLO may successfully claim nuisance if noise from the nightclub will depend on weighing the utility of the activity versus the harm. The empty bottles thrown by B's patrons constitute a trespass. P and OLO owner's strongest argument may be that Barb's proposed use of the adjoining parcel exceeds the scope of her easement as the volume of cars that will be using the easement vastly exceeds the parties' original expectations.

Answer:

Reciprocal covenants:

Since Phil (P) and the Other Lot Owners (OLO) probably would want to enforce this covenant against Barb (B) in equity (i.e., obtain a permanent injunction requiring B to use her parcel for residential, not commercial, purposes), V's implied promise should be analyzed as an equitable servitude (ES). Traditionally, for the burden of an equitable servitude to run with the land, (1) the promise had to be enforceable between the original parties, (2) the original parties must have intended it to be binding upon the covenantor's grantees, (3) the promise must touch and concern (i.e., affect the value or use of) the burdened parcel, and (4) the covenantor's grantee (in this instance, B) must have notice of the covenant.

Express covenant by V:

B could first contend that the words "To preserve high quality within this development" do not constitute a promise by V to restrict the remainder of the subdivision to residential dwellings. If this is what the earlier purchasers desired, they could have easily insisted upon clear language to that effect (e.g., "V hereby promises that all parcels within the development shall be restricted to residential dwellings"). P and the OLO will argue in rebuttal that they reasonably understood the language in question to be a covenant by V to limit the subdivision to residential use because this is the only means by which "high quality" could be preserved. However, without a plat map or similar document indicating that a uniform or comprehensive development scheme of residential housing was envisioned by V, B should prevail.

Assuming, however, that P and/or the OLO prevail on the foregoing issue, B might next contend that since there was no "successors and assigns" language in the deeds given to the OLO, there was no intention by the original parties that the ES run with the land. However, the plaintiffs could probably successfully argue in rebuttal that where a covenant affects the value or use of real property, most jurisdictions will presume that the original covenantor and covenantee intended it to be enforceable against subsequent possessors of the land.

In some states, a grantee is deemed to be on notice of all prior grants made by his grantor within the county. In such jurisdictions, B would be deemed to be on notice of the deeds pertaining to Lots 1-4 and 7-10 (and therefore would be on notice of V's purported promise to restrict subsequently sold parcels to residential uses). In other states, however, a grantee is only deemed to be on constructive notice of documents contained in his direct chain of title. In the latter type of jurisdiction, B would ***not*** be charged with knowledge of V's promise to the OLO.

Finally, B could contend that P should not be permitted to enforce the alleged express covenant by V since he was (or should have been) aware, at the time he purchased Lot 5, that B was not using her parcel for residential purposes. Therefore, he cannot now complain about B's use of Lot 6 for commercial purposes. P might have presumed, however, that since a zoning ordinance requiring single-family residential dwellings had been passed three months before P purchased Lot 5, B's compliance with the ordinance would be imminent. P reasonably could have assumed that B would not simply ignore the ordinance.

Implied reciprocal covenant:

If P and OLO cannot enforce the language in question as an express promise to restrict V's remaining parcels P and OLO could contend that a reciprocal covenant (limiting land in the rest of the subdivision to residential use) by V should be implied into the deed that B received. However, there would be little likelihood of success on this theory since, except for the language that appeared in the deeds themselves, the facts are silent as to any indicia that suggest that there was a common scheme pertaining to the development (i.e., a plat map, verbal statements made by V to purchasers of the lots, etc.).

Assuming there was an explicit restrictive covenant and P or the OLO could enforce it, B could also contend that it had been waived by reason of the inaction of the OLO. B has been engaged in her business for three years, and even P had purchased his lot one year ago. B could also argue that P and the OLO should be estopped from asserting the covenant now because P has purchased additional land from Farmer. B would seem to have a good chance of prevailing upon these arguments.

Even if an ES restricting the land to residential uses was found and was deemed to run with the land, equitable relief is always discretionary with the courts. Thus, B could argue that her use of Lot 6 as a nightclub should not be enjoined because (1) of laches (the facts discussed above with respect to waiver and estoppel would apply equally with respect to this theory); (2) on a balancing-of-hardships analysis; the economic loss that B would incur far outweighs any inconvenience that P and the OLO would be forced to endure; and (3) B's use of Lot 6 as a nightclub is consistent with the newly designated "commercial" rezoning of Lot 6. P could contend in rebuttal that the equities weigh against B since (1) she had used Lot 6 for commercial purposes at a time when to do so was completely contrary to the zoning ordinance, and (2) the discomfort suffered by P and the OLO outweighs the financial loss that will be suffered by B. However, it is unlikely that B would be obliged to convert her parcel into a residential dwelling at this late date.

Nuisance:

A nuisance occurs where the defendant has, in a nontrespassory manner, caused a substantial and unreasonable interference with the plaintiff's use and/or enjoyment of his land. (*See* Restatement (Second) of Torts §821B.) P and the OLO could contend that B's nightclub is causing them discomfort and inconvenience due to the loud music late at night. B could contend in rebuttal that the nightclub should not be considered a nuisance because (1) she is using the land in a manner authorized by the applicable zoning ordinance (although this fact ordinarily is not, *per se*, dispositive with respect to whether a nuisance is occurring); and (2) at least with respect to P, the fact that he purchased Lot 6 after B had established the nightclub would militate against a successful finding in P's favor or on P's behalf. The facts are silent as to precisely how loud the music from B's nightclub becomes and how late into the evening it can be heard. However, if it is played late into the evening (i.e., after 10 PM on weekday nights or 11 PM on weekend nights), at a volume sufficiently high to annoy a person of ordinary sensibilities, it is likely that P or the OLO would prevail (especially given the low utilitarian value of B's activity).

Even assuming that B's nightclub constituted a nuisance, an additional question exists as to what remedies are available to the plaintiffs. While P and the OLO probably would desire a permanent injunction, given that (1) to preclude B from using her land as a nightclub probably would result in substantial economic loss to her (especially since she has already purchased additional realty from Farmer), and (2) B has been using Lot 6 in the complained-of manner for three years without any litigation being commenced, it is likely that a court would enjoin B only from playing music at unreasonable hours and restrict her to acceptable noise levels. Also, P and the OLO should be able to recover damages equal to the decreased value of their land.

Trespass:

Since nuisance is generally limited to invasions by nonphysical forces, the occasional bottles thrown by B's customers probably do not constitute a nuisance. They may, however, give rise to a trespass claim. Trespass is an interference with the plaintiff's right to exclusive possession. Such invasions can be committed not only by the trespasser in person, but also by instrumentalities under his control, including objects left on plaintiff's land.

Spot zoning:

Zoning ordinances must be made in accordance with a comprehensive plan. Amendments that do not comply with such a plan are illegal (such ordinances are sometimes referred to as "spot zoning"). Since the County Commissioners advised P that Farmer's land was a likely shopping center site, they apparently have not prepared a comprehensive plan. P and the OLO therefore could contend that changing Lot 6 to "Commercial" was an invalid act and that Lot 6 should be returned to "Single Family Residential" use. However, most jurisdictions permit the appropriate governmental entity to develop the plan through a series of disconnected zoning ordinances. Since this is probably what is occurring in this instance, this attack by P and the OLO will probably ***not*** be successful.

Scope of B's easement:

P and the OLO could contend that B's proposed expansion will exceed the scope of her express easement. They would argue that the easement was merely for the use and benefit of Lot 6; it would be unduly burdensome to allow persons parking on the additional acre that B purchased from Farmer to use the easement. In addition, the volume of cars that will be using the easement vastly exceeds the original parties' expectations. B, however, could argue in rebuttal that (1) the easement is not being used by different parcel owners, but merely by additional guests of Lot 6; and (2) unless explicitly limited, easements are ordinarily interpreted to include uses that arise from the normal, foreseeable development of the dominant estate as long as the use does not impose an unreasonable burden on the servient estate. B probably would prevail on this issue, given that (1) the easement has been used by B's patrons for three years without formal complaint about the increased vehicular flow; (2) the misconduct by B's present customers appears to be isolated instances that are more properly dealt with by police authorities, rather than prejudicing B; and (3) the rock stars' funerals presumably would be relatively rare occurrences.

Summary:

It is unlikely that P or the OLO could impair B's business operations, except that unreasonably loud music played late into the night probably would be restrained.

Suggested Reading:

Equitable servitudes; ELO ch.9-IX(H)

Covenants; ELO ch.9-VIII(C)

Nuisance; ELO ch.13-I

Zoning; ELO ch.10-IV(D)

Easements, scope of; ELO ch.9-III

Answer to Question 13

Important aspects:

Title disputes, common law "first in time, first in right" rule, recording acts, nonconforming uses.

Summary:

Whether Baker ("B") or Charles ("C") will prevail in a quiet title action depends upon which party has a superior claim under the applicable recording act. Under the common law rule, first in time, first in right, B would prevail over C because Olga conveyed the property first to B and later conveyed the same property to C. C would prevail, however, in a pure notice jurisdiction where a subsequent grantee prevails over a prior grantee as long as the subsequent grantee took without notice. As for reopening the tavern, C could successfully argue that C should be able to continue its nonconforming use as long as C did not abandon the use.

Answer:

(1) The quiet title action between Baker (B) and Charles (C):

(a) Title disputes: common law:

Priority to the tavern will depend upon the type of recording act, if any, enacted in this jurisdiction. The common law rule was that the first person to receive his legal interest in the land had priority over subsequent grantees. Here, Olga (O) conveyed Harvard Place (HP) to B and later conveyed the same property to C. At common law, B prevails.

(b) Recording acts:

Recording acts allow subsequent grantees to prevail over the first in time grantee under certain limited circumstances. In a pure race jurisdiction, the first to record a clean chain of title from the grantor prevails over an earlier grantee. Here, B was both the earlier purchaser and the first to record. B prevails in a race jurisdiction.

In a pure notice jurisdiction, a subsequent grantee who acquires title to the land for value and without notice of the earlier conveyances has priority over earlier grantees. Here, C, the subsequent grantee prevails only if C took title to the land for value and without notice of B's prior interest. B could contend that C was on inquiry notice because C received a quitclaim deed. Here, O conveyed all of her "right, title and interest" in HP. A conveyancing document that states only that the grantor is conveying her "right, title and interest" is usually construed to be a quitclaim deed, and in a few jurisdictions, acceptance of a quitclaim deed charges the recipient with whatever facts would have been obtained from asking the grantor as to the validity of title to the land. However, C could probably successfully argue in rebuttal that (1) the majority view is that a quitclaim deed does ***not*** put the recipient on notice of any defect in the grantor's title to the land; and (2) even if he had asked O why only a quitclaim deed was being tendered, O probably would have not answered his inquiry honestly (i.e., since O was aware of her prior conveyance to B, she probably would have said she simply did not want to accept the risk of liability for a legal interest about which she was unaware). Assuming C is ***not*** deemed to have notice of B's interest by reason of his receipt of a quitclaim deed, C would prevail in a notice jurisdiction.

B probably would prevail in a race/notice jurisdiction. In a race/notice jurisdiction, a subsequent grantee for valuable consideration who has no notice of the prior conveyance at the time the deed is delivered to him and is the first to record a clean chain of title against the land in question has priority over earlier grantees. Even if C did not have notice of B's earlier interest (see discussion, above), nevertheless, B would prevail in a race/notice jurisdiction because C failed to record before B.

Finally, in the unlikely event that this jurisdiction has not adopted a recording statute, B would contend that because she received her interest before C, and because both parted with valuable consideration (B gave up a right of action against O for payment for medical services), she should have priority to the tavern. However, C could successfully contend in rebuttal that B should be equitably estopped from asserting her interest in the tavern vis-à-vis C, since B failed to record her deed for six-and-a-half months (which presumably could have been done quite easily), and that B allowed O to remain in possession of the premises (thereby making it possible for O to mislead a subsequent grantee of the land).

(2) May C reopen the tavern?

There are two bases upon which Waterbury (W) can contend that a reopening is prohibited: (1) while the zoning ordinance provided for continuation of any existing nonconforming use, since the tavern was closed at the time the ordinance became effective, the nonconforming use was not "in existence" on July 1, 2008, the effective date of the ordinance, and therefore the tavern's subsequent reopening was unlawful; and (2) because of the nine-month liquor license suspension, C's decision to close the tavern would constitute an "abandonment" within the meaning of the zoning ordinance.

(a) Nonconforming use:

As to the first contention, C would argue that (1) closing the tavern temporarily due to an injury did not cause it to cease to exist, especially since the merchandise and fixtures remained intact; (2) the equitable doctrine of laches applies, since W's failure to enforce the ordinance for three-and-a-half years resulted in substantial prejudice to C (C would not have purchased the tavern if he had any reason to believe that its operation would violate a three-and-a-half year old ordinance); and (3) W's construction of the statute would violate O's (and thereby derivatively C's) due process rights under the Fourteenth Amendment since it would amount to a taking of property (a substantial and unexpected diminishment of the value of land) without compensation. Because W does not appear to have a viable response to these arguments, C should prevail on W's first theory.

(b) Abandonment:

As to W's second theory (closing the tavern during the nine-month suspension would constitute an "abandonment"), C could (1) contend that the word "abandon" is ordinarily associated with a voluntary relinquishment of property, and therefore the word "voluntary" should be implied into the ordinance prior to the word "cessation" and (2) assert the due process argument described above. However, W would argue in rebuttal that (1) the plain meaning of the statute is clear, and there is no qualification of the word "cessation"; and (2) assuming the suspension procedure satisfied due process, there has been no"taking."Rather, C himself is responsible for the loss of the nonconforming use if he does not continue to operate the tavern (e.g., selling coffee and soft drinks) during the liquor license suspension. It is not clear at what point in the nine-month suspension this question is being asked. If less than six months has passed since C closed on January 19, 2012, C should be advised to reopen the tavern and sell something other than liquor to preserve the commercial use of the tavern. It is unknown whether C will again be able to serve liquor at the end of the nine-month license suspension, but at least C would not have lost all commercial rights. If, however, the nine-month suspension has already expired, W probably would prevail, based on the second theory discussed above, and it would be unlikely that C could legally reopen the tavern.

Suggested Reading:

Recording acts; ELO ch.12-II

Zoning; ELO ch.10-III

Answer to Question 14

Important aspects:

Adverse possession, trespass, riparian rights.

Summary:

Baker's rights. B likely obtained title through adverse possession based on B's occupation of the land.

Carla's rights. C is unlikely to have an action against B for the oil drilling as B, the owner of land overlaying the pool has an equal right as C to extract the oil. B, on the other hand, may have a claim against C to the extent that C trespassed on B's land to extract the oil.

Downstream Owners' rights. The rights of the Downstream Owners depend on the riparian rights doctrine adopted in their jurisdiction—reasonable use, natural flow, or prior appropriation. Under the reasonable use doctrine, B would be required to share the water equally with those DROS, whose use would also be considered artificial. Under the natural flow doctrine, B would have no liability for using the water for cultivating his crops but may be liable to the DROS for any financial loss they suffered due to the decrease in the river's flow because of the dam, but they could not prevent B from performing his contract with City. Under prior appropriation, B would not be liable for water used to cultivate his crops, but DROS could recover for the reduced flow attributable to the dam and perhaps could prevent B from performing the contract with City.

Answer:

(1) Baker's (B's) rights in the land:

Adverse possession:

The facts indicate that the statute of limitations period for real property actions in Myth is ten years. Thus, B could contend that he acquired title to the land by adverse possession (AP). The elements for AP are satisfied where the adverse possessor enters upon, continuously and exclusively occupies another's land in an open, notorious, visible, and hostile manner throughout the requisite statutory period. In many jurisdictions, the AP must also show that his possession is pursuant to a "claim of right." But most courts hold that the claim of right requirement is synonymous with the hostility requirement. In a few jurisdictions, the adverse possessor must also have paid the real property taxes pertaining to the land during the applicable period of time. Thus, B would assert that the combination of building a fence around the entire 400 acres, planting and harvesting crops on the land and paying the real estate taxes for 7 of the 11 years he was on the land constitutes open, notorious, and hostile conduct.

Able's daughter could argue that (1) some courts hold that the "claim of right" requirement is not satisfied unless the adverse claimant went upon the land with the belief, even if erroneous, that he was lawfully entitled to occupy it (which B did not, as evidenced by his statement to Carla); and (2) B's nonpayment of real estate taxes for 4 of the 11 years is a fatal flaw. As to the first contention, B would likely respond that most states adhere to the view that the "claim of right" element is satisfied as long as the adverse possessor is occupying the land without the owner's permission. However, if the minority view is followed in this jurisdiction, B has not acquired title to the land, and Able's daughter would still be the lawful owner. She would accordingly have a right against B for (1) *mesne* profits (i.e., the reasonable rental value of the land) for the period of time during which B grew crops on the land and (2) damages, to the extent that the land has been diminished in value as a result of B's activities. The daughter's second argument, about nonpayment of taxes, would probably not be persuasive since B paid the taxes for the majority of the years in question, although the facts do not indicate whether the four years of nonpayment were consecutive or intermittent (perhaps this could be viewed as an important distinction).

(2) & (4) Rights to the oil and the slant-hole well:

The majority view is that a landowner has a right to extract oil that is underneath the surface of her property. If in doing so the oil is drained from beneath the surface of a neighbor's land, the neighbor has no recourse against the extractor (since there is always the possibility that oil could naturally seep into the adjacent land). In addition, it is often impossible to prove how much oil was extracted from beneath each party's real property. If this view is adhered to in Myth, neither B nor Carla (C) has any rights against the other with respect to the oil they have each extracted from beneath their lands. However, B probably would have a right to recover damages from C to the extent that oil was obtained through the slant-hole well, since it encroached onto B's tract. In the slant-hole situation, C is deliberately withdrawing oil from beneath another's land interest (i.e., the oil is not merely "escaping" into C's land). Thus, C would have committed a trespass (an intentional intrusion upon, beneath, or above the surface of another's land) vis-à-vis B's right to the oil underneath B's land.

There is, however, a minority view whereby oil in its underground state is viewed as unowned, similar to an animal *ferae naturae.* In such a jurisdiction, oil becomes the property of anyone who has obtained possession of it without actually going upon another's land. If this view were followed here, B would have a right of action against C only for the oil obtained through the one well that encroached upon the substrata of B's tract, but would have no action against C for the oil obtained through those wells that do not trespass on B's land.

(3) Rights of downstream owners against B:

There are three actions for which B may be liable in this instance. First, B appropriated 100,000 cubic feet per day from the river for the irrigation of his crops. Second, B created the dam that reduced the flow of water to the downstream riparian owners (DROs). Finally, he entered into the recent contract with City to sell it water from the water wells.

(a) Reasonable use doctrine:

Under the "reasonable use" doctrine (which is probably the prevailing view in the United States), a riparian owner may make any reasonable use of a waterway abutting her land (including the sale of water to a nonriparian party) provided that (1) such use does not significantly interfere with a similar or more beneficial use of the water by DROs, and (2) there is no permanent depletion of the waterway (since public policy usually desires the preservation of existing streams, rivers and lakes). In deciding what constitutes a reasonable use, the courts distinguish between "artificial" and "natural" uses and also consider whether due regard has been given to the rights of other riparian owners. Here B used the river water to irrigate his crops on a large expanse of land, and this type of large-scale irrigation is generally held to be an artificial use. Thus, B would be required to share the water equally with those DROs whose use would also be considered artificial. And B would not be allowed to take any water for artificial uses until the needs of those DROs requiring water for natural uses had been satisfied.

It is unclear from the facts whether the DROs who relied upon the waterway for manufacturing purposes were significantly injured by B's dam. However, given the above restrictions placed on B's artificial use of the water, the DROs probably could obtain an injunction requiring B to remove the earthen dam and they also probably could recover for damages resulting from B's action, particularly if the reduced flow rendered the DROs' businesses more expensive or less productive. On the other hand, since the facts seem to indicate that as much as six years have elapsed since B created the dam, B could argue, perhaps successfully, that there has not been a substantial interference with the DROs' operations. If this conclusion is accurate, then B may not have any liability for damages to the DROs as a result of the dam.

Finally, no liability would lie with respect to the diminution of the water table unless the DROs could show that the water wells constructed for City's benefit ultimately would result in depletion of the waterway. If DROs could show that the wells inevitably would deplete the waterway, the DROs probably could enjoin B from performing his contract with City.

(b) Natural flow doctrine:

Under the "natural flow" doctrine (the second most popular doctrine), a riparian owner can use as much water as necessary for commercial purposes, except that (1) a DRO can restrain any use that results in a material diminution in the quantity or quality of water flowing to him (regardless of whether he is harmed), and (2) nonriparian uses are ***not*** permissible. Under this view, B would have no liability with respect to the water used to cultivate his crops. However, to the extent that B's dam has caused a material decrease in the river's flow to the DROs, the DROs could enjoin continued use of the dam even if they cannot show they suffered any financial loss. However, since the dam appears to have been in existence for six years apparently without any complaint by the DROs, the DROs may now have difficulty contending that the river's flow has been seriously diminished by the dam. The DROs, however, probably could prevent B from performing his contract with City, since nonriparian uses are not permitted.

(c) Prior appropriation doctrine:

Numerous western states follow the "prior appropriation" doctrine, whereby water rights (both riparian and nonriparian) are determined by priority of beneficial use, subject to an earlier user's right to compensation when her water flow is diminished by a subsequent, higher priority usage. Under this theory, B would not be liable for water used to cultivate his crops since this conduct resulted in no diminution to the uses being made of the waterway by other parties. Both irrigation of a large tract of land and using water for manufacturing purposes would be classified as "commercial" uses, and therefore neither usage would have priority.

As to the reduced flow attributable to the dam, the DROs probably could obtain an injunction and recover for any financial loss that resulted to their prior operations. Whether the DROs could impede performance by B of his contract with City would depend upon whether (1) the court viewed the furnishing of water to City as a higher priority than manufacturing purposes, and (2) the DROs could prove that the water basin would eventually be depleted. In the absence of such proof, B probably would not be restrained from furnishing water to City. If providing water to City were deemed to be a higher priority than manufacturing, the DROs would be entitled to compensation for their inevitable loss. If the manufacturing processes, however, were deemed to constitute a more beneficial use and if it could be demonstrated that the water basin would eventually be depleted, the DROs probably could restrain B from performing the contract with City.

Finally, there are a few jurisdictions that overlay the "reasonable use" and "natural flow" theories with the "prior appropriation" doctrine. In these states, the rights that were vested at an earlier point in time are entitled to compensation from the party whose use of the waterway has been given priority.

Suggested Reading

Adverse possession; ELO ch.3

Water rights; ELO ch.13-III(B)

Answer to Question 15

Important aspects:

Title disputes, common law "first in time, first in right" rule, recording acts, bona fide purchasers, the shelter doctrine, deed covenants.

Summary:

B v. D. B will likely win his action against D as B has superior claim to title of Blackacre under a race-notice recording act. Under a race notice act, D, the subsequent purchaser, must establish that she was the first to record and did not have notice of the prior conveyance. Although D recorded the deed she received from C prior to B, she was not the first to "duly record." Many jurisdictions require the subsequent purchaser to be the first to record a clean chain of title. To perfect the chain of title, D would have had to record the A-to-C deed and then record the C-to-D deed. The omission of the last six words from the statute would convert the statute into a notice statute, which would change the outcome. D would prevail over B as D took without notice of any prior interest in the land.

B v. A. If B loses, B would have no rights against A based on the covenants in the deed but might have recourse against A under a negligence theory.

Answer:

(1) B v. D:

Title disputes: common law:

B will claim priority of title over D. The common law rule was that the first person to receive his legal interest in the land had priority over subsequent grantees. Here, A conveyed to B before A conveyed to C (who later conveyed to D).

Title disputes: recording acts:

The recording acts allow a subsequent grantee to prevail over the first in time grantee under certain limited circumstances. In this case, the jurisdiction has adopted a race/notice recording statute. In a race/notice jurisdiction a subsequent grantee for valuable consideration who takes without notice of the prior conveyances and is the first to record a clean chain of title against the land in question has priority over earlier grantees. B will contend that D does not come within the description of the recording statute because (1) D was not a good faith purchaser, (2) D did not take for "valuable consideration," and (3) D was not the first to "duly record."

Good faith purchaser:

B's first contention is that D was not a "good faith" purchaser because she received a quitclaim deed from C. In some jurisdictions, receipt of a quitclaim deed automatically results in a denial of bona fide purchaser (BFP) status. In others, it places the recipient upon inquiry notice (i.e., the grantee is charged with notice of whatever facts a reasonable inspection of, and inquiry at, the premises would have revealed). In a majority of jurisdictions, however, a quitclaim deed does not put the purchaser on notice of anything. In this case, even had D gone to the premises, she would have learned nothing about B's purported interest in Blackacre (B/A) since the tract of land was vacant. In addition, even had D searched the grantor/grantee index at the time D acquired the land, she would not have learned of B's interest (since B did not record his deed until December 1). Thus, unless this is one of the few jurisdictions that equates receipt of a quitclaim deed with knowledge of all prior interests in land, D would be deemed to have acquired her interest in B/A in "good faith."

Valuable consideration:

B would alternatively contend that D had not acquired her interest in B/A for "valuable consideration" since D did not part with any new monetary value in obtaining title to B/A. However, D could probably successfully rebut this contention by pointing out the contemporaneous consideration of D relinquishing a prior claim against C in exchange for the deed to B/A. Thus, D's acquisition of B/A in satisfaction of an antecedent debt would probably be deemed to constitute valuable consideration.

The shelter doctrine:

In addition, many states employ the "shelter rule." Under this theory, a purchaser or transferee from a BFP, in effect, steps into the shoes of the BFP. Since C received a warranty deed and paid a fair cash price for B/A, there appears to be no question that C is a BFP. Thus, if this jurisdiction adheres to the "shelter rule," D would be sheltered under C's BFP status, even if D was not a BFP on her own.

First to record:

B would alternatively contend that D did not "duly record" her deed to B/A first. B would claim that one has not duly recorded until she has perfected a clean chain of title involving the subject land. Although D recorded the deed she received from C on November 2, prior to the time B recorded his deed from A (December 1), D did not perfect her chain of title until

February 1 of the following year (when D recorded the deed from A to C). Before February 1, D had what is often referred to as a "wild" deed in B/A. The deed was "wild" because a search of the grantor/grantee index looking for transactions by A involving B/A would not have discovered D's interest because the deed between A and C was not recorded. In fact, to perfect the chain of title properly with respect to B/A, D would have to rerecord the C-to-D deed after having recorded the A-to-C deed on February 1. D does not appear to have a good rebuttal to this argument, and B probably would have priority to B/A under the statute.

However, D might contend that B should be equitably estopped from asserting a superior interest in B/A because it was as a result of B's failure to promptly record A's deed that D was not able to discover B's prior interest in B/A. (Had C searched the grantor/grantee index immediately before receiving A's deed, B's interest would ***not*** have appeared.) However, B could probably successfully argue in rebuttal that despite B's delay in recording A's deed, D could have still protected herself by requiring C to have recorded A's deed before she (D) accepted C's deed. Therefore, D's loss of priority to B/A was not due to B's failure to promptly record the deed from A.

(2) Omission of last six words from statute:

Omission of the last six words from the recording statute would convert the statute into a "notice" statute. Based upon the ***B v. D*** discussion above, D would prevail in this instance because the property was acquired by C (and D) in good faith, for a valuable consideration, and without notice of any prior interests in the land.

(3) B's recourse against A:

B might contend that the typical warranty deed contains covenants of warranty, quiet enjoyment, and future assurances (i.e., that the grantee will not be disturbed in his enjoyment of the land by anyone with superior title, and that in the event the grantee is evicted, the grantor will indemnify the grantee for attorneys' fees and costs expended in attempting to protect title to the land). However, A could probably successfully contend in rebuttal that these warranties protect against claims by third parties in existence on the date of the conveyance. Here, D's claim arose after B acquired B/A. Thus, B would have no rights against A based upon the deed (even assuming B had given value to A).

A might nevertheless be liable to B under a negligence theory. It should have been reasonably foreseeable to A that, by conveying the property to a subsequent party such as C, a title dispute might result between the transferees. Thus, B should be able to recover for any actual losses occasioned by A's subsequent transfer of B/A to C.

Suggested Reading

Recording statutes; ELO ch.12

Covenants for title; ELO ch.11-F

Answer to Question 16

Important aspects:

Marketable title, Statute of Frauds, adverse possession, equitable conversion, and the risk of loss.

Summary:

Vendor's rights and obligations. It is unlikely that Vendor would be able to provide marketable title as it appears that Vendor purported to convey the property to his daughter prior to the conveyance to Purchaser. Although the conveyance to Daughter did not comply with the Statute of Frauds and does not appear to fall within one of the exceptions to the Statute, Vendor would likely be estopped from raising the Statute of Frauds as a defense to defeat Purchaser's claim that Vendor lacked marketable title. Assuming, however, Vendor was deemed to be able to convey marketable title, since the property was damaged prior to closing, in most jurisdiction Purchaser would bear the risk of loss and therefore Vendor could enforce the contract against Purchaser.

Daughter's rights and obligations. Daughter's rights depend upon whether she gained title to the land either because the oral conveyance from Vendor fell within an exception to the Statute of Frauds of whether she otherwise gained title through adverse possession. The oral conveyance from Vendor to Daughter does not appear to fall within any exception to the Statute of Frauds, and Daughter is unlikely to satisfy the requirements for adverse possession. Daughter does not appear to have any rights in the property.

Purchaser's rights and obligations. Purchaser had the right to back out of the contract for sale if he can show that Vendor was unable to provide marketable title at closing or, once the premises were destroyed by fire, the risk of loss fell upon Vendor. As discussed above, it appears that Vendor would be estopped from raising the Statute of Frauds to support his claim of marketable title. On the other hand, in most jurisdictions, the risk of loss would fall on the purchaser. Therefore, the destruction of the building would not be grounds for Purchaser to avoid the contract.

Answer:

Vendor's Rights and obligations:

Vendor was obliged to provide marketable title to Purchaser at closing. Whether Vendor satisfied this obligation depends upon the effect of the Vendor's purported gift to his Daughter and the zoning conflict. Even if V was deemed to be able to convey marketable title, since the property was damaged prior to closing, V's right to enforce the contract depends upon which party bears the risk of the loss.

Marketable title:

Implicit in transactions for the sale and purchase of real estate is that the vendor will have, at the closing, marketable title to the land that is being sold. Marketable title means that which would be acceptable to a reasonably prudent buyer (i.e., free from reasonable doubt).

Oral conveyance of land:

The issue here is whether Vendor's (V) gift to his daughter rendered his title unmarketable. V could contend that since the purported grant to Daughter (D) was verbal, it is unenforceable by reason of the Statute of Frauds (i.e., transfers of land must be embodied in a writing that contains the essential terms and is signed by the party against whom enforcement is sought). Thus, V would argue that he retained marketable title to the land.

Part performance:

Purchaser (P), however, could argue in rebuttal that, in many states, where a grantee does acts that are "unequivocally referable" to a transfer of the land by the grantor, the grantee is entitled to prove that a conveyance was made (despite the Statute of Frauds). Since D lived on the land for six years and made substantial improvements thereto, P would contend that the "unequivocally referable" standard is satisfied. The facts are silent as to whether D also paid the real property taxes with respect to the land. If she did, P's position would be strengthened. If D were V's only child, V could respond that D's conduct was ***not*** "unequivocally referable" to a transfer of the real property since D's actions could have been in anticipation of her likely inheritance of the land. In other words, D would have had reason to improve and maintain the land, even if a transfer had not occurred. However, it is likely that D would be asked to testify about the conveyance to her, and P probably would prevail on this issue.

Equitable estoppel:

P could also contend that V might be estopped to assert the Statute of Frauds as to D since D foreseeably and justifiably relied upon V's gift in making "substantial improvements" to the land at "considerable expense." While V could argue in rebuttal that since D had lived on the land for six years on a rent-free basis, she suffered no detriment, P probably would prevail on this issue.

Adverse possession:

Alternatively, P could claim that D might be able to assert ownership to the land by adverse possession (assuming the statute of limitations for real property actions is six years or less). The elements for AP are satisfied where the adverse possessor enters upon, continuously and exclusively occupies another's land in an open, notorious, visible, and hostile manner throughout the requisite statutory period. In many jurisdictions the AP must also show that his possession is pursuant to a claim of right. But most courts hold that the claim of right requirements is synonymous with the hostility requirement. P could contend that since D entered the land under a claim of right (i.e., with the belief that she was the lawful owner of it) and committed acts that were consistent with exclusive ownership (i.e., occupying and making substantial improvements), D has acquired title to the real property. Even if this were one of those jurisdictions requiring such a showing, since V gave D permission to live in the house and provided her the keys to the house, it is unlikely that D satisfies the "hostile" element so as to claim ownership by adverse possession.

Based upon the foregoing, it does not appear that V had marketable title to the land. The facts are silent as to the type of deed that V was required to deliver to P at the closing. If it were a quitclaim deed, V could conceivably contend that he had promised only to convey to P whatever interest, if any, he might have in the land. However, even where the parties have stipulated to a quitclaim deed, most courts nevertheless imply an obligation to transfer marketable title (at least to the extent of any adverse interests of which the seller was aware).

Equitable conversion:

Assuming that V was deemed to be able to convey marketable title, P might contend that he is entitled to cancel the agreement based on the destruction of the house. However, the majority view is that risk of loss that is neither party's fault and that occurs after a contract has been signed rests with the vendee, subject to the obligation of the seller to reduce the purchase price by the amount of any insurance proceeds received as a result of the damage. If this view is adhered to here, the building's destruction would not be grounds for P to avoid the contract. There is, however, a minority view (sometimes referred to as the "Massachusetts" rule) that usually places the burden of loss upon the seller until legal title is conveyed. Thus, a contract for the sale of land is deemed to be cancelled when there is ***substantial*** damage to the land prior to the closing. V could also argue that since P had indicated his intention to raze the building anyway, the "damage" to P is insignificant. Because P is attempting to avoid the contract primarily because he wants to buy other land (rather than because of the house being destroyed), V should prevail under these facts even if the Massachusetts view is followed in this jurisdiction.

D's rights and obligations:

Daughter's rights depend upon whether she gained title to the land either because the oral conveyance from Vendor fell within an exception to the Statute of Frauds of whether she otherwise gained title through adverse possession. As discussed above, D probably cannot claim title to the premises. The oral conveyance from V to D does not appear to fall within any exception to the Statute of Frauds, and D is unlikely to satisfy the requirements for adverse possession.

P's rights and obligations:

P had the right to back out of the contract for sale if he can show that Vendor was unable to provide marketable title at closing or, once the premises were destroyed by fire, the risk of loss fell upon Vendor. As discussed above, it appears that V would be stopped from raising the Statute of Frauds to support his claim of marketable title. On the other hand, in most jurisdictions, the risk of loss would fall on the purchaser. Therefore, the destruction of the building would not be grounds for P to avoid the contract.

Remedies:

If V could prevail on both the marketable title and equitable conversion issues described above, he probably could obtain a judgment against P for the balance of the purchase price (conditional upon his delivery of a valid deed to the land when the full amount was tendered). In a number (not a majority) of jurisdictions, however, an aggrieved vendor is entitled to recover only his out-of-pocket expenses if the seller attempted to convey, in good faith, an unmarketable title. If the latter view is followed here, V would still prevail, only if P acted in bad faith; if a court decided that he acted in good faith, V would be able to receive only out-of-pocket expenses.

If V were not successful on the marketable title dispute, P would be entitled to cancel the agreement and recover his deposit (i.e., the failure of V to furnish marketable title is a precondition to sale, entitling P to rescind the contract). If the deposit could be located, P probably would be entitled to impose a constructive trust upon it since V would be unjustly enriched if he were permitted to retain it.

Finally, D could institute a successful "quiet title" action to require V to give her a deed to the land. If V refused to execute a deed, D probably could obtain a court order transferring ownership of the land to her.

Suggested Reading

Marketable title; ELO ch.11-I(D)

Statute of Frauds; ELO ch.11-I(B)

Adverse possession; ELO ch.3

Equitable conversion; ELO ch.11-I(H)

Answer to Question 17

Important aspects:

Estoppels by deed, recording acts, bona fide purchasers, adverse possession.

Summary:

Able appears to have a superior claim to Greenacre over Owens and Charlie. Although Owens did not have title at the time Owens conveyed Greenacre to Able, Owens later acquired title as a devisee under his grandmother's will. Under a theory of estoppel by deed, when Owens acquired title to Greenacre, the title automatically vested in Able. Charlie's strongest argument is that he has a superior claim to Greenacre by operation of the recording act as he is a bona fide purchaser for value who took without notice of Able's interest and was the first to record. But Able would nevertheless have priority to Greenacre despite the recording act because Able appears to have satisfied the requirements to obtain title through adverse possession.

Answer:

Owen's rights to Greenacre:

Owen received title to Greenacre as a devisee in his grandmother's will, but appears to have conveyed away any rights he had to Greenacre.

Able's Rights to Greenacre:

Able's rights in Greenacre depend upon whether Able received valid title from Owens. O purported to convey G/A to Able before O had clear title to the land. Later, O purported to convey G/A to Charlie. A may also have gained title to G/A through adverse possession.

1. Estoppel by deed:

Charlie (C) would first contend that Able (A) has no interest in Greenacre (G/A) because at the time Owens (O) purported to transfer the land to A, O had no interest therein. Since the initial purported transfer to A was void, C would argue that he is the only party with an interest in G/A. However, A could probably successfully contend that most jurisdictions recognize the common law doctrine of estoppel by deed. Under this theory, where a grantor purports to transfer real property that he does not then own, but later acquires title to the property, his subsequently acquired title automatically operates to vest ownership in the earlier grantee. If this jurisdiction recognizes this doctrine, title in G/A would have passed to A immediately upon O's grandmother's death three years ago, when she left G/A to O in her will.

2. Recording statute:

Even if the estoppel-by-deed theory exists in this jurisdiction, C could contend that, under the recording statute, he still has priority to G/A because he is a subsequent taker for value and without notice. A could claim, however, that C does not satisfy the elements of the recording statute since (1) the prior conveyance to A was recorded, (2) C did not give new value to O at the time G/A was conveyed to him, and (3) C was not "without notice" because a purchaser of land is ordinarily charged with whatever notice a reasonable inspection of the property would have disclosed (in this instance, it would have revealed the metallic sign posted by Bank, indicating the summer home had been built by A). However, C could argue in rebuttal that (1) A's initial recording would not satisfy the statute since it was outside the chain of title under the grantor/grantee indexes and therefore should be deemed "unrecorded" for purposes of the legislation;

(2) C gave O present value since O was relieved of an outstanding obligation to C; and (3) there was no inquiry notice because, even had C seen the sign that was posted by Bank, he would have assumed the cabin was built by A before it was transferred to O. Finally, it appears that A built the cabin 22 years ago, and thus it is possible that Bank's sign had become so obliterated over time that it would be impossible to read. If this were the case, then C may be able to use this fact to strengthen his assertion that he had no inquiry notice of A's prior claim.

Assuming the metallic sign was readable, A could argue in rebuttal that C should have asked O whether anyone else had an interest in G/A since A's name would not have appeared in the grantor/grantee indexes. However, C might have reasonably assumed that A was simply a prior lessee of the property. In addition, C could contend that even if he had asked O about other grantees, O would have denied A's interest in G/A since O conveyed a second deed to G/A with full knowledge of A's prior interest. C probably will be deemed to satisfy the recording statute and therefore would have priority to G/A on this basis.

3. Adverse possession:

Assuming C prevails with respect to the foregoing issues, A could alternatively assert priority to G/A under the adverse possession (AP) doctrine. The elements for AP are satisfied where the adverse possessor enters upon, continuously and exclusively occupies another's land in an open, notorious, visible, and hostile manner throughout the requisite statutory period. In many jurisdictions the AP must also show that his possession is pursuant to a claim of right. But most courts hold that the claim of right requirement is synonymous with the hostility requirement. In a minority of jurisdictions, the possessor must also pay real estate taxes pertaining to the land, which A here has done.

A went upon G/A believing he had a valid deed from O. At the time of the conveyance O did not have title. Where a person enters into adverse possession pursuant to a defective instrument, he is said to enter under color or title. Such color of title is generally sufficient to meet the hostility and the claim of right requirements. If this jurisdiction has adopted this view, then A has satisfied this element. The open and notorious requisites of A's AP claim are satisfied as well. A undertook actions (building a summer home, paying the taxes) that evidenced to the world his exclusive ownership of the land. The requisite statutory period would appear to be satisfied since A has been in possession of the land for 22 years; the applicable period of time is ordinarily no longer than 21 years (and sometimes as short as 5 or 10 years). The fact that O's grandmother was unaware that A had constructed a summer home on G/A would not diminish A's assertion of AP.

C might contend, however, that the "open" and "notorious" elements are not satisfied because A occupied G/A for only one month each year. A could argue in rebuttal, however, that the "continuous" element is satisfied if the adverse possessor uses the land in a manner similar to that which would be made of it by the legal occupant. Since the parcel was located in a mountainous area that was inaccessible by road for six months of the year, the use of the land solely as a summer home would be appropriate. C might argue that a summer cottage should be occupied two or three months a year, but most people have a vacation period of, at most, only one month. A's occupancy of G/A for that period of time should be sufficient. It therefore appears that A should have priority to G/A despite the recording statute because A can claim to have obtained title to G/A as an adverse possessor.

Charlie's rights to G/A:

As discussed above, C would have priority over A under the recording acts, but would lose under the operation of the doctrine of adverse possession, which operates outside the recording acts.

Suggested Reading

"Chain of title" problems; ELO ch.12-II(K)(3)(d)(i)

Adverse possession; ELO ch.3

Answer to Question 18

Important aspects:

Deed conveyancing, statute of frauds, deed delivery, concurrent ownership, recording statutes, adverse possession.

Summary:

Mark would likely be declared the owner of Greenacre and should begin eviction proceedings against Ruth and sue Ruth for reasonable rental value of Greenacre for the period Ruth was in occupation. Henry likely transferred a future interest in joint tenancy in Greenacre to Paula and Mark. Henry's transfer was likely valid even though Henry handed the deed to a third person and did not specifically identify the land to be conveyed or the last names of the grantees. The language was probably precise enough to identify the property and the parties and the deed delivered, albeit through a third party. Since Mark held title as a joint tenant with Paula, at Paula's death, Mark succeeded to the entire future interest and the interest became possessory at Henry's death. In this case, Ruth cannot seek the protection of the recording acts as she knew of the earlier grant to Mark and Paula. Nor can Ruth claim title through adverse possession as time would not have begun to run against Mark until his estate became possessory.

Answer:

Mark should begin eviction proceedings against R and sue R for reasonable rental value of G/A for the period R was in occupation.

(1) Henry (H) likely made a valid transfer of G/A to Paula (P) and Mark (M) 12 years ago.

Deed formalities:

A valid conveyance occurs where there has been a delivery (completion of a valid deed together with the grantor's intention that the instrument be immediately operative) and acceptance by the grantee. Where the purported transfer is a gift, acceptance ordinarily will be presumed and will relate back to the time of delivery. Statutes in some states require a deed to be witnessed by one or more persons and acknowledged before a notary public. If this jurisdiction requires such additional steps, the purported deed to P and M likely would be invalid as there are no facts to suggest the deed was witnessed or acknowledged, and M would have no interest in G/A. Many states have enacted legislation that cures the absence of witnesses or acknowledgments if no dispute arises over the document within a specified time after recordation. However, even if such legislation exists in this jurisdiction, it might not apply here because H's deed to P and M was not recorded until just recently.

Deed: land description:

A valid deed must reasonably identify the land conveyed and the grantees. Ruth (R) could contend that the deed was not valid since (1) there was not a sufficient description of the real property being transferred (it merely referred to unspecified land in Utopia), and (2) the last names of P and M were not stated. However, M could probably successfully contend in rebuttal that (1) the land that H owned in Utopia was easily identifiable (it would require only checking the county records of all counties within Utopia) since the grant extends to ***all*** of H's property within that state; and (2) assuming P and M were H's only niece and nephew with those first names, the precise grantees are certainly determinable. It therefore appears that H's transfer of G/A to M is valid.

Deed: delivery:

R might next contend that delivery did not take place since it appears that H did not intend the deed to be immediately operative since (1) he handed the deed to JoAnn (J), a friend from whom H could presumably later recover the deed if he chose to do so; and (2) he later sold G/A to R (presumably, H would not fraudulently sell land that he did not own). The facts seem to indicate that H sold the land to R because he no longer wanted M to have it, but there is no indication that H ever communicated this to any third party. M could argue in rebuttal that (1) delivery to J was unequivocal (i.e., H did not attach any conditions to delivery of the deed to P and M or otherwise advise J that he might demand the deed back), and (2) the fact that H gave R a quitclaim deed demonstrates that his recognition that he might not have any further rights in G/A. Since H made absolutely no provision for re-obtaining the deed from J, it is likely that the conveyance of a future interest to P and M had occurred (i.e., H gave a future interest to P and M while preserving a life estate in himself).

(2) Assuming G/A was conveyed to P and M, M became the sole owner of it when P died.

Joint tenancy: right of survivorship:

When a joint tenant dies, his interest passes automatically to the surviving joint tenants. M would contend that since G/A was conveyed to P and M as "joint owners," they received a joint tenancy estate and, thus, M succeeded to sole ownership of G/A when P died. P's heirs or devisees (whoever succeeded to her interest in G/A) could argue in rebuttal, however, that there is a judicial preference to construe ambiguous grants as tenancies in common rather than joint tenancies. In fact, some jurisdictions will refuse to conclude that a joint tenancy was intended unless the words "with right of survivorship" are contained in the grant. However, where the grantees have a consanguinary relationship (M and P may have been siblings), many courts presume that the grantor would not have desired one grantee to be able to force the other to permanently share land with a complete stranger (as would be the case if the property were conveyed as a tenancy in common). Thus, M probably became the sole owner of G/A when P died.

(3) R did not obtain a superior interest to M based on the recording act.

Title dispute: common law:

The common law rule is that the first person to receive his legal interest in land has priority over any subsequent grantee. Here, H conveyed to M before H conveyed to R.

Title dispute: recording act:

The recording acts allow a subsequent grantee to prevail over the first in time grantee under certain limited circumstances. If Utopia is a pure race state (i.e., the first to record a complete chain of title has priority to that parcel), then R would have a superior interest to G/A since she recorded her deed before M. If the jurisdiction adheres to a race/notice or notice recording statute, R could not claim priority to G/A since she had actual knowledge of the earlier grant to M and P. (The fact that R believed the transfer was invalid does not detract from her awareness of the earlier transfer.)

(4) R did not obtain a superior interest in G/A by adverse possession (AP).

If this jurisdiction has a relatively short statute of limitations for real property actions (seven years or less), R would contend that she has, under color of title, entered upon, continuously and exclusively occupied G/A in an open, notorious, visible, and hostile manner throughout the requisite statutory period. Building a home and living on land certainly would constitute open, notorious, and hostile possession of the land. However, where an AP claimant commences her occupation between the time a future interest has been given and the right of possession by such future interest holder vests, the AP period does not begin to run against the holder of the future interest (here M) until his estate becomes possessory. Since H died only three months ago, M presumably would be entitled to commence eviction proceedings against R. (No equitable argument in the nature of laches could be successfully asserted against M since he has learned only recently of his interest in G/A.)

(5) M would likely be entitled to evict R and sue R for rent but offset by the value of R's improvements.

Relations between co-tenants:

Assuming M prevailed upon the foregoing issues, he could claim ownership of G/A (including the home that R has constructed) and sue R for *mesne* profits (i.e., the reasonable rental value of G/A throughout the period the land was occupied by R). In many jurisdictions, however, where one in good faith (i.e., believing the land belongs to her) enters upon real property belonging to another and makes improvements thereon, the latter may be required to make restitution to the former for those improvements. Given R's belief that she owned the land, a court probably would allow R to offset the reasonable value of the home she constructed (and possibly also the taxes she paid on that property) against any rent due to M.

Suggested Reading

Deed formalities; ELO ch.11-III(A)-(E)

Joint tenancy; ELO ch.7-I

Recording statutes; ELO ch.12-I, II

Adverse possession; ELO ch.3

Answer to Question 19

Important aspects:

Statute of Frauds, deed delivery and acceptance, common law "first in time, first in right," recording statutes.

Summary:

Elk Mortgage Co's action for declaratory relief. The issue here is which of the multiple claimants to title has a superior claim. E's rights are derivative of Cap's rights. Each of Art, Bill, and Cap can argue that Ollie intended to convey Goldacre to each of them. As Ollie's conveyance to Art was likely valid, then at common law, Ollie had no interest to convey to Bill or Cap. Nevertheless, Bill or Cap may establish title priority over Art if either is protected by the recording statute. If this jurisdiction has adopted a race statute, Cap (and therefore E) would prevail as Cap was the first to record a deed from Ollie. In a notice jurisdiction, neither Bill nor Cap would be protected. In a race-notice jurisdiction, neither Bill nor Cap would be protected.

Answer:

The rights of Elk Mortgage Co. (E) are derivative through Cap (C). Thus, E's rights turn upon whether C would have priority to Goldacre (G/A) vis-à-vis Art (A) and Bill (B).

A's Rights in G/A:

(1) O likely validly conveyed G/A to A.

A conveyance occurs when there has been a delivery (completion of a valid deed together with the grantor's intention that the instrument be immediately operative) and acceptance by the grantee. A will argue that (1) there was a valid delivery and Ollie's statement ("If I die before you") is thus of no effect; (2) there is a presumption that if a deed is manually tendered to a grantee, the grantor intended it to be immediately operative (the fact that one's possessory interest in land will not vest until some point in the future does not prevent a delivery from having occurred if the grantor has relinquished any right to withdraw the grant); and (3) the statement by Ollie (O) should be construed as a condition subsequent (i.e., A had a future interest in G/A subject to the condition that he survive O). However, B and C could contend in rebuttal that (1) extrinsic evidence is admissible for the purpose of showing that the grantor did not intend the deed to be immediately operative, and O's statement in this instance indicates clearly that the purported transfer was ***not*** effective unless A survived O; and (2) even though O did not expressly reserve the right to revoke the deed, O obviously did ***not*** intend the conveyance to be immediately operative since she subsequently changed her mind and gave deeds pertaining to G/A to B and C (which she would not have done if she believed that she no longer had any interest in G/A). However, A would contend in rebuttal that O's subsequent purported transfers of G/A are of no consequence because O (a layperson) did not recognize that she no longer had any interest in G/A. A probably will prevail on this issue because O's statement did not establish her right to revoke the deed. However, if no conveyance occurred, then A never acquired any rights in G/A.

Acceptance:

There appears to be no question that all of the possible grantees accepted their deeds. Acceptance is ordinarily presumed where no objection is made by the grantee when he learns of the delivery.

(2) A likely has priority to G/A in notice and race-notice jurisdictions but not in a pure race jurisdictions.

Common law: first-in-time, first-in-right:

Priority to G/A would depend upon which type of recording statute applies in Lotus. The common law rule was that the first person to receive his legal interest in the land had priority over any subsequent grantee. Here, O conveyed to A before O conveyed to B or C.

Recording act:

Recording acts allow a subsequent grantee to prevail over the first in time grantee under certain limited circumstances.

Race jurisdiction. If this is a pure race state where a subsequent grantee who is the first to record a clean chain of title has priority over an earlier grantee, then C (and through C, E) would prevail because C was the first party to record a deed from O.

Notice jurisdiction. If Lotus is a pure notice jurisdiction where a subsequent grantee who acquires title to land for value and without notice of any prior grantees has priority over the prior grantees, neither B nor C is protected by the recording statute. B would have been on constructive notice of A's prior recordation, and C had actual notice of A's and B's prior interests since C was present when O purportedly made a transfer of G/A to B and since O told C she had revoked her deeds to A and B. C might contend that since O specifically told him that she had revoked the deeds to A and B, he believed that his interest was superior to either of theirs. However, B could probably successfully argue in rebuttal that C was at least upon inquiry notice to (1) ask A and B what interest, if any, either claimed in G/A and (2) verify independently that O was capable of revoking her prior deeds. Had C done this, he would have learned that O had already conveyed G/A both to A and to B.

Race/notice jurisdiction. If Lotus is a race/notice jurisdiction where a subsequent transferee for value, who has no notice of conflicting claims at the time of the conveyance and is the first to record a clean chain of title against the land, has priority vis-à-vis earlier grantees, the result would be the same as in a notice jurisdiction. Since C is deemed to have had notice of both A's and B's prior interests in G/A at the time of the conveyance to him, his interest would be subordinate to both A's and B's (even though C was the first to record his interest). B's interest would not succeed against A's interest because A recorded his deed first; under the race/notice statute, the subsequent grantee must be the first to record a clean chain of title.

(2) B's rights in G/A:

The conveyance from O to B was valid only if the earlier conveyance from O to A failed. If no conveyance occurred between O and A, then A never acquired any rights in G/A and B likely obtained a future interest in G/A, which B became possessor on O's death.

B will contend that the conveyance from O was valid because O intended the deed to him to be immediately operative. E, C, and A would argue in rebuttal that (1) since O kept the deed (she only showed it to B but did not give it to him), there is a presumption against delivery; (2) B was not to obtain physical possession of G/A until O died (which suggests that O intended the transfer to be effective only at that time); and (3) O would not have sold G/A to C if she believed that she no longer had any interest in G/A. B could probably successfully respond that (1) since he had the combination to the safe (with O's blessing), the deed was virtually in his possession; (2) the words by O ("I am now giving Goldacre to you") evidence an intention that the deed be immediately operative; and (3) as contended by A above, when O subsequently deeded G/A to C, O probably did not understand that she had already conveyed her interest in G/A. In short, O probably made a present conveyance of a future interest to B and simply retained a life estate in G/A. In a dispute between B and C, B would prevail under the common law first-in-time theory, but C would prevail under the recording acts.

C's rights:

If neither the conveyance to A or B was valid, there seems to be little doubt that O intended the deed to C to be immediately operative, as evidenced by the fact that she accepted "valuable consideration" for the sale of G/A to C.

Suggested Reading

Deeds; ELO ch.11-III(A)-(E)

Recording statutes; ELO ch.12-I, II

Answer to Question 20

Important aspects:

Deed delivery to a third party escrow agent, equitable estoppels.

Summary:

Art v. Dale. Dale will likely prevail in the quiet title action. Art is likely estopped from challenging the validity of Barb's conveyance to Dale, a bona fide purchaser who would not have Barb wrongfully obtained the deed before escrow was complete.

Art and Dale v. Carl. Carl, the escrow agent, likely breached his contract with Art by sending the deed to Barb before all of the escrow conditions were met.

Answer:

(1) Dale would likely prevail in a quiet title action with Art.

In an action by Dale (D) to quiet title to Greenacre (G/A) against Art (A), A will contend that Barb (B) could not have conveyed G/A to D because no conveyance of G/A was made to B, and thus B had nothing to transfer to D. A conveyance occurs when there has been a delivery (completion of a valid deed together with the grantor's intention that the instrument be immediately operative) and acceptance by the grantee. Where an escrow has been established, there is usually a presumption that the grantor intended the deed ***not*** to be operative until the conditions of the escrow have been satisfied. Since the condition precedent to the deed being operative (the payment of $5,000 by B) never occurred, B never acquired title to G/A that she could have transferred to D.

D, however, could contend that A should be equitably estopped from asserting that the transfer to D was invalid. Some states have adopted the rule that where a grantee wrongfully acquires a deed from an escrow holder chosen by the grantor and then conveys the land to a bona fide purchaser (BFP), the grantor is estopped from denying the validity of the transfer against the BFP. Assuming D parted with present consideration to acquire G/A (the facts are silent on this point), D would seem to be a BFP (since the land was vacant, a visit to G/A would not have put D upon inquiry notice of A's ownership interest). Also, since A had prepared a warranty deed for B (as opposed to a quitclaim deed), D would have no reason to investigate B's title beyond a search of the grantor/ grantee index.

Assuming D was a BFP, D would additionally contend that there is a maxim in the law that where one of two innocent parties must suffer, the loss should fall upon the more blameworthy person. Here, A is more blameworthy because (1) A chose Carl, who mistakenly parted with possession of the deed; and (2) by giving Carl a "clean" deed (one with no conditions upon the face of it), A should have realized that it would be possible for B, if she ever obtained the deed from Carl, to "sell" G/A. A might contend in rebuttal that escrows are a common device for transferring ownership of land and that Carl, as a real estate broker, should have been well aware of the potential for harm if the deed left his possession. Assuming D paid value for G/A, D should prevail in her quiet title action against A (even though no actual conveyance took place).

(2) If Art (A) loses against Dale, Art can likely recover against Carl (C).

A probably would sue C for breach of contract and negligence. With respect to the breach of contract claim, C could contend that he has no liability because (1) no contract ever arose between him and A (it appears that C did not receive any consideration); and (2) in any event, the Statute of Frauds (which pertains to the sale of land) was never satisfied (C never signed the statement prepared by A). However, it probably would be implied into the A-C arrangement that C would receive reasonable compensation for his efforts on behalf of A and B. In addition, A can probably successfully assert equitable estoppel to overcome these contentions since A detrimentally relied upon C to act as escrow agent.

If C were found to have breached his contract with A, C might next assert that A's damages are limited to $5,000 (the amount he would have received if the escrow had closed), rather than the enhanced value of the land. However, A should be able to successfully argue in rebuttal that since the conditions for the close of escrow were never satisfied, he would have been able to recover the deed (there was never a valid contract between A and B for the sale of land). Therefore, A should be able to recover the present fair market value of G/A from C.

A would also contend that C, by agreeing to act as escrow agent, assumed a duty to A that he would not deliver the deed to B unless B gave C the $5,000 cash purchase price within a month. When C sent the deed to B (so that B allegedly could show the deed to a bank), C breached his duty to A and became liable to A for negligence. C might contend that he could only foresee damages of $5,000. A could probably successfully argue in rebuttal that C should have foreseen that, if B transferred the deed to G/A to another party without fulfilling the conditions of escrow, A would not be able to recover the deed and benefit from an enhanced market value of G/A.

Suggested Reading

Deed, delivery of; ELO ch.11-III(D)

Deed, estoppel by; ELO ch.11-III(F)(7)

Answer to Question 21

Important aspects:

Adverse possession under color of title, option agreements and the rule against perpetuities; risk of loss and equitable conversion doctrine, term of years tenancy.

Summary:

Alex probably cannot claim ownership based on the deed she purchased from Swindler because Swindler did not own Flatacre at the time of the sale. Even if Alex cannot make a claim to title based on the deed itself, she can make a claim of title based on adverse possession under color of title. As for Bill, since the option to purchase did not violate the Rule Against Perpetuities, it became a binding contract of sale upon Bill's valid exercise of the option. Here, Bill probably cannot enforce the option because he has not yet paid the purchase price. If Bill did not validly exercise the option, Bill may owe Alex rent for the balance of the lease term.

Answer:

Title to Flatacre (F/A):

(1) Alex's (A) claim to title:

(a) Bona fide purchaser:

Since Owen (O) is the owner of record of F/A, to prevail, A must show she has a superior claim to title. A probably cannot claim ownership based on the deed she purchased from Swindler because Swindler did not own F/A at the time of the sale. A deed obtained by fraud or forgery will not divest the true owner of title vis-à-vis the grantee. Forged deeds are absolutely void and therefore transfer no interest to the grantee. On the other hand, a deed obtained by fraud is merely voidable. Once the property has passed to a bona fide purchaser without notice of the fraud, the conveyance can no longer be rescinded. Here, the facts do not state how Swindler obtained the deed. If Swindler forged the document, then the deed is void and O keeps title to the property. If Swindler fraudulently induced O to sign over the deed, then O cannot rescind the deed after it was transferred to A, a bona fide purchaser for value who took without notice.

(b) Adverse possession (AP):

Even if A cannot make a claim to title based on the deed itself, she can make a claim of title based on AP under color of title. The elements of AP are satisfied where the adverse possessor enters upon and continuously and exclusively occupies another's land in an open, notorious, visible, and hostile manner for the statutory period. Here, A built a home and resided there openly for three years. A's occupation satisfies the open, notorious, and visible elements. There are no facts to suggest that, for the time she was living on the property, A shared the property with the true owner or the public in general. Therefore, A's possession appears to meet the exclusive element. A did not have the owner's permission to occupy the land. A's possession was adverse and hostile. Further, since A possessed the property under color of title (pursuant to a defective written instrument purporting to give her title), such color of title is virtually always sufficient to meet the hostility requirement.

O will likely argue that A has not been in actual and continuous possession for the statutory period since A only resided on the land for three of the required five years before leasing to Bill (B). A's claim is not necessarily defeated, however, because the adverse possessor does not necessarily have to be in possession of the property personally, but can tack on the possession of those with whom she is in privity. Here, A transferred her possession to B, a tenant. B's possession should suffice for meeting the continuity requirement. Normally, an adverse possessor acquires title only to that property actually occupied. Here, the facts do not indicate how much of the land A actually used. In this case, however, since A entered under color of title, she would gain title to the entire area described in the defective deed, even if she only occupied a portion of it.

B's claim to title: option to purchase:

B will contend that he validly exercised an option to purchase and has the right to compel A to complete the sale of F/A. An option to purchase is a right to buy property for a stated price at some point in the future. It is akin to an executory interest and therefore ordinarily is subject to the Rule Against Perpetuities (RAP), although some courts do not apply the RAP to options in leases. Under the RAP, executory interests are void unless they must vest, if at all, within 21 years after an ascertainable life in being at the time the interest was created. The Third Restatement, however, recommends changing the rule so that options are not subject to the RAP. (*See* Rest. 3d Prop. (Servitudes), §3.3.) Here, even assuming that the RAP applies to options to purchase, the RAP is not violated. The agreement states that the option must be exercised during A's life. Since A is a life in being at the time the interest was created, the option does not violate the RAP.

When an option is exercised it becomes a binding contract of sale. Here, B will argue that he validly exercised the option because he sent timely notice to A. While A may contend that she did not actually receive notice because the letter was misplaced, Norma would likely be considered B's agent and have authority to receive correspondence on his behalf. But, while B has sent notice of his intent to exercise the option, B has not yet paid the price for the property. It is unlikely that the option is enforceable. On the other hand, if B validly exercised the option, he may have a claim of equitable ownership of F/A under the doctrine of equitable conversion. Under the doctrine of equitable conversion, the signing of an enforceable land sale contract is viewed as vesting in the purchaser equitable ownership of the land. An option to purchase gives rise to an equitable conversion claim when the option is validly exercised because upon due exercise of the option, the landlord-tenant relationship ends and the parties become vendor and vendee. Even if B validly exercised the option, his claim to title rests on the strength of A's claim. As discussed above, if Swindler forged the deed, A cannot claim ownership based on the deed itself.

A v. B for nonpayment of rent:

If B did not validly exercise his option to purchase, B may owe A for five months' rent. As discussed above, it does not appear that B can enforce the option because he has not yet paid the purchase price. Therefore, A can pursue B to recover unpaid rent for the balance of the lease term. The lease between A and B created a two-year term of years because the lease was for a fixed period of time. The lease commenced on January 1 and continued for a period of two years. While a term of years tenancy expires by its terms at the end of the term and no notice of termination is required, B left after 19 months, 5 months before the lease expired. B would owe rent for the five-month period.

Suggested Reading

Adverse possession; ELO ch.3

The rule against perpetuities; ELO ch.5-IX

The equitable conversion doctrine; ELO ch.11-I(H)

Landlord and tenant; ELO ch.8-II(B)

Answer to Question 22

Important aspects:

Breach of the implied warranty of habitability, latent defects, misrepresentation, equitable mortgages.

Summary:

Petra's rights. Petra may be able to make out a claim for breach of the implied warranty of habitability but probably cannot make out a claim of misrepresentation against Olivia. Although the implied warranty of habitability usually operates between the builder and the original owner, modern courts have shown a willingness to allow subsequent purchasers to pursue claims against the builder as long as the defect was latent and the claim is brought within a reasonable time. Petra's misrepresentation claim may fail as Olivia made no express representations regarding the house, Petra agreed to buy the house "as is," and even if Petra had a duty to disclose latent defects not readily observable, the facts suggest that Olivia was not aware of the dry wall problem.

Petra v. Second Chances. Petra's deed is not likely subject to any interest of Second Chances. At most, Second Chances had an equitable mortgage in the property, which mortgage was subordinate to that of Lender. If the court interprets the agreement between Olivia and Second Chances as a lease, then Second Chances may be liable for breach of the implied warranty of habitability. On the other hand, if the agreement is treated as an equitable mortgage rather than a lease, then Second Chances cannot simply evict Olivia, but must follow steps to properly foreclose the mortgage.

Olivia v. Second Chances. If the court interprets the agreement between Olivia and Second Chances as a lease, then Second Chances may be liable for breach of the implied warranty of habitability for the drywall problem during the time Olivia was in possession.

Answer

Drywall Problem:

Petra's rights with respect to the drywall depend upon whether P can make a claim for breach of the implied warranty of habitability or for misrepresentation.

(1) Implied warranty of quality:

No implied warranty of habitability existed at common law. A home buyer, like any other purchaser of real property, had only the benefit of those covenants that he could induce the seller to place into the deed. Today, however, most states hold that a builder/vendor makes a warranty of quality of skillful construction. Here, the warranty was violated because inferior materials were used in the interior walls. Therefore, O, the original buyer, would have a claim against B. Most courts also allow a purchaser of a used home to sue the original builder for breach of the IWH if the defect was latent when the purchaser bought and the defect appears within a reasonable time after construction. Here, Petra purchased the house at a short sale, approximately five years after the initial sale.

(2) Misrepresentation:

A seller of property who misrepresents the condition of the property will normally be liable to the buyer for damages. The buyer must show (1) the seller made a false statement concerning a material fact; (2) the seller knew that the representation was false; (3) the seller intended that the buyer rely on the statement; and (4) the buyer was injured. The common law traditionally did not make the seller liable for merely failing to disclose material defects, but many courts reject the common law approach and now hold the seller liable for failing to disclose material defects of which he is aware. But, generally the seller's duty to disclose is limited to material defects the buyer could not reasonably have discovered by reasonable diligence. Here, O will contend that she (O) made no representations whatsoever and that P agreed to accept the property "as is." P, on the other hand, would argue that the drywall problem was a defect that she was unlikely to discover even had she hired an inspector. O would contend that the unpleasant odor provided notice of the problem and that P should have inquired further. O would also argue that even if she had a duty to disclose, the duty was extinguished once she transferred the deed to O. Traditionally, sellers were often insulated from liability by the doctrine of merger. Under the doctrine of merger, a contract of sale merges into the deed and the deed becomes the final expression of the parties' agreement. Therefore, even if the seller made representations or gave warranties in the contract, these obligations would be extinguished when the buyer closed on the deal and took the deed. However, the majority of courts hold that misrepresentation claims are not extinguished when the deed is conveyed. If O misrepresented the condition of the property (see discussion, above), then the claim was not destroyed by merger when P accepted the deed.

O's claims against Second Chances:

O's claims against Second Chances (SC) depends on whether O is considered a tenant or a mortgagor.

Implied warranty of habitability:

If the agreement between SC and O created a landlord-tenant relationship, O can raise SC's possible breach of the implied warranty of habitability as a defense to the eviction action. At common law, no IWH existed; the position taken was "tenant beware." Since most all states now impose some type of IWH on landlords of residential property, the implied warranty likely applies here. The IWH implies a continuing duty on the part of the landlord of residential property to maintain the premises in habitable condition. If the implied warranty of habitability is breached, the tenant is permitted to (1) terminate the lease and recover damages, although tenant must generally provide reasonable notice to the landlord; (2) withhold rent; and (3) repair the defect and deduct the cost of the repairs from the rent.

O would contend that cracks beginning to form in the walls and the sulfur odor rendered the house uninhabitable, thus giving O the right to stop paying rent. SC would argue (1) O effectively waived any rights to repair because, under the lease, O undertook all responsibility for maintaining and repairing the property, even structural repairs; (2) even if O did not waive her rights, the premises had not become uninhabitable since O continued to live there and failed to notify SC of the defect and give SC an opportunity to repair; and (3) even if the premises are currently uninhabitable, the defective conditions existed prior to the lease, and O knew or should have known about the defect. SC's first argument will probably fail. Often courts will not enforce an attempted waiver of the breach of the implied warranty of habitability or will only enforce the waiver if it is set forth in a separate writing signed by the parties and supported by adequate consideration, which was not the case here. SC's second argument will likely fail because the sulfur-based gases that are corroding the air conditioning coils and computer wiring would seem to render the premises unsafe and perhaps hazardous. While SC could argue that O failed to give notice of the problem and denied SC an opportunity to repair, considering the serious health and safety concerns, lack of notice probably will not defeat O's action. Finally, SC could contend that the defect was one that O either knew about or should reasonably have discovered. After all, O was the original owner of the house. O has resided on the premises for five years and was aware of the sulfur odor well before SC purchased the property from her. While some courts hold that there is no implied warranty against patent defects (a defect the tenant either knows about or should reasonably have discovered), this principle likely will not apply here as it is not clear that the odor alone would have been enough to reveal the extent of the problem, even if O had conducted a reasonable inspection.

Equitable mortgage:

O will argue that SC cannot enforce the lease agreement against her because the agreement was a mortgage in disguise and therefore SC's only remedy is to foreclose the mortgage. A transfer of a deed will be treated like an equitable mortgage where the transfer was intended merely to provide security for a loan rather than a sale of the property. Generally courts look at whether a debt exists, the relationship of the parties, whether legal assistance was available, the sophistication and circumstance of each party, the adequacy of the consideration, and who retained possession of the property. (*See, e.g., Bernstein v. New Beginnings Trustee, LLC,* 988 So. 2d 90 (Fla. App. 2008).) The transaction between O and SC appears to meet this standard. O was delinquent in her mortgage payments when SC approached her. No facts suggest that O was a sophisticated buyer. The amount she received from SC ($24,000) was a good deal lower than the value of her house. And, O remained in possession of the property; SC never even asked for a key. Therefore, SC will not succeed in its eviction action because a court is more likely to treat the agreement as a mortgage rather than a lease.

Second Chances' rights:

Generally a purchaser of property takes subject to existing liens and mortgages. In this case, Second Chance could argue that it had a valid mortgage against the property. (see discussion, above). But Second Chances' mortgage interests, if any, would have been subordinate to Lender's interest. When a senior mortgage is foreclosed, the property is sold free and clear of the senior mortgage and any junior mortgage. Therefore, Second Chances did not likely retain any interest in the property following the sale. As for the money from the sale, the money would have been applied first to satisfy Lender's outstanding $24,000 mortgage and any amount over that would be paid to the junior lien holders, including Second Chances (assuming the court treated the agreement between Second Chance and O as a mortgage rather than a lease) and any surplus would be due to O.

Suggested Reading

Builder's implied warranty of habitability; ELO ch.11-III(G)

Misrepresentation and concealment; ELO ch.11- III(H)

Landlord's implied warranty of habitability; ELO ch.8-IV

Mortgages; ELO ch.11-II

Answer to Question 23

Important aspects:

Eminent domain, lost vs. mislaid property, unreasonable restraints on alienation.

Summary:

Holdout v. City. City will likely prevail over Holdout. City's condemnation action is probably within City's powers of eminent domain.

Victor v. Nonprofit. Nonprofit will likely have a superior claim to the currency than Victor (the finder) as the currency would likely be classified as mislaid rather than lost because it is unlikely that someone would unintentionally leave a large sum of money in a ceiling tile. As between a finder and the owner of the premises, mislaid property generally belongs to owner.

Nonprofit v. Owner. The resale provision is likely unenforceable as an unreasonable restraint on alienation. While the restraint furthers an important public policy, the failure to include at time limit for the duration of the restraint and failure to include a mechanism for terminating the restriction may render the restriction unreasonable.

Answer

(1) Holdout v. City: eminent domain:

A government entity may condemn property if it does so for the public good as long as it pays just compensation.

(a) Public use:

Holdout will argue that City improperly exercised its powers of eminent domain because it did not take her property for a "public use," but for a private benefit. Holdout will argue that since only two of the six parcels will be dedicated to parks and other public spaces, overall the proposed development project serves the interests of private homeowners and business rather than the general public. City, on the other hand, will argue that the proposed development does benefit the public and, therefore, meets the "public use" requirements.

A "public use" must be for a public good. A use is considered for the public good as long as it is rationally related to a conceivable public purpose. Economic development projects can be for public purposes because they can lead to urban renewal, stimulate job creation, and expand the tax base. Courts often defer to a government entity's determination that a taking of private property for economic development purposes is justified by a public need. (*See Kelo v. City of New London, Conn.*, 545 U.S. 469 (2005).)

Even if economic development can be an appropriate public use, Holdout will likely contend that condemnation for economic development purposes should be limited to economically blighted properties, not her well-maintained lot. While Holdout's individual lot is not blighted, City probably need only show that the surrounding area is blighted; a court would likely defer to City's determination that the area was sufficiently distressed to warrant redevelopment. Where, as here, the government entity acts pursuant to an integrated development plan, the entity's determination that the taking is for a public use would likely be upheld. City is probably within its rights to exercise its power of eminent domain for economic development purposes.

(b) Just compensation:

Holdout will likely argue that while $50,000 may represent the market value of the property, it does not adequately compensate her for the loss of her home and will not sufficiently compensate her for the cost of rebuilding somewhere else. Holdout's argument will likely fail. While a government entity must pay just compensation, just compensation generally means fair market value at the time of the taking. It does not usually include compensation for the property owner's emotional attachment to the land or the increased cost of rebuilding elsewhere. City appears to have paid "just compensation" for the condemned property.

(2) Victor v. NonProfit: finders:

Victor, the volunteer, will argue that he has a superior claim to the money over NonProfit, the owner of the land where the money was found. The outcome of this dispute will turn on whether the property is categorized as

(1) abandoned property, (2) lost property, or (3) mislaid property. Property is considered "abandoned" where the owner intentionally and voluntarily relinquishes his ownership claim. Abandoned property is generally awarded to the finder. Here, however, a court would likely conclude that the condition under which Victor found the money (in a cardboard box concealed in the ceiling) suggests that the owner did not intend to abandon the property; rather, the owner intended to keep the property safe in its hiding place.

Alternatively, Victor would argue that the property was probably lost by its owner and should be awarded to him, the finder, over NonProfit, the owner of the premises where the money was found. NonProfit can make several rebuttal arguments. First, NonProft would argue, whether the property was "lost" or "mislaid" is irrelevant because Victor cannot lay claim to the money because he was trespassing at the time of his find. In a dispute between a landowner and a finder, many courts award the property to the landowner if the finder was trespassing at the time of the find under the theory that a trespasser should not be rewarded for his bad acts. Here, Victor was on the property as part of a group of volunteers to clear the vacant land of debris. NonProfit would argue that Victor did not have permission to be in the apartment building; thus, he exceeded his license and was trespassing at the time he made his find. Victor, on the other hand, would argue that his license was explicitly limited to the vacant lot but reasonably included access to and from the lot and its surroundings. The facts, however, do not suggest that Victor needed to enter the apartment building as an incident to his license. NonProfit will likely prevail on this issue.

Second, even if Victor was not trespassing at the time of the find, NonProfit will argue that its claim is superior because the property was "mislaid" rather than "lost." Where the finder is not trespassing at the time of the find, many courts award"lost"property to the finder but"mislaid"property to the landowner. Lost property is property that the owner unintentionally parts with and does not know its whereabouts. Mislaid property is property that the owner sets down with intent to retrieve it but forgets where he left it. NonProfit would argue that the property was "mislaid" rather than "lost" because it is unlikely that someone would "unintentionally" leave a large sum of money in a ceiling tile. More likely, the money was intentionally placed in the ceiling tile but the owner forgot to retrieve it. NonProfit will likely prevail on this issue.

(3) NonProfit v. Owner: restraints on alienation:

Owner will argue that the resale provision is void as a direct restraint on alienation because the resale provision limits sale to other low- or moderate-income persons. At common law, direct restraints on alienation upon a fee simple estate were considered void as inconsistent with the nature of a fee estate. Some modern courts have relaxed the common law position and sometimes will uphold partial restraints on alienation of fee estates. Partial restraints on alienation are restraints that either last for a limited time or limit the transfer of property to certain class of persons. A total restraint prohibits any transfer of the estate for an unlimited time.

The resale provision contained in Owner's deed is a partially disabling restraint. The resale provision does not prohibit all transfers, but it limits to whom the property may be transferred. In this case, the restraint permits the owner to transfer the property to a limited number of buyers, other low-income persons. NonProfit would further argue that the prohibition has a legitimate public policy purpose: fostering stable and affordable housing in neighborhoods.

Partial restraints are generally subject to a rule of reasonableness. Reasonableness is determined by weighing the utility of the restraint against the injury caused by its enforcement. (Some jurisdictions follow the approach suggested in the Restatement (Third) and subject all direct restraints to a rule of reasonableness.) (*See* Rest. 3d Prop. (Servitudes), §3.4.) Here, the utility of the restraint is substantial. The restraint furthers an important public policy purpose: to provide continued access to affordable housing. But enforcement of the restraint causes substantial harm, as it severely limits the market of possible buyers for the property. On the whole, failure to include a time limit for the duration of the restraint and failure to include a mechanism for terminating the restriction likely renders the restriction unreasonable, and the restriction would be stricken. Owner likely can sell her unit for more than the purchase price.

Suggested Reading

Eminent domain; ELO ch.10-VIII

Finders of lost articles; ELO ch.2-I(C)

Restraints upon alienation; ELO ch.5-X

Answer to Question 24

Important aspects:

Encroachment, boundary settlement, relative hardship doctrine, statutory period for adverse possession, spite fences.

Summary:

Both Betty and Arthur appear to have valid claims against the other. It appears that Arthur trespassed on Betty's property when Arthur tore down the fence separating their properties. However, the trespass may be rendered moot if Arthur can show that he gained title to the land based on adverse possession. Arthur's success on this point may depend upon the statutory period for adverse possession in this jurisdiction as Arthur has only been in possession for five years. Alternatively Arthur could probably succeed in showing that the new fence should be recognized as the agreed upon boundary. Even if Arthur's fence does encroach on Betty's party there is a strong likely hood that while he may have to pay Betty for the loss in the value of the land, it is unlikely that Arthur would be forced to take on the expense of tearing down and relocating the fence to the property boundary. On the other hand, Betty was likely within her rights to cut the branches of Arthur's pecan tree and perhaps recover for the damages she sustained to her roof as a result of the falling pecans. Arthur's rights against Betty with respect to Betty's fence would depend upon whether Betty's fence would be declared a spite fence (built solely to interfere with Arthur's use and enjoyment). But Betty can likely show that a non-malicious reason for the fence—to block the view of Arthur's security cameras.

Answer:

(1) Betty v. Arthur:

(a) Arthur's fence:

Betty will contend that Arthur trespassed when he tore down the old fence separating their properties. A trespass occurs when the defendant intentionally intrudes upon, beneath, or above the surface of the plaintiff's land. (*See* Restatement (Second) of Torts, §159.) Here, Betty claims that the old fence that Arthur tore down was on her property. If true, then Arthur trespassed on her property when he entered her property without her consent and removed the fence. Although Arthur may claim that he did not intend to trespass, but mistakenly believed that he was on his own property, his mistaken belief is irrelevant. The intent element for trespass is satisfied by Arthur's conscious, intentional act of removing the fence.

Arthur will claim, even if the fence is technically on Betty's property, that he has gained title to that strip of land by adverse possession, or in the alternative, that the fence is located on an agreed-upon boundary. The elements for adverse possession are satisfied where the adverse possessor enters upon and continuously and exclusively occupies another's land in an open, notorious, visible, and hostile manner throughout the requisite statutory period. The building of a fence is generally sufficient to satisfy the open, notorious, continuous, and exclusive requirements. Arthur also can likely satisfy the hostility requirement. Most courts hold that one who possesses an adjoining landowner's land, under the mistaken belief that he has only possessed up to the boundary of his own land, meets the hostility requirement. A minority of courts, on the other hand, hold that a mistake as to the boundary does not satisfy the hostility requirement. In most jurisdictions, Arthur satisfies the hostility requirement. Arthur, however, may have trouble satisfying the time requirement for gaining title through adverse possession. While the statutory period for which the adverse possessor must maintain possession varies from state to state, two-thirds of the states require the adverse possessor to be in possession for 15 years or longer. The facts do not state the statutory period that applies in this jurisdiction, but they do make clear that Arthur has only been in possession for five years. Arthur would likely lose his adverse possession claim because he has not been in possession long enough to satisfy the statutory period.

Alternatively, Arthur can argue that the court should recognize his fence as the new boundary between the two properties because both parties had always treated the fence line as the boundary between their properties. When neighboring owners are uncertain as to the precise location of a boundary, courts will, in certain circumstances, recognize an informal agreed-upon boundary, even if the agreement has the effect of placing a boundary somewhere other than at its "true" location. Here, there are no facts to suggest the parties orally agreed to the boundary. However, even absent an express oral agreement between Arthur and Betty as to the location of the boundary, Arthur can argue that the boundary should be located at the fence line based on acquiescence or by estoppel. Arthur would argue that Betty acquiesced to the boundary by her long recognition and acceptance of the boundary. Arthur could also argue that Betty should be estopped from challenging the boundary, as she did not object to the fence and he relied on the understood boundary to his detriment. Betty, on the other hand, would argue that she is not estopped, as she never represented to Arthur that she agreed that the fence line was the boundary. Although it's a close question, the facts favor Arthur on this point. Both parties acted as though the fence line was the boundary between their properties.

Moreover, even if the court concludes that Arthur's fence encroaches on Betty's property, Arthur could argue that he should not be ordered to remove the fence. A majority of states recognize the relative hardship doctrine. In these states, courts refuse to order removal of an innocent encroachment that causes minimal harm and would be expensive to remove. Here, the facts do not state how much the fence encroaches on Betty's property; nor do they state the cost to Arthur of removal. Nevertheless, it is unlikely that Betty can show that the fence causes more than minimal harm. Betty never objected to the old fence, which Arthur's fence replaced. On the other hand, to the extent that the fence lowers Betty's property value, Arthur may have to pay Betty to compensate her for the loss in value, or he may be forced to buy the land on which the fence stands.

(b) Arthur's pecan tree:

Betty will argue that the branches of Arthur's pecan tree that overhang her yard constitute a trespass upon her property. A trespass can occur beneath or above the surface of the land. Here, the overhanging branches intrude upon Betty's property. But some courts hold that a landowner cannot recover in a trespass action merely because the branches overhang her property, although such courts would agree that Betty has the right to engage in self-help and trim the branches back from her property. Therefore, while Betty was within her rights to cut the branches, it is unlikely that she will recover damages for trespass.

Alternatively, Betty can argue that the pecan tree is a nuisance. A nuisance occurs when a defendant has, in a nontrespassory manner, caused an unreasonable and substantial interference with, or impairment of, the plaintiff's use and enjoyment of her land. However, according to most courts, encroaching trees are not a nuisance merely because they cast shade or drop leaves or fruit. Encroaching trees, however, may be regarded as a nuisance when they cause actual harm to neighboring property. In such circumstances, the owner of the tree may be held responsible for any harm caused. Here, Betty can show that the pecans are filling the gutters along her roof and causing water to back up, resulting in damage to her roof. Betty should be able to recover for damages sustained as a result of the falling pecans.

(2) Arthur v. Betty: Betty's fence:

Arthur will argue that Betty's fence interferes with the flow of light and air across his property. Absent an express agreement to the contrary, a property owner has no right to the free flow of light and air across his property. In many jurisdictions, however, spite fences—fences constructed for the purpose of blocking a neighbor's light and air or to hurt the neighbor—are deemed a nuisance. Here, Arthur will argue that Betty's fence was constructed in retaliation for his installation of a security camera. Betty, on the other hand, could successfully argue that she had a legitimate, non-malicious reason for building the fence: to block the view of Arthur's security camera. Betty will likely prevail on this issue.

Suggested Reading

Adverse possession; ELO ch.3

Nuisance; ELO ch.13-I

Easements; ELO ch.9-II(C)(6)

Answer to Question 25

Important aspects:

Easement implied from prior use, easement by necessity, bona fide purchaser, inquiry notice.

Summary:

Easements implied by necessity and from prior use were likely created in Westley's favor. Since Westley does not have a permanent right of way to access his land, except over Old Logging Road, a court would most likely find that he has an easement by necessity across Eastacre. Moreover, Buyer is likely bound by the easements and must allow Westley access across the Old Logging Road because Buyer was likely on inquiry notice of Westley's interest.

Answer:

Westley's rights to old logging road depend upon whether an easement was created and whether the burden of the easement runs to Buyer.

(1) Easement: creation:

(a) Implied by necessity:

Westley will argue that an easement by necessity arose by operation of law when Orson divided the land and conveyed Westacre to Westley. An easement by necessity arises where land previously owned in common is severed, and access to a public road can only be gained via a right of way over the other parcel. Here, Eastacre and West acre were once commonly owned by Orson. When Orson severed the tract, Westacre was rendered landlocked.

Buyer will argue that Westacre is not landlocked because Westley has access over neighboring properties using Schoolhouse Road. While it is true that Westley currently has access to his property over Schoolhouse Road, his right to use Schoolhouse Road is pursuant to a revocable license. Since Westley does not have a permanent right of way to access his land, except over Old Logging Road, a court would most likely find that he has an easement by necessity across Eastacre.

(b) Implied from prior use:

Westley could also claim that an easement implied from prior use was created when Orson divided the tract if Westley can show that, prior to severance, Orson used the road that is now part of Eastacre to access the land that is now Westacre. An easement can be implied from prior use if (1) the common owner of two or more adjoining parcels used one parcel to gain access to the other; (2) such prior use was apparent, continuous, visible, and permanent; and (3) continued use of the servient parcel is reasonably necessary for the use and enjoyment of the dominant estate.

Here, the facts do not explicitly state that Orson used Old Logging Road to access the western portion of his property. However, this was likely the case. At the time of Westley's purchase, Old Logging Road appeared to be the only way Orson could reach the cabin, which was the only structure on the land. Orson's prior use was also apparent, continuous, visible, and permanent. Old Logging Road, which was made of dirt and gravel, was in an affixed and permanent location on the land and apparently was visible to anyone visiting the property, since both Westley and Esther saw the road on their visits to the property. Westley can also show that use of Old Logging Road is reasonably necessary for Westley's enjoyment of the property.

While Westley can easily traverse Old Logging Road, Schoolhouse Road covers difficult-to-traverse hills and is sometimes impassable.

(c) By estoppel:

Westley might also argue that an easement was created by estoppel since he relied on access to Old Logging Road to his detriment. Buyer would argue that Westley had at most a license, which Buyer later revoked. A license is generally revocable at the will of the licensor. However, some courts hold that where a licensee has made substantial expenditures in reasonable reliance on the license with the licensor's knowledge, the license is irrevocable.

Here, the facts do not indicate whether Westley expressly was given permission to use Old Logging Road before Buyer purchased Eastacre from Esther. However, the facts do indicate at least tacit approval was given. Orson and Esther, the prior owners of Eastacre, were aware that Westley was using Old Logging Road. Orson mentioned to Esther that Westley would probably like to continue using the road. Orson and Esther saw Westley using the road to bring building materials to his land. These facts suggest that the licensor was aware of the use and took no steps to prevent it. Buyer, on the other hand, would argue that Esther never approved Westley's use of the road. But Westley could successfully counter that Esther never indicated to him any intent to revoke the license.

Alternatively, Westley could argue that an easement by estoppel was created when Buyer gave Westley a key to the lock across Old Logging Road and explicitly gave Westley permission to use Old Logging Road except during deer hunting season. But, since no facts suggest that Westley made any substantial expenditures in reliance on that license, it is unlikely that Westley will succeed on this claim.

(d) By prescription:

Alternatively, Westley could argue that he has an easement by prescription across Eastacre. An easement by prescription arises where a plaintiff can demonstrate adverse use that is open, notorious, continuous, and uninterrupted for the statutory period.

Here, two defects undermine Westley's claim. First, he may have difficulty showing that his use was adverse (at least up until Buyer obstructed his access to the road). As discussed above, Westley's use may have been with the consent of the prior owners, Orson and Esther. On the other hand, since the facts do not indicate that the owner of Eastacre either expressly granted or expressly denied Westley access to the road, Westley would argue that his possession should be presumed nonpermissive. In any event, even if his use was adverse to Orson and Esther, it appears that Westley's use was not adverse to Buyer. Buyer explicitly gave Westley permission to use Old Logging Road.

Second, while the facts do not state how long the use must be adverse to establish an easement by prescription, as with adverse possession, most jurisdictions require that adverse use continue for a period of time governed by statute. The facts do not indicate the length of time indicated in the statute in this jurisdiction. While the statutory period varies from state to state, most states require more than five years of adverse use. It is unlikely that Westley can prevail on this claim.

(2) Easement: transferability:

Even if an easement was created, Buyer will argue that he should not be burdened by the easement because he had no notice of it. The burden of an easement will run automatically with the burdened land unless the land is purchased by a bona fide purchaser for value without notice (actual, inquiry, or record) of the easement. In this case, Buyer is probably a bona fide purchaser for value. Although the facts do not state how much Buyer paid, as long as it was more than a nominal amount, courts will generally consider Buyer a purchaser for value. This case will likely turn on whether Buyer had notice of the easement. Buyer will argue that he also did not have notice of Westley's interest. First, he did not have actual notice, as no facts suggest that anyone told Buyer about Westley's easement. Second, since the easement arose by operation of law, there was no document to record, so Buyer could not have been on constructive notice. Buyer, however, may be charged with inquiry notice. Old Logging Road was made of gravel, which suggests it was of a permanent nature. It also appears from the facts that the road was visible to visitors and occupants of Eastacre. While Buyer may argue that because he did not reside on the property full time, he never saw Wesley use Old Logging Road, his argument will likely fail. Whether or not an owner actually saw the adverse use is irrelevant. Inquiry notice is presumed where the use is sufficiently visible to put a reasonable owner on notice. Buyer could argue that even a reasonable owner would not be on notice because most owners did not reside on the land full time, but this argument will likely lose because it appears that the road was visible even to the infrequent visitor.

(3) Easement: termination:

If the court were to hold that Eastacre was burdened by the easement, Buyer will argue that the easement terminated. Generally an easement by necessity terminates when the necessity no longer exists. Buyer will argue that Westley has alternative access over Schoolhouse Road and no longer needed to use Old Logging Road. But, as discussed above, Westley's access to Schoolhouse Road can be revoked at any time. A court is likely to determine that the necessity continues to exist, even though it may currently lie dormant.

Buyer could also argue that the easement terminated by prescription because he blocked Westley's access to the road. It does not appear, however, that Buyer has interfered with Westley's access long enough to satisfy the applicable statute of limitations. At most, Buyer's interference began a year ago. One year is not long enough to satisfy the statutory period in any jurisdiction.

Suggested Reading

Easements, creation of; ELO ch.9-II

Licenses; ELO ch.9-VI(D)(2)

Transfer and subdivision of easements; ELO ch.9-IV

Notice; ELO ch.12-II(I)-(L)

Easements, termination; ELO ch.9-(V)(E)

Answer to Question 26

Important aspects:

Condemnation, eminent domain, public use.

Summary:

City will likely prevail because the taking would likely be construed as for a public use and will have to pay fair market value for the land.

Answer:

A government entity may condemn property if it does so for the public good as long as it pays just compensation.

(a) Public use:

Jack will argue that City improperly exercised its powers of eminent domain because it did not take his property for a "public use," but for a private benefit. Jack will argue that since less than 10 percent of the proposed development will be dedicated to parks and other public spaces, overall the proposed development project serves the interests of a private business rather than the general public. City, on the other hand, will argue that the proposed development does benefit the public because it will likely create jobs and generate tax revenue from ticket, souvenir, and concession sales and therefore meets the "public use" requirements.

A "public use" must be for a public good. A use is considered for the public good as long as it is rationally related to a conceivable public purpose. Economic development projects can be for public purposes because they can lead to urban renewal, stimulate job creation, and expand the tax base. Courts often defer to a government entity's determination that a taking of private property for economic development purposes is justified by a public need. (See *Kelo v. City of New London, Conn.*, 545 U.S. 469 (2005).)

Even if economic development can be an appropriate public use, Jack will likely contend that condemnation for economic development purposes should be limited to economically blighted properties, not his lot, which serves as a natural habitat. Although after *Kelo*, some jurisdictions prohibit or restrict takings related to economic development, most jurisdictions allow takings for economic development purposes. The City's determination that the taking is for a public use would likely be upheld. City is probably within its rights to exercise its power of eminent domain for economic development purposes.

(b) Just compensation:

Jack will likely argue that he should receive $1,000,000 for revenue lost if the sanctuary is closed. While $10,000 may represent the market value of the property, it does not adequately compensate him for the loss of his home and business and will not sufficiently compensate him for the cost of rebuilding somewhere else. Jack's argument will likely fail. While a government entity must pay just compensation, just compensation generally means fair market value at the time of the taking. It does not usually include compensation for the property owner's emotional attachment to the land or the increased cost of rebuilding elsewhere. City appears to have paid "just compensation" for the condemned property.

Suggested Reading:

ELO ch10-VIII(A)(1); ch10-VIII(B)(1); ch 10 VIII(C)(1)

Answer to Question 27

Important aspects:

Interpreting ambiguous conveyancing, Rule Against Perpetuities, easements created by implication and necessity.

Summary:

Thoroughbred Racing Society of America (TRSA) can stop Out-to-Pasteur (OTP) from selling to the developer but cannot claim title to the Tom's house and surrounding ten acres. The condition on the conveyance to the fraternity violates the Rule Against Perpetuities (RAP) and would be stricken, meaning the fraternity would own the house and surrounding ten acres in fee simple absolute. TRSA can stop OTP from selling to Developer because, while the condition on the conveyance to OTP violates the Rule Against Perpetuities, it falls within the charity-to-charity exception.

Answer:

Out-To-Pasteur (OTP)'s Rights:

OTP will argue that the devise to TRSA violates RAP and therefore the gift to TRSA should be stricken, leaving OTP with a fee simple absolute and allowing OTP to dispose of the property as it sees fit. TRSA, however, will successfully contend that its interest is valid as it falls within the charity-to-charity exception to the RAP.

Upon Tom's death, the devise from Tom to OTP would be classified as a fee simple subject to executory limitation with an executory interest in The Thoroughbred Racing Foundation of America (TRFA). The interest in the OTP is a defeasible fee (a present interest that terminates at the happening of a specified event). When the future interest in a defeasible fee belongs to someone other than the grantor, the present interest is called a fee simple subject to executory interest and the future interest is called an executory interest. Because an executory interest creates a contingent future interest in a third party, it is subject to RAP.

The Rule states "No interest is good unless it must vest, if at all, not later than 21 years after some life in being at the creation of the interest." Because the gift is to a corporation and not a human being, the perpetuities period runs for 21 years from the effective date of the conveyance (i.e., 21 years from Tom's death). Ordinarily a gift such as this would violate the Rule as it is possible that the farm may cease to be used as a thoroughbred refuge more than 21 years after the interest was created. However, because both the possessory estate (OTP) and the future interest (TRSA) are given to charities, an exemption applies and the Rule Against Perpetuities does not apply. Therefore, the future interest to TRSA is valid.

TRSA's Rights:

As discussed above, TRSA can successfully prevent the sale by OTP. As a result of OTP's violation of the condition in Tom's will, title to the property reverted to TRSA. However, whether TRSA can take over the house and surrounding acres depends upon whether the condition on Tom's gift to the fraternity violates the RAP.

Tom's devise of the remaining 10 acres of land to TRSA may be invalid under the RAP unless the fraternity is considered a charitable organization for RAP purposes. Generally nonprofit fraternities and sororities are not organized and operated exclusively for charitable purposes, but they often operate charitable foundations. If the gift was given to a charitable foundation exclusively for charitable purposes, then it may fall within the charity-to-charity exception. If the gift to the fraternity is not a charitable gift, which it does not appear to be, the gift violates RAP. The devise from Tom to the fraternity would be classified as a fee simple subject to executory limitation with an executory interest in TRSA. The interest in the fraternity is a defeasible fee (a present interest that terminates at the happening of a specified event). When the future interest in a defeasible fee belongs to someone other than the grantor, the present interest is called a fee simple subject to executory interest and the future interest is called an executory interest. The executory interest is subject to the Rule Against Perpetuities. The Rule states, "No interest is good unless it must vest, if at all, not later than 21 years after some life in being at the creation of the interest." Because the gift is to a corporation and not a human being, the perpetuities period runs for 21 years from the effective date of the conveyance (i.e., 21 years from Tom's death). The gift violates the Rule, as it is possible that the property may be used for hazing more than 21 years after the interest was created. Therefore, the future interest in TRSA would be void, the language stricken, resulting in the fraternity having a fee simple absolute. If the fraternity is a charitable entity and the gift was for a charitable purposes, then the gift would fall within the charity-to-charity exception, as discussed above.

The fraternity's rights:

As discussed above, the fraternity has a fee simple absolute in the land because the gift to TRSA violated the RAP. The fraternity will be successful in its suit to have the barrier removed because an easement across the 90acre lot was likely created by implication and necessity.

An easement by implication arises where (1) land was previously held by a common grantor; (2) the servient tenement was used for the purpose for which the easement is now being claimed before the severance of the dominant and servient parcels, (3) such use was reasonably apparent and continuous at the time of the severance, and (4) the easement is reasonably necessary to the enjoyment of the dominant tenement. Here, Tom owned the entire 100-acre parcel, and he built a road over the 90-acre parcel to gain access to the 10-acre parcel. The paved road was visible, and its use reasonably necessary for the enjoyment of the 10-acre parcel.

The fraternity could also successfully argue an easement was created by necessity. An easement by necessity arises if a common grantor previously owned the land; the necessity for the easement existed at the time the dominant and servient tenements were severed, and the easement is strictly necessary. Here, Tom once owned both parcels, but the parcels were severed as a result of Tom's will, and without access to the road, the fraternity's parcel would be effectively landlocked. On the other hand, if the condition on the gift to the fraternity does not violate RAP, then TRSA would own both parcels, and under the doctrine of merger the easement would terminate.

Suggested Reading

ELO ch4-II (B)(4), Ch.5-IX (B), ch.9-II(C)

Answer to Question 28

Important aspects:

Finder's, first possession, abandonment.

Summary:

Adam likely has a superior claim to the ring. While Jack can establish a claim to the box, mere possession of the box would not establish Jack's claim to the ring inside.

Answer:

The diamond ring:

As between two parties both claiming possession, the first possessor has the superior claim. To establish possession one must show an intent to possess and an act of possession.

Here, Jack found the box, but mere discovery is not enough. Jack must also show he took possession of the property with an intent to exercise dominion and control over the object. Jack clearly took possession by removing the box from the place of discovery and transporting it to his house. Jack has probably done enough to establish intent to claim the box, but not the ring inside. Adam will argue that possession of the box does not entitle Jack to possession of the ring. Ownership of a container generally is not sufficient to establish ownership of the contents of the container. In this case, however, Jack would argue by shaking the box and hearing the ring rattle inside, he has also established an intent to take possession of the ring. Adam would likely prevail as Jack's only evidence of his intent is his own self-serving statement.

Even if Jack could establish intent to own the ring, Adam would argue that Jack cannot prevail because he entered the vacant house without permission. This argument would likely fail. Even if Jack was trespassing at the time, this fact would be relevant in a dispute between Jack and the homeowner, but not between Jack and Adam.

Adam would likely argue that he was the first to possess the ring. He physically removed the ring from the box and removed the ring from the place of discovery. (He took it to the park to present it to his girlfriend). Jack would argue, however, that by returning the ring to the box, Adam either did not fully establish possession, or Adam abandoned the ring when he returned it to the box under Jack's bed.

Jack would argue that Adam did not establish first possession as he merely "borrowed" the ring. Jack's argument would fail, however, because it appears Adam exercised sufficient dominion and control to establish a claim for possession. His conversation with his girlfriend seems to affirm Adam's belief that the ring was his to give away. Although Adam is no longer in physical possession of the ring, if he can establish he had possession, he will nevertheless prevail over Jack. Once a finder has established possession, even if he later loses possession, he nevertheless has a superior claim to a subsequent possessor.

Jack would also argue that Adam abandoned the ring. Property is considered "abandoned" where the owner intentionally and voluntarily relinquishes ownership. Abandoned property is generally awarded to the finder. Here, Adam has relinquished physical possession of the ring, but his intent is ambiguous. This is a close question but likely favors Adam as Jack would have the burden of proving Adam intended to abandon the ring.

The Gold Watch:

The outcome of this dispute will likely depend on whether the watch is characterized as lost or mislaid property and the location where the watch was discovered.

In this case the facts state the watch was located on the "walk leading up to Fran's house," which could indicate the public sidewalk or a private walk. If the watch was located on the public sidewalk, Jack would have a superior claim to Fran. On the other hand, if the property was located on Fran's private walk, the outcome may depend on where the object was found and whether the property was lost or mislaid. When lost or mislaid property is found on someone's premises, even by one invited to the premises, courts are divided. Some courts look to whether the object was found in a private home or a place open to the public. Here, the watch was located at Fran's private home but in an area visible and open to any passerby. Some courts hold the owner of the premises has a superior right to mislaid, but not lost, property. Property is mislaid if the owner intentionally put it in the place where it was found with an intent to retrieve it later. Property is lost where it is found in a place where the owner would be unlikely intentionally to leave it with an intent to retrieve it later. Courts reason that the true owner of mislaid property is more likely to return to the premises where the object was lost to claim it but not necessarily know where to search for lost property. Here, the watch is likely lost rather than mislaid because it is unlikely that someone would intentionally leave a valuable watch on the walk. This is a close question, but court would likely award the watch to Jack because it was likely lost rather than mislaid and because it was discovered in an open area on Fran's property.

Suggested Reading

ELO ch.2-9(C)

Answer to Question 29

Important aspects:

Deed delivery, Rule Against Perpetuities, recording acts, restraints on alienation, restrictive covenants.

Summary:

1. Title to the property:

The deed to Chanel is likely invalid as it was not delivered. Even if the deed to Chanel was valid, based on the operation of the recording act in this jurisdiction, Wesson likely has a superior claim to title to Chanel. ITAWV likely has no claim to the property as the condition placed on Chanel's deed likely violates the Rule Against Perpetuities (RAP). Since Chanel likely has no interest, neither does SSNG.

1. The Re-sale provision

Re-sale provision operates as a restrictive covenant and would bind any successor with notice of the restriction, including Chanel and Wesson. Although the re-sale provision severely limits the number of potential buyers of the property, the restriction is a valid, reasonable restraint on alienation as its purpose is to provide affordable housing.

Answer:

Chanel's Rights:

Chanel will claim that she has title to the property based on the deed from her grandmother. Wesson will argue that the purported conveyance to Chanel was invalid. A valid deed must comply with the Statute of Frauds. It must identify the parties, contain the material terms, and be signed by the grantor. Here, there are no facts to suggest any deficiency in the written instrument. However, statutes in some states require a deed to be witnessed by one or more persons and acknowledged before a notary public. If this jurisdiction requires such additional steps, the purported deed likely would be invalid as there are no facts to suggest the deed was witnessed or acknowledged.

Wesson could also argue the deed is void as it was not properly delivered. For a deed to be effective it must be delivered to, and accepted by, the grantee. The delivery requirement does not mean that the deed must necessarily be manually given to the grantee. Instead, the delivery requirement is satisfied by "words or conduct of the grantor which evidence his intention to make his deed ***presently operative***." If the grantor retains possession, there will be a presumption that delivery was ***not*** intended. For example, where a grantor executes a deed and places it in a box where it is discovered after the grantor's death, no delivery has occurred. Here, Mrs. Smith showed Chanel the box but kept the box in her own possession. By retaining the box, a court would likely find the deed was not delivered.

Further, Wesson would argue that Smith's verbal instructions to Chanel that Chanel only open the box if something happened to her (Smith) indicate that the document was intended as a testamentary document. Where the text of the deed, or surrounding circumstances, may show an intent on the part of the grantor that the deed not become effective until her death, the court will likely treat the document as an attempt to create a will, rather than a deed. However, since the conditions do not appear on the face of the deed, most courts would likely hold the deed sufficient to pass title and disregard Smith's verbal restrictions. If the verbal instructions are upheld, the deed likely passed a future interest to Chanel (a vested remainder subject to divestment), following Smith's life estate.

Finally, even if the deed was delivered, delivery did not occur until Smith died, which occurred after Smith conveyed the property to Wesson.

Most courts hold that a deed will not transfer title until it is not only delivered, but accepted by the grantee. Where the purported transfer is a gift, acceptance ordinarily will be presumed and will relate back to the time of delivery. Some courts hold a grantee need not even show she knew of the deed or was aware of its delivery. Some courts, however, might hold no delivery has occurred where the grantee does not immediately learn of the conveyance, and in the meantime, a third party has obtained rights.

Wesson's Rights:

Even if a court determined that Smith validly conveyed the property to Chanel, Wesson would nevertheless prevail under the recording statute. At common law the first claimant prevailed under theory that grantor retained no interest to convey to a subsequent purchaser. The recording acts, however, operate as an exception to the common law rule. Under the recording acts, a subsequent grantee can prevail if that grantee meets the requirements of the recording act.

Wesson would prevail under San Angeles' race notice statute. A race-notice jurisdiction protects the subsequent purchaser only if he meets two requirements: (1) he records before the earlier purchaser records, and (2) he takes without notice of the earlier conveyance. Here, at the time he purchased the property, Wesson had no notice of Chanel's interest and was the first to record.

It Takes A Whole Village (ITAWV):

ITAWV likely has no claim to the property as the condition placed on Chanel's deed ("to my granddaughter, Chanel, but if the property is ever used for commercial purposes, then to It Takes A Whole Village") likely violates the Rule Against Perpetuities (RAP). The devise from Smith to Chanel would be classified as a fee simple subject to executory limitation with an executory interest in ITAWV. The interest in ITAWV is a defeasible fee (a present interest that terminates at the happening of a specified event), and the future interest an executory interest. The executory interest is subject to RAP. The Rule states, "No interest is good unless it must vest, if at all, not later than 21 years after some life in being at the creation of the interest." The gift violates the Rule, as it is possible that the property may be used for commercial purposes more than 21 years after the death of the lives in being on the effective date of the grant (i.e., Smith and Chanel). Therefore, the future interest in ITAWV would be void, the language stricken, resulting in the Chanel having a fee simple absolute.

Stop-Shop-N-Go:

Stop-Shop-N-Go's (SSNG) rights are derivate of Chanel's rights. Since Chanel likely has no interest, neither does SSNG. However, if the conveyance to Chanel is upheld, SSNG could claim at least an equitable interest based on a theory of equitable conversion, which holds that once parties have entered into a contract that equity would enforce, the buyer obtains an equitable interest in the property.

The re-sale provision:

Chanel and Wesson would argue that PPS cannot enforce the re-sale provision as (1) the burden of the restriction does not run to either of them and (2) the restriction is an unreasonable restraint on alienation.

Chanel and Wesson's first argument would fail. For the burden of a restrictive covenant to run with the land, the promise must be enforceable between the original parties, the original parties must have intended it to run with the land, the burden must touch and concern the burdened land and the subsequent grantee must have been on notice. Traditionally, the enforcer would also have to show horizontal and vertical privity. Here, all the elements are met. The re-sale provision was enforceable between the original parties. Although the restriction did not expressly state that it was binding upon successors and assigns, most court will conclude that by limiting those who could inherit the property, the restrictions were intended to bind successors to the land. Further, the restriction touches and concerns the land as it restricts occupancy to the homeowner and those who succeed to her interest. The privity requirements are also met. Horizontal privity requires a transfer of an interest of land between the original covenanting parties. Here, the sale from PPS to Smith would satisfy that requirement. Vertical privity requires a conveyance between the original party and the successor. Here, Smith purported to convey her entire interest (either to Chanel or Wesson), so the conveyance would satisfy the strictures of strict vertical privity. Finally, Chanel and Wesson were on constructive notice of the restriction as the restriction was recorded.

Chanel and Wesson's second argument would also likely fail as a court would likely find the re-sale provision reasonable. The deed to Smith contains a partial disabling restraint on a fee simple. Traditional common law held restraints on fee estates void as repugnant to the fee. Modern courts, however, apply a rule of reasonableness to partial restraints on fee estates. Here, the re-sale restriction does not prohibit all sales; rather, it limits the number of persons who can purchase the property. Although partial restraints are generally invalid where, like here, the group of potential buyers is so small, a court would likely hold this restraint to be reasonable in light of the city's purpose of providing affordable homes for low- and moderate-income persons.

Suggested Reading

ELO ch.5-IX(C)(5); ch.9-IX(H); ch.11-III; ch.12-I, II

Multiple-Choice Questions

1. Anna found a valuable tennis bracelet on the ground after entering a coffeehouse. She showed it to the manager, who told her to leave it with him so he could display the item in the hope that its owner would claim it. Several weeks later, Anna returned and asked about the bracelet. The manager told her that no one had claimed it, and that he had given it to his wife as a birthday present.

   Based on the foregoing, Anna's rights are best described as

   A. superior to rights of the true owner, the shopkeeper, and his wife.

   B. superior to rights of the true owner, but inferior to rights of the shopkeeper and his wife.

   C. inferior to rights of the true owner and the shopkeeper's wife, but superior to rights of the shopkeeper.

   D. inferior to rights of the true owner, the shopkeeper, and his wife.

2. Anna found a valuable tennis bracelet on the sidewalk as she was entering a coffeehouse. She showed it to the manager, who told her to leave it with him. He said he would display the item, hoping that its owner would claim it. Several weeks later, Anna asked about the bracelet. The manager told her that no one had claimed it, and that he had sold the bracelet to a customer for $200, the best offer he received. The bracelet's fair market value was actually $1,000.

   Based on the foregoing, it is most likely that Anna may

   A. recover the bracelet from the customer who purchased it.

   B. recover $1,000 from the shopkeeper, but not the bracelet from the customer.

   C. recover $200 from the shopkeeper, but not the bracelet from the customer.

   D. recover neither the bracelet, nor its true value, nor the consideration paid for it.

3. Cory took his radio to a local repair shop to have it repaired. The manager of the store gave him a receipt for the radio and told him to come back in a week. The receipt contained a provision that stated as follows: "Repair shop shall have no liability for damage to the item delivered, regardless of cause." When Cory returned to pick up his radio, he was told that a repairman had accidentally knocked it off a counter where it was being fixed and had broken it beyond repair.

Based on the foregoing, if Cory seeks to recover the value of his radio from the repair shop, it is most likely that

A. the repair shop is liable to Cory since it was a gratuitous bailee.

B. the repair shop is liable to Cory if it failed to exercise ordinary care.

C. the repair shop is liable to Cory because it is an insurer of his property while the bailment exists.

D. the repair shop is not liable to Cory because it expressly limited its liability.

4. Anna wished to give some jewelry to her friend, Kate, who was on a trip through Asia. She telephoned her best friend, Gina, and asked her to come to Anna's house. When Gina arrived, Anna told her that she had some jewelry that she wanted to leave to her friend, Kate, but that she had never made a will. Anna asked Gina to take the jewelry and see that it was delivered to Kate upon Anna's death. Gina took the jewelry to her own home and kept it for Kate. When Anna died six months later, Gina delivered the jewelry to Kate. Anna was survived by her mother, who was her only heir.

Based on the foregoing, if Anna's mother sues Kate to recover the jewelry:

A. Anna's mother should recover the jewelry because the gift was not complete.

B. Anna's mother should not recover the jewelry because the gift was complete.

C. Even if the gift was complete, Anna's mother should recover the jewelry because the gift was *causa mortis.*

D. Anna's mother should not recover the jewelry because Anna's intent was clear.

5. Edward received an inheritance from his father. He wanted to retain access to the funds during his lifetime, but wanted the balance at his death to go to John, his son from a prior marriage. He deposited the funds in an account at First National Bank. The account was entitled "Edward, in trust for John." When Edward died recently, it was discovered that Edward's will left all of his property to his second wife, Emma, who is not John's mother. Emma has made claim to the funds on deposit at First National Bank.

Based on the foregoing, it is most likely that

A. the funds pass to Emma because the account at First National Bank did not constitute a formal trust.

B. the funds pass to John because the account constituted a valid gift to John during his lifetime.

C. the funds pass to John because Edward manifested a testamentary intent that John have the funds at his death.

D. the funds pass to Emma because Edward retained control of the account until his death.

6. Ann and Maryellen bought adjoining tracts of land. Maryellen built a house on her property. The house encroached 12 feet onto Ann's land. Maryellen used the house sporadically as a vacation home. Since Maryellen worked and had an inconsistent vacation schedule, her visits were infrequent and sometimes as much as four to seven months apart. Ann discovered the encroachment 12 years after the house was built, when she had a new survey made of her property. She told Maryellen to move the house from her land, but Maryellen replied, "That house has been there for more than 10 years, and I'm not moving it."

Based on the foregoing, in a jurisdiction which has a 10-year statute of limitations for the recovery of land, it is most likely that

A. Ann may force Maryellen to remove the house because Maryellen was not continuously in possession.

B. Ann may force Maryellen to remove the house because Maryellen was not exclusively in possession.

C. Maryellen will not have to remove the house since the house was built 12 years ago.

D. Maryellen will not have to remove the house if she built it in good faith.

7. Todd purchased a large residential lot from Barbara. The deed gave the boundaries of a tract of land that contained 1.7 acres. Unfortunately, the description in the deed mistakenly included 0.5 acres that Barbara did not own. The 0.5 acres belonged to Chad, who lived in another state and who had bought the property adjacent to Barbara's as an investment. Todd built a house on the parcel that he purchased from Barbara, but he also landscaped and gardened on the 0.5 acres owned by Chad. Todd has lived there for 15 years.

Based on the foregoing, in a jurisdiction that has a ten-year statute of limitations for the recovery of land:

A. Chad can evict Todd since Todd's house did not encroach on the 0.5 acre tract.

B. Chad can evict Todd because Todd's claim occurred by a mistake and is therefore not "hostile."

C. Chad cannot evict Todd because Todd took possession of the land under color of title.

D. Chad cannot evict Todd because Todd has had hostile and continuous possession for the requisite statutory period.

Questions 8-10 are based on the following fact situation:

O, the owner of Blackacre, conveyed the land in the following manner:

> To A for life, remainder to B and his heirs, but if B ceases to use the property for residential purposes, to C and her heirs.

8. Following this conveyance, it is most likely that A's interest is

A. a fee simple absolute.

B. a fee simple determinable.

C. a life estate determinable.

D. a life estate.

9. Following this conveyance, it is most likely that B's interest is

A. a vested remainder in fee simple determinable.

B. a vested remainder in fee simple on condition subsequent.

C. a vested remainder subject to divestment.

D. a vested remainder in fee simple because the restriction on B's use of the property is unlawful.

10. Following this conveyance, it is most likely that C's interest is

A. a contingent remainder in fee simple absolute.

B. a contingent remainder in fee simple determinable.

C. a shifting executory interest in fee simple absolute.

D. a springing executory interest in fee simple absolute.

11. Gene was the owner of a large tract of land called Blueacre. He conveyed the land by deed "to my son, Bill, for life, then to my son's oldest surviving child and his heirs." At the time of this conveyance, Bill had no children.

Based on the foregoing, the most likely present state of title of Blueacre is

A. Bill has a life estate, there is a contingent remainder in Bill's oldest child who survives Bill in fee simple absolute, and Gene has a reversion in fee simple absolute.

B. Bill has a life estate, there is a vested remainder in Bill's oldest child who survives Bill in fee simple absolute, and Gene has a reversion in fee simple absolute.

C. Bill has a life estate, and Gene has a reversion in fee simple absolute.

D. Bill has a life estate, Gene has a reversion in fee simple subject to executory limitation, and Bill's oldest child who survives Bill has a springing executory interest in fee simple absolute.

12. Toni conveyed 200 acres of land "to the Parks and Recreation District, its successors and assigns, so long as the property is used for park purposes."

Based on the foregoing, it is most likely that

A. if the Parks and Recreation District uses the property for purposes other than a park, Toni must sue the District to recover title to the land.

B. if the Parks and Recreation District ceases to use the property for purposes other than a park, it is a trespasser and Toni may evict the District.

C. if the Parks and Recreation District ceases to use the property for purposes other than a park, Toni may not recover the land, but may sue it for damages.

D. the interest of Toni following this conveyance is a reversion in fee simple absolute.

13. Sherri is the owner of Blackacre. She conveyed the land as follows: "To my daughter, Ann, for life; remainder to her eldest child, if such child reaches age 25." At the time of the conveyance, Ann had no children.

Based on the foregoing, following this conveyance, Blackacre is most likely held in which manner?

A. Life estate in Ann; contingent remainder in Ann's eldest child; reversion to Sherri.

B. Life estate in Ann; vested remainder in fee simple absolute in Ann's eldest child.

C. Fee simple absolute in Ann.

D. Life estate in Ann; reversion to Sherri in fee simple absolute.

14. Arthur owned Greenacre. He conveyed it as follows: "To my son, Roger, for life; remainder to my grandchildren when they reach 21." At the time of the conveyance Arthur had two sons, Roger and Ted. Roger and his wife have two minor children who were alive at the time of Arthur's conveyance.

Based on the foregoing, Greenacre is most likely held in which manner?

A. Life estate in Roger; contingent remainder in Arthur's grandchildren; reversion in Arthur's heirs.

B. Life estate in Roger; vested remainder in Arthur's grandchildren; reversion in Arthur's heirs.

C. Life estate in Roger; reversion in Arthur's heirs.

D. Life estate in Roger; contingent remainder in Arthur's grandchildren.

15. Oliver, the owner of Blackacre, conveyed it to his to friends, "to Anna and Staci, equally." Soon afterwards, Anna conveyed "all my right, title, and interest in Blackacre to John." Thereafter, Anna died. Anna was survived by Staci and by Anna's mother, who is Anna's only heir.

Based on the foregoing, Blackacre is most likely held in which manner?

A. Blackacre is owned by Staci by right of survivorship.

B. Blackacre is owned by John and Staci as tenants in common.

C. Blackacre is owned by Anna's mother by right of inheritance.

D. Blackacre is owned three-fourths by Staci and one-fourth by Anna's mother.

16. John owned a 200-acre tract of land. He devised this realty by will to "my sisters, Jeanne, Joan, and Jonni, as joint tenants, with right of survivorship." Jeanne conveyed her interest to her husband, Ted. Joan died survived only by her son, Bill.

Based on the foregoing, it is most likely that the land is held in which manner?

A. Ted, Bill, and Jonni are tenants in common.

B. Ted, Bill, and Jonni are joint tenants, with right of survivorship.

C. Ted and Jonni are tenants in common.

D. Ted and Jonni are joint tenants, with right of survivorship.

17. Moira and Colin owned Blackacre as joint tenants with right of survivorship. Blackacre consisted of 100 acres of land on which two houses were situated. Colin began farming the 100 acres. Moira moved into one of the houses and rented the other to Ian.

Based on the foregoing, it is most likely that

A. Colin must pay Moira one-half of the reasonable rental value of the land he farmed, and Moira must pay Colin one-half of the reasonable rental value of the house she occupied.

B. Colin must pay Moira one-half of the reasonable rental value of the land he farmed; Moira must pay Colin one-half of the reasonable rental value for the house that she occupied and one-half of the rents she received from Ian.

C. Colin must pay Moira one-half of the actual profit he received from the land he farmed; Moira must pay Colin one-half the reasonable rental value of the house she occupied and one-half of the rents she received from Ian.

D. Moira must pay Colin one-half of the rents that she received from Ian.

18. John and Rita held title to Blackacre as joint tenants with right of survivorship. Each year, John made the mortgage payments out of his earnings and paid the taxes out of his savings account. Rita maintained the premises and made all necessary repairs to Blackacre at her own cost.

Based on the foregoing, it is most likely that

A. John and Rita may seek immediate contribution from each other for a proportionate share of the expenditures made by the other.

B. John is permitted to seek immediate contribution from Rita for her proportionate share of the mortgage and tax payments; Rita is permitted to seek contribution only in an accounting for rents or partition.

C. John is permitted to seek contribution only in an accounting for rents or partition; Rita is permitted to seek immediate contribution from John for his proportionate share of the repairs.

D. neither John nor Rita is permitted to seek immediate contribution from the other, but each may seek contribution in an accounting for rents or in partition.

19. Landlord leased a commercial building to Tenant for a term of three years. The lease commenced on August 1 and concluded on July 31 three years later. Rent was stated to be "$24,000 annually, payable in monthly installments, due on the first of each month, of $2,000." About one year after Tenant commenced occupancy, Tenant wrote to Landlord giving the latter 30 days' written notice of her intent to terminate the lease.

Based on the foregoing, it is most likely that

A. since this is a month-to-month periodic tenancy, the notice terminated the lease at the end of the succeeding month.

B. since this is a year-to-year periodic tenancy, one year's notice is required to terminate the lease.

C. since this is a year-to-year periodic tenancy, six months' notice is required to terminate the lease.

D. since this is a term of years tenancy, notice is ineffective to terminate the lease.

20. Landlord leased her home to Tenant for one year. The lease commenced on January 1 and concluded on December 31, with rent being payable monthly. On January 1 following the end of the term, Tenant was still in possession and tendered to Landlord a check for one month's rent. Landlord refused to accept the check and sued to evict the Tenant.

Based on the foregoing, it is most likely that

A. Landlord may evict Tenant and recover the reasonable rental value of the property for the time of Tenant's holdover.

B. Landlord may evict Tenant and recover the rent stipulated in the original lease for the time of Tenant's holdover.

C. Landlord may evict Tenant and recover the reasonable rental value of the property for the time of Tenant's holdover, or hold Tenant to an additional one-year's term.

D. Landlord may evict Tenant and recover the rent stipulated in the original lease for the time of Tenant's holdover, or hold Tenant to an additional one-year term.

21. Landlord leased an apartment to Tenant on a month-to-month basis for $1,000 per month. When the lease commenced on June 1, Tenant attempted to move into the premises, but was prevented from doing so by the previous occupant, who was wrongfully holding over.

Based on the foregoing, it is most likely that

A. if the so-called English rule is followed in the jurisdiction, Tenant may sue Landlord for breach of the lease agreement and may also recover damages arising out of the lease, but Tenant may not sue the holdover tenant to evict him.

B. if the so-called American rule is followed in the jurisdiction, Tenant may sue Landlord for breach of the lease agreement and may also recover damages arising out of the lease, but Tenant may not sue the holdover tenant to evict him.

C. if the so-called English rule is followed in the jurisdiction, Tenant may sue Landlord for breach of the lease agreement and may also recover any damages arising out of the lease; Tenant may also sue the holdover tenant to evict him.

D. if the so-called American rule is followed in the jurisdiction, Tenant may sue Landlord for breach of the lease agreement and may also recover any damages arising out of the lease; Tenant may also sue the holdover tenant to evict him.

22. Landlord leased an apartment to Tenant for $500 per month. Landlord orally explained to Tenant that he normally received $700 per month; but since there were "some problems with the place," he would reduce the rent if Tenant would take the premises "as is." Tenant agreed, and the written, signed lease so provided. Upon moving in, Tenant found that the toilets did not work, there was no hot water, and the apartment was infested with rats and cockroaches. Tenant requested that Landlord cure these deficiencies, but Landlord refused, citing their agreement.

Based on the foregoing, in most jurisdictions (which imply a warranty of habitability into lease agreements), it is most likely that

A. Landlord is liable for these conditions since Tenant cannot waive the warranty of habitability.

B. Landlord is liable for these conditions since Tenant did not effectively waive the warranty.

C. Tenant is liable for these conditions since he accepted the premises in an "as is" condition.

D. Tenant is liable for these conditions since he accepted the premises in an "as is" condition for specifically agreed upon consideration.

23. Landlord leased an apartment to Tenant for $500 per month. Landlord explained to Tenant that he normally let the apartment for $700 per month; but since there were "some problems with the place," he would reduce the rent if Tenant would take the premises "as is." Tenant agreed. Upon moving in, Tenant found that the toilets did not work, there was no hot water, and the apartment was infested with rats and cockroaches. Tenant requested that Landlord cure these deficiencies, but Landlord refused, citing their agreement. Assume that Landlord is responsible for the conditions on the premises and that Tenant has given Landlord reasonable notice.

Based on the foregoing, it is most likely that Tenant's remedies are

A. Tenant may treat the lease as breached and move out.

B. Tenant may treat the lease as breached and move out, or Tenant may remain in possession and withhold rent.

C. Tenant may treat the lease as breached, move out, and sue for consequential damages; or Tenant may remain in possession and withhold rent.

D. Tenant may treat the lease as breached, move out, and sue for consequential damages; or remain in possession without any further liability for rent.

24. Landlord leased a house to Tenant for ten years commencing on January 1. Rent was payable in advance annually on January 1 of each year. Two years later, Tenant transferred possession of the house to Ben "for a period of two years from the date hereof" at a stated annual rental payable in advance to Tenant on January 1. (You may assume that Ben was not aware of the Landlord/Tenant lease.) Ben paid the first year's rent, but failed to pay rent for the second year. Tenant did not pay any rent to Landlord for two years.

Based on the foregoing, under real property principles, it is most likely that

A. Landlord may hold Tenant and Ben jointly and severally liable for the unpaid rent for the two-year period.

B. Landlord may hold Tenant liable for the unpaid rent for the two-year period, but may not hold Ben liable for the rent.

C. Landlord may hold Ben liable for the unpaid rent, but may not hold Tenant liable for the rent.

D. Landlord may hold Tenant liable for the rent for the two-year period, but may hold Ben liable only for one-year's unpaid rent.

25. Landlord leased an apartment to Jill for two years with an annual rental payable in monthly installments. The lease agreement provided that Jill could not "assign the lease without the prior written consent of Landlord. Any such assignment is void and entitles Landlord to terminate Tenant's interest in the premises." Jill recently has been transferred to another city and wishes to transfer the balance of the lease (less one month) to a coworker.

    Based on the foregoing, it is most likely that

    A. the agreement is enforceable as written, and Jill may not put another tenant into possession.

    B. the agreement is unenforceable as written, and Jill may put another tenant into possession.

    C. Jill may sublease the apartment, but not assign the lease to another tenant.

    D. Landlord would be able to enforce the agreement against an assignee from Jill, whether or not the Landlord acted reasonably.

26. Albert, the owner of Blackacre, approached Brad, the owner of Whiteacre, to request that Brad allow Albert to cross Whiteacre in order to get to a public road that bordered Whiteacre. Brad told Albert that Albert could cross Blackacre "anytime you want." Three years later, Brad decided to fence his land and, in doing so, closed off Albert's access to Whiteacre. Albert sued Brad to establish his right to cross Whiteacre.

    Based on the foregoing, it is most likely that

    A. Albert has an easement across Whiteacre, and Brad cannot block Albert's access.

    B. Albert has an easement across Whiteacre, but Brad may block Albert's access.

    C. Albert has an easement by necessity across Whiteacre, which Brad may not block.

    D. Albert has no easement across Whiteacre, and Brad may block Albert's access.

27. Okie, the owner of Blackacre, a 200-acre tract of land, sold the back half of Blackacre to Purchaser. Okie retained the front half, which abutted the county road. The back half of Blackacre was surrounded by other tracts of land owned by persons other than Okie or Purchaser, and was thus landlocked.

Based on the foregoing, it is most likely that

A. Purchaser has an easement by necessity that will exist only so long as the necessity exists; Okie may decide the location of the easement.

B. Purchaser has an easement by necessity in perpetuity; Okie may decide the location of the easement.

C. Purchaser has an implied easement based on prior use; but Purchaser may decide the location of the easement.

D. Purchaser has no right to an easement since the land was presumably purchased with knowledge of its condition.

28. Jim owned Tract A on which he operated a used car lot. He obtained from Ken a written easement "for purposes of ingress and egress" across Tract B, which abutted Tract A on its west side. Subsequently, Jim expanded his business by purchasing Tract C, which abutted Tract A on its east side. He then moved the used car business to Tract C and built a repair shop on Tract A.

Based on the foregoing, it is most likely that

A. Jim may continue to use the easement for ingress and egress to Tracts A and C.

B. Jim may continue to use the easement for ingress and egress to Tract A.

C. Jim may not continue to use the easement for ingress and egress to Tract A.

D. Jim may not continue to use the easement for ingress and egress to Tracts A or C.

29. April owned a one-acre tract of land. After some negotiation, Barbara granted, in writing, to April a specific easement across Barbara's land for ingress and egress to April's one-acre tract. However, this writing was not recorded. Several years later, April divided her tract of land into two half-acre tracts, built houses on each, and sold one lot to Chris and the other to Colleen. The road that April had used runs solely to the land now owned by Chris. However, Chris is willing to permit Colleen to cross his land to have ingress to, and egress from, her house.

Based on the foregoing, it is most likely that

A. Chris may use the road, but Colleen may not since Colleen's house is located on a nondominant estate.

B. neither Chris nor Colleen may use the road since neither one owns a dominant estate.

C. neither Chris nor Colleen may use the road since the easement was given to April and not to Chris or Colleen.

D. both Chris and Colleen may use the road since both own dominant estates.

Questions 30-31 are based on the following fact situation:

Staci and Shelley owned adjoining lots. They both wanted to build rather expensive single-family dwellings on their lots, but were concerned that the other might convert her lot to a different use. They entered into a written agreement in which each promised the other that her property would be devoted exclusively to a single-family residential dwelling, and that no structure inconsistent with that use would be erected. This agreement was not recorded, but each retained a copy of it.

30. Assume that Staci built a single-family home on her lot, but that Shelley sold her lot to Bill after telling him about the agreement. Assume, also, that Bill commenced construction of a commercial building on his tract.

Based on the foregoing, it is most likely that

A. Staci may not enforce the covenant by injunction against Bill because the agreement was not recorded.

B. Staci may enforce the covenant by injunction against Bill, even though the agreement was not recorded.

C. Staci may not enforce the covenant by injunction against Bill because the agreement was not recorded, but may sue Bill for damages.

D. Staci may not enforce the covenant against Bill by either injunction or damages.

31. Assume that Shelley had not sold her home to Bill, but that she herself began construction of a commercial building on her tract.

Based on the foregoing, it is most likely that

A. Staci may enforce the covenant by injunction or recover damages against Shelley.

B. Staci may enforce the covenant by injunction, but may not recover damages, against Shelley.

C. Staci may recover damages, but not secure an injunction, against Shelley.

D. Staci may not enforce the covenant against Shelley because there is no horizontal privity.

32. Rod owned a commercial building in which Lon was a tenant under lease for a term of 15 years. The lease contained a provision that stated as follows: "Tenant covenants and agrees that Tenant will not use the leased premises for an auto repair business." The lease was recorded. Three years after the date of the lease, Lon transferred "all my right, title, and interest in and to the premises leased from Rod" to Sarah for "a term of five years from date hereof." Sarah neither requested nor was given a copy of the Rod-Lon lease. Sarah immediately began using the premises for an automobile repair business.

    Based on the foregoing, if Rod commenced an action against Sarah, it is most likely that

    A. Rod may sue Sarah for damages or for an injunction since there is both horizontal and vertical privity, and Sarah took with notice.

    B. Rod may sue Sarah for damages or for an injunction, without regard to whether Sarah had notice.

    C. Rod may not sue Sarah for damages or for an injunction since there was no horizontal or vertical privity.

    D. Rod may not sue Sarah for damages but may sue for an injunction.

33. Chad owned a house and lot that he orally agreed to sell to Lynn for $230,000. Lynn paid Chad a deposit of $25,000. After several weeks of unsuccessfully trying to find a lender who would loan her the balance of the money to buy the house, Lynn finally called Chad and said: "The deal is off. Send my deposit back." Chad refused to do so.

    Based on the foregoing, if Lynn sued Chad to recover her $25,000 deposit, the most likely result will be that

    A. Chad must repay the $25,000.

    B. Lynn will not be able to compel Chad to return the $25,000 since there was an enforceable agreement.

    C. Lynn will not be able to compel the return of the $25,000 since the agreement is enforceable because of part performance (i.e., her down payment to Chad).

    D. Lynn cannot compel the return of the $25,000, but can recover her actual damages.

34. Kyla owned a house and lot in a residential neighborhood. She entered into a written contract with John to sell him the house for $200,000. The contract provided that Kyla would deliver "marketable title" to John on the closing date. In examining title, John discovered that the

property was covered by residential restrictions that were also imposed on the other houses in the subdivision. He thereafter refused to perform the agreement.

Based on the foregoing, the most likely result will be that

A. Kyla may compel specific performance of the agreement or sue for damages since the restrictions presumably enhance the property's value.

B. Kyla may sue for damages since the restrictions benefit the property, but may not compel specific performance.

C. Kyla may not compel specific performance or sue for damages since the title is not marketable.

D. Kyla may not compel specific performance since the title is not marketable, but may sue for damages.

35. Bob purchased a vacant residential lot. He built a house on the lot that violated a municipal ordinance setback requirement of three feet from adjoining side lot lines. After building the house, Bob contracted with Carol to sell her the house and lot for $150,000 and to deliver "marketable title, but subject to all covenants, conditions, and restrictions of record." Subsequently, Carol had a survey made of the property and discovered the violation of the setback ordinance. She refused to complete the purchase of the house.

Based on the foregoing, if Bob commences an action against Carol, it is most likely that

A. Bob may compel specific performance of the contract or sue for damages.

B. Bob may compel specific performance of the contract or sue for damages without regard to the marketability of title since Carol agreed to accept the land subject to restrictions of record.

C. Bob may not compel specific performance of the contract or sue for damages since the mere existence of a setback ordinance makes his title unmarketable.

D. Bob may not compel specific performance of the contract or sue for damages since violation of the setback ordinance makes his title unmarketable.

Questions 36-37 are based on the following fact situation:

Amy owned a house and lot that she contracted to sell to Jennifer for $200,000. Jennifer made a $20,000 deposit at the time the contract was signed and took possession of the house. While Jennifer was examining the title and arranging for financing, lightning struck the house and burned it to the ground.

36. In a majority of jurisdictions,

A. the risk of loss was on Amy.

B. the risk of loss was on Jennifer.

C. the risk of loss was on Jennifer because she had taken possession of the house.

D. the risk of loss is allocated 10 percent to Jennifer and 90 percent to Amy since Jennifer has paid 10 percent of the purchase price.

37. Assuming Amy had an insurance policy that covered the house against risk of loss by fire for $180,000, it is most likely that

A. the risk of loss is allocated to Amy since she had insured the premises.

B. the risk of loss is allocated to Jennifer, and Amy may keep the insurance proceeds.

C. although the risk of loss is allocated to Jennifer, Amy must credit the insurance proceeds against the purchase price.

D. the risk of loss is allocated to Jennifer, but Amy must rebuild the house to the extent permitted by the insurance proceeds.

38. Ted purchased Blackacre from Olivia. He paid $20,000 of the $200,000 purchase price in cash, and gave Olivia a promissory note for $180,000. The note was secured by a first mortgage lien on Blackacre. Ted then sold his interest in Blackacre to Mary for $30,000. Although Mary advised Ted that she would satisfy the first mortgage, she failed to pay the mortgage, and Blackacre was conveyed to her "subject to an outstanding indebtedness in favor of Olivia in the amount of $180,000, secured by a first mortgage lien on Blackacre." Mary subsequently defaulted on payment of the indebtedness due Olivia. There is still an unpaid balance of $180,000 under the promissory note. The property is now worth $150,000.

Based on the foregoing, if Olivia forecloses, it is most likely that

A. Olivia may foreclose on Blackacre and hold Mary and Ted personally responsible for the difference between $180,000 and the foreclosure sale price.

B. Olivia may foreclose on Blackacre, but not hold Mary or Ted personally responsible for the difference between $180,000 and the foreclosure sale price.

C. Olivia may foreclose on Blackacre and hold Mary personally responsible for the difference between $180,000 and the foreclosure sales price.

D. Olivia may foreclose on Blackacre and hold Ted personally responsible for the difference between $180,000 and the foreclosure sales price.

39. Ron, the owner of Blackacre, executed a deed conveying Blackacre to his son, Ben, as a gift. The deed was not acknowledged and was not recorded. However, Ron immediately delivered it to Ben. Several months later, Ron told Ben that he (Ron) had received an excellent offer for Blackacre and would like to sell it. Ben retrieved the deed and handed it back to his father, saying, "Here, Blackacre is all yours."

Based on the foregoing, it is most likely that

A. Blackacre is presently owned by Ron since no consideration was paid by Ben.

B. Blackacre is presently owned by Ron because Ron did not execute an acknowledgment to the deed.

C. Blackacre is presently owned by Ron since Ben returned the deed to him before it was recorded.

D. Blackacre is presently owned by Ben.

Questions 40-41 are based on the following fact situation:

Norma owned Blackacre. She entered into a written contract with Nikki to sell Blackacre to the latter for $100,000. Nikki paid $20,000 down. The balance was due in cash upon closing. Norma executed a deed conveying Blackacre to Nikki and deposited it with an escrow agent, pending Nikki's payment of the balance of the purchase price. By mistake, the escrow agent mailed the deed to Nikki before the price was paid. Nikki promptly recorded it.

40. Based on the foregoing, it is most likely that

A. title to Blackacre is still in Norma, and she may sue to have the recorded deed set aside.

B. title to Blackacre is vested in Nikki.

C. title to Blackacre is vested in Nikki, but Norma has an equitable lien on Blackacre for the unpaid purchase price.

D. title to Blackacre is vested in Nikki, but Norma has a cause of action against the escrow company for negligence.

41. Assume that Nikki went into possession of the land and then sold the property to her sister, Angela, for $80,000 cash. Assume that Nikki delivered a deed to Angela, who had no notice of Norma's interest and believed that Nikki had paid Norma in full.

Based on the foregoing, it is most likely that

A. title to Blackacre is still in Norma, and she may sue to have both deeds set aside.

B. title to Blackacre is vested in Angela.

C. title to Blackacre is vested in Angela; however, Norma has an equitable lien against Blackacre for the unpaid purchase price.

D. title to Blackacre is vested in Nikki since the conveyance to Angela was ineffective.

Questions 42-44 are based on the following fact situation:

Shelley owned Whiteacre. She conveyed Whiteacre to Gary by general warranty deed for $20,000. Gary went into possession, but subsequently discovered that there was an outstanding mortgage on Whiteacre in favor of First National Bank. This mortgage had been recorded prior to the sale. Shelley has been making payments on the mortgage, so First National is not threatening foreclosure.

42. Based on the foregoing, it is most likely that

A. Shelley has breached the covenant of seisin.

B. Shelley has breached the covenant against encumbrances.

C. Shelley has breached both the covenant of seisin and the covenant against encumbrances.

D. Shelley has not breached either the covenant of seisin or the covenant against encumbrances since there is no assertion by Bank of its right to foreclose.

43. Assume that Gary, prior to actually having notice of the outstanding lien, sold Whiteacre for consideration, by general warranty deed, to Randy.

Based on the foregoing, it is most likely that

A. Randy may sue Shelley and Gary for breach of the covenant against encumbrances.

B. Randy may sue Shelley, but not Gary, for breach of the covenant against encumbrances.

C. Randy may sue Gary, but not Shelley, for breach of the covenant against encumbrances.

D. Randy may not sue Gary or Shelley for breach of the covenant against encumbrances.

44. Based on the foregoing, it is most likely that the measure of damages in Randy's suit against Gary will be

A. the value of the property at the time Randy discovered the outstanding lien.

B. restitution of the purchase price paid by Randy to Gary.

C. the difference between the value of the property at the time of trial and the unpaid balance of the debt.

D. the unpaid balance of the debt, plus accrued interest.

Questions 45-46 are based on the following fact situation:

Louis owned Blackacre in fee simple absolute. He conveyed Blackacre to Tim by quitclaim deed several years ago. However, Tim did not record the deed or go into possession. Recently, Louis conveyed Blackacre to Marsha by general warranty deed. Marsha was aware of Tim's purported interest, but did not believe that it was valid. Marsha promptly recorded her deed from Louis. Tim so far has made no claim to the land.

45. Based on the foregoing, it is most likely that

A. Louis has breached the covenant of seisin and the covenant of quiet enjoyment.

B. Louis has breached the covenant of seisin, but has not breached the covenant of quiet enjoyment.

C. Louis has breached the covenant of quiet enjoyment, but has not breached the covenant of seisin.

D. Louis has not breached the covenant of seisin or the covenant of quiet enjoyment.

46. Assume that Marsha conveyed Blackacre to Amy by quitclaim deed, and that Amy then conveyed Blackacre to Laura by general warranty deed. All of the transferees had notice of Tim's purported interest. Tim then asserted his interest in the property.

Based on the foregoing, it is most likely that

A. Laura may sue Louis, Marsha, and Amy for breach of the covenants of seisin and quiet enjoyment.

B. Laura may sue Louis and Amy for breach of the covenant of seisin.

C. Laura may not sue Louis for breach of covenants because of the quitclaim deed, but may sue Amy for breach of the covenants of seisin and quiet enjoyment.

D. Laura may sue Amy for breach of the covenant of seisin, and Amy and Louis for breach of the covenant of quiet enjoyment.

47. Seller delivered a deed to Purchaser conveying Blackacre. The deed was not acknowledged by Seller before a notary, although acknowledgment is a requirement for recordation of deeds in the state where Blackacre is located. The recording clerk did not notice the lack of an acknowledgment and recorded the deed. Soon thereafter, Seller sold Blackacre again. This time, the sale was to Buyer. Buyer did not examine the record and had no actual notice of Purchaser's claim. The state in which Blackacre is located is a "notice" jurisdiction (a purchaser who takes without notice of a prior claim is protected against it).

Based on the foregoing, it is most likely that

A. Purchaser's interest is superior to that of Buyer since the recording of the deed constituted notice of Purchaser's prior interest.

B. Buyer's interest is superior to that of Purchaser since Buyer had no notice of Purchaser's prior interest.

C. Purchaser's interest is superior to that of Buyer, without regard to whether Buyer had inquiry notice of Purchaser's prior interest.

D. Buyer's interest is superior to that of Purchaser, without regard to whether Buyer had inquiry notice of Purchaser's prior interest.

48. Abbot conveyed Greenacre to Bill, as a gift, by general warranty deed. Bill did not immediately record his deed. Abbot subsequently conveyed Greenacre to Cliff, for consideration, by general warranty deed. Cliff recorded his deed. Subsequently, Bill recorded his deed. Greenacre is located in a jurisdiction that has a "race-notice" recording statute.

Based on the foregoing, it is most likely that

A. Cliff's interest is superior to Bill's; however, Abbot is liable to Bill for breach of the covenant of seisin.

B. Cliff's interest is superior to Bill's.

C. Bill's interest is superior to Cliff's, and Abbot is liable to Cliff for breach of the covenant of seisin.

D. Bill's interest is superior to Cliff's, and Abbot is liable to Cliff for breach of the covenant of quiet enjoyment.

49. Marlo conveyed Blackacre to Amy, for consideration, by general warranty deed. Amy did not immediately record her deed. Subsequently, Marlo conveyed Blackacre to Connie, for consideration, by general warranty deed. Connie did not record her deed. Then, Connie conveyed Blackacre to Debbie, for consideration, by general warranty deed. Debbie immediately recorded her deed. Finally, Amy recorded her deed. Blackacre is located in a jurisdiction that has a "race-notice" recording statute that protects subsequent purchasers who take in good faith and are the first to record their interest.

Based on the foregoing, it is most likely that

A. Amy's interest is superior to that of Debbie; however, Connie is liable to Debbie for breach of the covenant of seisin.

B. Amy's interest is superior to that of Debbie; however, Connie is liable to Debbie for breach of the covenant against encumbrances.

C. Debbie's interest is superior to that of Amy since Debbie recorded first.

D. Debbie's interest is superior to that of Amy; however, Marlo is liable to Amy for breach of the covenant of seisin.

50. Ed conveyed Blackacre to Adam, for consideration, by general warranty deed. Adam did not immediately record. Subsequently, Ed conveyed Blackacre to Baker, for consideration, by general warranty deed. Baker had no knowledge of Adam's interest in Blackacre. Shortly thereafter, Adam recorded his deed. Baker then conveyed Blackacre, by general warranty deed and for consideration, to Carl. Carl promptly recorded his deed. Blackacre is located in a jurisdiction that has a "notice" recording statute. This legislation protects subsequent purchasers who take in good faith and without notice.

Based on the foregoing, it is most likely that

A. Adam's interest is superior to Carl's, if Carl had actual knowledge of Adam's interest at the time Carl purchased.

B. Adam's interest is superior to Carl's since Carl had constructive notice of Adam's interest.

C. Adam's interest is superior to Carl's, without regard to whether Carl had actual or constructive notice of Adam's interest.

D. Carl's interest is superior to Adam's since Carl is treated as a bona fide purchaser without notice.

51. Steve conveyed a 200-acre tract of land to Elise, for consideration, by general warranty deed. He gave her an owner's policy of title insurance that stated that marketable title was in Elise. The policy contains an exclusion from coverage for the "rights of parties in possession that are not a matter of record." Prior to this conveyance, Joan had filed suit against Steve to quiet title to 15 acres of Steve's tract on the basis of adverse possession, but the suit had not yet been tried. When Joan added Elise as a defendant in the suit, Elise discovered Joan's claim for the first time.

Based on the foregoing, it is most likely that

A. the title company is liable to Elise if Joan prevails in her suit to quiet title since Steve did not have title to the 15 acres at the time of conveyance.

B. the title company is liable to Elise for negligent examination of the title to the property, if Joan prevails in her suit to quiet title.

C. the title company is not liable to Elise, but Steve has breached the covenant of seisin if Joan prevails in her suit to quiet title.

D. neither the title company nor Steve is liable to Elise, if Joan prevails in her suit to quiet title.

52. Peter operated a small automobile repair business in the garage at his home. His home was located in a neighborhood zoned for residential use only. Peter was employed elsewhere during the day, and he repaired the automobiles at night. In making these repairs, Peter made significant noise, which disturbed his neighbors' sleep. When they complained to Peter, he responded: "A guy's gotta make a living."

Based on the foregoing, if Peter's neighbors commence a nuisance action to compel him to discontinue his automobile repair business, it is most likely that

A. Peter is not liable for interfering with his neighbor's sleep since he did not make noise for the purpose of disturbing them.

B. Peter is not liable for interfering with his neighbor's sleep since his actions were not unreasonable.

C. Peter is strictly liable for interfering with his neighbor's sleep since his actions violated applicable zoning laws.

D. Peter is liable since he knew that his actions substantially interfered with his neighbor's sleep.

53. Rick owned a lot on which he intended to build a home. Lita purchased the adjoining lot. She began excavating her lot in order to build a house. In order to protect Rick's lot, she built a retaining wall on her property on the side adjacent to Rick's lot. However, the retaining wall did not hold, and a slide occurred. As a result, part of Rick's lot slid onto Lita's lot.

Based on the foregoing, it is most likely that

A. Lita is strictly liable to Rick for damage caused by the failure of the retaining wall.

B. Lita is liable to Rick for damage caused by the failure of the retaining wall, only if Rick can prove Lita was negligent in the excavation of her lot.

C. Lita is liable to Rick for damage caused by the failure of the retaining wall since her withdrawal of lateral support to his land was negligent per se.

D. Lita is not liable to Rick for damage caused by the failure of the retaining wall, if she was making a reasonable use of her land.

54. Seller owned a residential lot that Buyer wanted to purchase. Since Buyer had a poor credit rating, Seller agreed to sell the lot to Buyer by an installment sales contract. They executed a written contract, which provided that Buyer had paid 5 percent of the purchase price and agreed to pay the balance due in equal monthly installments over a three-year period. The contract contained a provision that "in the event that Buyer shall default in the payment of the amount due hereunder, Seller has the right to forfeit Buyer's interest in this property and retain all amounts previously paid as liquidated damages." Buyer made one payment, but was then unable to make any further payments to Seller.

Based on the foregoing, it is most likely that

A. Seller may forfeit Buyer's interest in the property and retain the amount paid as liquidated damages.

B. Seller must judicially foreclose upon Buyer's interest in the property.

C. Seller must give Buyer a reasonable period of time to pay the balance due on the contract and, if Buyer fails to do so, may forfeit Buyer's interest in the property and retain the amount paid as liquidated damages.

D. Seller must give Buyer a reasonable period of time to pay the past due amounts on the contract and, if Buyer fails to do so, may forfeit Buyer's interest in the property and retain the amount paid as liquidated damages.

55. Erin owns a restaurant in a relatively unpopulated area of City. She has operated the restaurant for almost seven years. City recently amended its general plan to provide that the area of City in which Erin's restaurant is located shall be "used for residential purposes only." In fact, the City Council recently enacted an ordinance that zones Erin's property for single-family residential use only.

Based on the foregoing, it is most likely that

A. the City Council's action is a per se Fifth Amendment taking for which Erin must be paid just compensation.

B. the City Council's action will not be a Fifth Amendment taking, provided that it grants Erin the right to continue her nonconforming use indefinitely.

C. the City Council's action will not be a Fifth Amendment taking, if it grants Erin a substantial period of time in which to continue her nonconforming use.

D. despite the ordinances, Erin has the constitutional right to continue her preexisting use of the premises indefinitely.

56. Alice conveyed Twinoaks Farm "to Barbara, her heirs and assigns, so long as the premises are used for residential and farm purposes, then to Charles and his heirs and assigns." The jurisdiction in which Twinoaks Farm is located has adopted the common law Rule Against Perpetuities unmodified by statute.

As a consequence of the conveyance, Alice's interest in Twinoaks Farm is

A. nothing.

B. a possibility of reverter.

C. a right of entry for condition broken.

D. a reversion in fee simple absolute.

Questions 57-60 are based on the following fact situation:

Thirty years ago, Owen, owner of both Blackacre and Whiteacre, executed and delivered two separate deeds by which he conveyed the two tracts of land as follows: Blackacre was conveyed "to Alpha and his heirs so long as it is used exclusively for residential purposes, but if it is ever used for other than residential purposes, to the American Red Cross." Whiteacre was conveyed "to Beta and his heirs so long as it is used exclusively for residential purposes, but if it is used for other than residential purposes within the next 20 years, then to the Salvation Army." Twenty-five years ago, Owen died, leaving a valid will in which he devised all of his real estate to his brother, Bill. The will had no residuary clause. Owen was survived by Bill and by Owen's son, Sam, who was Owen's sole heir.

For the purpose of this set of questions, it may be assumed that the common law Rule Against Perpetuities applies in the state where the land is located and that the state also has a statute providing that "all future estates and interests are alienable, descendible, and devisable in the same manner as possessory estates and interests."

57. Twenty years ago, Alpha and Sam entered into a contract with Joan whereby Alpha and Sam contracted to sell Blackacre to Joan in a fee simple. After examining title, Joan refused to perform on the ground that Alpha and Sam could not give good title. Alpha and Sam joined in an action against Joan for specific performance. Their action for specific performance will be

   A. granted, because Alpha and Sam together own a fee simple absolute in Blackacre.

   B. granted, because Alpha alone owns the entire fee simple in Blackacre.

   C. denied, because Bill has a valid interest in Blackacre.

   D. denied, because the American Red Cross has a valid interest in Blackacre.

58. Twenty-nine years ago, the interest of the American Red Cross in Blackacre could best be described as

   A. a valid contingent remainder.

   B. a void executory interest.

   C. a valid executory interest.

   D. a void contingent remainder.

59. Twenty-four years ago, the interest of Bill in Blackacre could best be described as

   A. a possibility of reverter.

   B. an executory interest.

   C. an executory interest in a possibility of reverter.

   D. none of the above.

60. Twenty-seven years ago, a contract was entered into whereby Beta and the Salvation Army contracted to sell Whiteacre to Yates in fee simple absolute. After examining title, Yates refused to perform on the ground that Beta and the Salvation Army could not convey a fee simple. Beta and the Salvation Army joined in an action for specific performance. Their action for specific performance will be

   A. denied, because Beta and the Salvation Army cannot convey a fee simple without Owen joining in the deed.

   B. granted, because Beta and the Salvation Army together own a fee simple absolute in Whiteacre.

C. granted, because the attempted restrictions on the use of Whiteacre are void as a violation of the Rule Against Perpetuities.

D. granted, because the attempted restrictions on the use of Whiteacre are void as a violation of the rule against restraints on alienation.

Questions 61-62 are based on the following fact situation:

Al, who is in possession of and who owns Redacre in fee simple absolute, conveyed Redacre by deed "to my daughter, Bea, for so long as she may live, then to Carla, only child of my deceased son Sam, and her heirs, but if Carla should ever enroll in law school, then to the Legal Aid Society."

61. What interest has Carla received in Redacre?

A. Remainder absolutely (i.e., indefeasibly) vested.

B. Vested remainder subject to complete divestment.

C. Executory interest.

D. Contingent remainder.

62. What interest has the Legal Aid Society received in Redacre?

A. Contingent remainder.

B. Fee simple subject to a condition subsequent.

C. Executory interest.

D. Vested remainder.

Questions 63-66 are based on the following fact situation:

Ten years ago, Alex paid for and received a deed to Flatacre from Steve, who, unbeknownst to her, was a swindler who did not own Flatacre. Alex immediately moved onto Flatacre, built a home, and resided there openly for the next three years. Alex then entered into a written lease of Flatacre with Bill. The terms of that lease gave Bill a one-year tenancy, and thereafter a month-to-month, all at an agreed rental. The agreement also gave Bill the option to purchase Flatacre during Alex's life at a price to be set following an appraisal by a mutually selected appraiser. Bill took possession of Flatacre and faithfully paid rent to Alex for 19 months. Bill then sent Alex timely notice of his desire to purchase Flatacre. However, unbeknownst to Bill, Alex had recently embarked on a trip around the world and had left instructions with her neighbor, Norma, to receive and deposit rent checks for Alex. Norma received Bill's letter but misplaced it.

Six months later, having patiently awaited a response from Alex, Bill, who had paid no rent since sending the letter to Alex, became disgusted and vacated Flatacre, taking his belongings with him. When Alex returned one year later (six months after Bill left) and observed that Flatacre was vacant, she moved back in and has resided there to date.

Owen, the true owner of Flatacre, has just learned of both Steve's conveyance to Alex and that Alex and Bill had occupied Flatacre. He now seeks to recover possession of Flatacre. The applicable statute of limitations is five years, and there is no requirement concerning the payment of property taxes.

63. If Owen were to bring an action to eject Alex,

A. Owen would prevail because Alex's right of adverse possession has not vested.

B. Owen would prevail because he never was aware that Flatacre was being occupied by other persons.

C. Alex will prevail because she has occupied Flatacre for more than five years.

D. Alex will prevail because she may tack Bill's possession of Flatacre onto her own.

64. If the local school district were now to acquire title to Flatacre by eminent domain, to whom would the district be obliged to pay "just compensation"?

A. Alex and Bill, in appropriate proportions.

B. Bill only.

C. Alex only.

D. Owen only.

65. Assume for this question that Flatacre consisted of four acres of land and that only one acre (upon which the house was located) had been occupied by Alex and Bill. If Owen's ejectment action was ***not*** successful, Alex could claim ownership to

A. none of Flatacre.

B. the one acre of Flatacre that had been occupied.

C. all of Flatacre.

D. the house and an easement of ingress onto and egress from Flatacre.

66. Assume for this question that Owen was successful in his ejectment action against Alex. Bill would owe rent to

A. no one, since Alex was an adverse possessor and Owen was unaware of Bill.

B. Steve, since he was the original vendor of Flatacre.

C. Alex, since their contract called for payment on a month-to-month basis.

D. Owen, because Alex never became owner of Flatacre under the adverse possession doctrine.

Questions 67-68 are based on the following fact situation:

Forty years ago, Owens, the owner in fee simple of Barrenacre, a large, undeveloped tract of land, granted an easement to the Water District "to install, inspect, repair, maintain, and replace pipes" within a properly delineated strip of land 20 feet wide across Barrenacre. The easement permitted the Water District to enter Barrenacre for only the stated purposes. The Water District promptly and properly recorded the deed. One year later, the Water District installed a water main that crossed Barrenacre within the described strip; the Water District has not entered Barrenacre since then.

Thirty-five years ago, Owens sold Barrenacre to Peterson, but the deed, which was promptly and properly recorded, failed to refer to the Water District easement. Peterson built her home on Barrenacre that year, and since that time has planted and maintained, at great expense in money, time, and effort, a formal garden area that covers, among other areas, the surface of the 20-foot easement strip.

Recently, the Water District proposed to excavate the entire length of its main in order to inspect, repair, and replace it, to the extent necessary. Peterson objected to the Water District plans.

67. Peterson asked her attorney to secure an injunction against the Water District and its proposed entry on her property. The best advice that the attorney can give is that Peterson's attempt to secure injunctive relief will be likely to

A. succeed, because Peterson's deed from Owens did not mention the easement.

B. succeed, because almost 40 years have passed since the Water District last entered Barrenacre.

C. fail, because the Water District's plan is within its rights.

D. fail, because the Water District's plan is fair and equitable.

68. Assume that Peterson's injunction was not granted, and after the Water District had completed its work, Peterson sued for $5,000 in lost profits she suffered by reason of the disruption to her garden caused by the Water District's entry. Peterson's action probably will

A. succeed, because her deed from Owens did not mention the easement.

B. succeed, because of an implied obligation imposed on the Water District to restore the surface to its condition prior to entry.

C. fail, because of the public interest in maintaining a continuous water supply.

D. fail, because the Water District acted within its rights.

69. Bill, owner of Redacre, granted to Jane, owner of adjoining Blackacre, an easement for a right of way across Redacre. After Bill went to live in Europe for a while, Jane moved into possession of Redacre and used it openly and exclusively, paying the taxes, for 20 years. She did not use her easement during this period. Bill returned and tried to evict Jane from Redacre. The court held that Jane had acquired title to Redacre by adverse possession. Jane then sold Redacre back to Bill, who immediately put a chain across the easement. Jane has now brought an action to remove the chain. In most jurisdictions, Jane will

A. lose, because she had become the owner of Redacre.

B. lose, because she did not use her easement for the statutory period of 20 years.

C. lose, because it had become unnecessary to use the easement due to her possession of Redacre.

D. win, because mere nonuse of an easement does not extinguish it.

70. The following events took place in a state that does not recognize common law marriage. The state does recognize the common law estate of tenancy by the entirety, but has no statute on the subject.

Wade Sloan and Mary Jones, who were never married, lived together over a seven-year period. During this time, Mary identified herself as "Mrs. Sloan" with Wade's knowledge and consent. Wade and Mary maintained several charge accounts at retail stores under the names Mr. and Mrs. Wade Sloan, and they filed joint income tax returns using the same names. During this period, Wade decided to buy a home. The deed was in the proper form and identified the grantees as "Wade Sloan and Mary Sloan, his wife, and their heirs and assigns forever as tenants by the entirety." Wade made a down payment of $10,000 and gave a note and mortgage for the unpaid balance. Both Wade and Mary signed the note and mortgage as husband and wife.

Wade made the monthly payments as they became due until he and Mary had a disagreement and he left her and the house. Mary then made the payments for the next three months. She has now brought an action against Wade for partition of the land in question.

The prayer for partition should be

A. denied, because a tenant by the entirety has no right to partition.

B. denied, because Wade has absolute title to the property.

C. granted, because the tenancy by the entirety that was created by the deed was severed when Wade left Mary.

D. granted, because the estate created by the deed was not a tenancy by the entirety.

71. Talbot and Rogers, as lessees, signed a valid lease for a house. Lane, the landlord, duly executed the lease and delivered possession of the premises to the lessees.

During the term of the lease, Rogers verbally invited Andrews to share the house with the lessees. Andrews agreed to pay part of the rent to Lane, who did not object to this arrangement despite a provision in the lease that provided that "any assignment, subletting, or transfer of any rights under this lease without the express written consent of the landlord is strictly prohibited, null and void." Talbot objected to Andrews moving in, even if Andrews were to pay a part of the rent.

When Andrews moved in, Talbot brought an appropriate action against Lane, Rogers, and Andrews for a declaratory judgment that Rogers had no right to assign the lease. Rogers's defense was that she and Talbot were tenants in common for a term of years, and that she had a right to assign a fractional interest in her undivided one-half interest. In this action, Talbot will

A. prevail, because a co-tenant has no right to assign all or any part of a leasehold without the consent of all interested parties.

B. prevail, because the lease provision prohibits assignment.

C. not prevail, because she is not the beneficiary of the nonassignment provision in the lease.

D. not prevail, because her claim amounts to a void restraint on alienation.

72. Ted agreed to rent a yogurt shop from Lin on a year-to-year basis beginning January 1, 2011, at an annual rental of $3,600, to be paid in advance.

On June 30, 2011, Ted sent a valid legal notice to Lin informing her that he was terminating his tenancy as of December 31, 2011. However, Ted did not actually vacate because the new space he had rented as of January 1, 2012, had been painted, and he didn't want to move in until the paint odor had dissipated.

On January 2, 2012, Ted received notice from Lin that his annual rent of $3,600 was overdue. Is Ted liable for the sum in question?

A. Yes, because Ted held over after the original lease term had expired.

B. Yes, because Ted failed to give Lin prior notice of his temporary holdover.

C. No, because a holdover tenant is liable for rent only in monthly increments.

D. No, because a holdover tenant is liable for rent only on a pro rata basis.

Questions 73-76 are based on the following fact situation:

Landlord owned grocery store, but leased grocery store to Tenant. The lease provides:

> Commencing November 1, 2010, Landlord rents his grocery store on Main Street in Crosstown to Tenant for four years. The rent shall be $100 per month, payable on the first day of each month.
>
> /s/ "Landlord"
>
> /s/ "Tenant"

On January 31, 2011, Landlord conveyed the grocery store and lease to Owner for consideration. Tenant had no notice of the conveyance and continued paying rent to Landlord until June 30, 2012, when he learned of the sale. That same day, Tenant assigned his entire interest in the lease to Assignee without Owner's knowledge. Tenant vacated the premises, and Assignee took over the premises, but paid no rent.

73. If Owner sued Assignee for the rent due under the lease for the months of July, August, September, October, and November 2012, she would collect

A. because one can never occupy land without being obliged to pay the rightful owner for such right.

B. if Assignee had notice of the conveyance to Owner.

C. because they stood in privity of estate.

D. if the assignment by Tenant to Assignee was in writing.

74. In the absence of an applicable statute, the assignment of the lease by Tenant to Assignee was

A. effective, regardless of whether it was in writing.

B. effective, because the lease did not prohibit an assignment.

C. not effective, because leasehold interests cannot ordinarily be assigned.

D. not effective, because Tenant failed to give notice thereof to Owner.

75. Assume Assignee dies testate before the lease expires. Assignee's interest in the lease

A. is terminated, because a leasehold estate cannot survive the death of the lessee.

B. is terminated, unless the land is located in a state that has a statute abolishing the distinction between freehold and nonfreehold estates.

C. survives for the remaining portion of the term and is dealt with as a part of Assignee's estate.

D. reverts to Tenant for the remaining portion of the term.

76. For purposes of this question, assume that Tenant (1) transferred to Assignee his interest in the lease only for the next two years, and (2) reserved the right to reenter the premises if Assignee was in default under the lease. In the absence of an applicable statute, which of the following statements is most accurate?

A. Tenant could not enforce his sublease because it was not authorized by the lease.

B. Tenant could enforce the sublease because it was not prohibited by the lease.

C. Tenant's position would be the same as that of an assignee.

D. Assignee would be liable to Owner for rent because of his privity of estate with Owner.

Questions 77-79 are based on the following fact situation:

After Allen had built a four-story building on his own land, an accurate survey revealed that one of the eaves extended about six inches over the land of Bates, his neighbor. The gutters and spouts were constructed so that no water from the house fell on Bates's land. Bates's land was unoccupied and unimproved at the time, but shortly thereafter Bates began to build a two-story building on her land. In doing so, she excavated several feet down—up to but not over the line between the two properties. Bates did not give Allen any advance notice of the excavation. The excavation was performed in a careful manner, except that no steps were taken to shore up Allen's building. As a result of the excavation, Allen's building settled and cracked and was seriously damaged before Allen knew about the excavation.

77. Bates sued Allen in trespass, praying for damages caused by the overhanging eaves. Judgment will likely be for

A. Allen, because Bates has suffered no damages.

B. Allen, because Allen was unaware of the overhang until after the building was completed.

C. Allen, because the overhang does not interfere with any present or contemplated use of Bates's land.

D. Bates, without regard to whether Bates is able to show any actual harm to herself.

78. Allen sued Bates for damages to his building as a result of Bates's failure to provide lateral support, but was unable to show that there would have been any settling of Allen's land if it had been in its natural condition without the weight of Allen's four-story building on it. Judgment will likely be for

A. Allen, because he is entitled as a matter of right to lateral support from adjoining lands.

B. Allen, because of Bates's failure to give Allen notice of the excavation.

C. Bates, because a landowner has no obligation to provide support to artificial structures on her neighbor's land.

D. Bates, because her duty extends no further than to perform the excavation in a careful manner.

79. Assume for this question that in an action brought by Allen against Bates for damage to Allen's building as a result of Bates's failure to provide lateral support, it was shown that even if there had been no building on Allen's land, it would have subsided as a result of Bates's excavation. This was because of an especially pliable clay soil condition of which Bates had no reason to be aware prior to the excavation. Judgment will likely be for

A. Allen, because he is entitled to support for his land in its natural condition.

B. Allen, because he is entitled to support for his land in its improved condition.

C. Bates, because she is not liable for the peculiar condition of the soil.

D. Bates, because there was no showing of malice or ill will toward Allen.

Questions 80-81 are based on the following fact situation:

West is the owner and operator of an oil well on her ranch. West is now, and has been for the past year, dumping waste from the oil well into a slush pit about a quarter of a mile from East's property. East has just begun raising chickens commercially on his property. As the waste is dumped, it settles into the ground and eventually percolates into a small stream that runs through East's property. East had intended to obtain water from this stream for his chickens. If the pollution of the stream is not stopped, East will have to import water for his chickens at a substantial expense. Also, last year West erected bright lights around her oil well that go on at dusk and off at dawn to discourage people from stealing her oil. East lives near his chicken operation with his wife and five-year-old son.

80. West's activities are probably

A. a nuisance, because they have interfered with a commercial enterprise (East's chicken business).

B. a nuisance, because they unreasonably interfere with East's use of his property.

C. not a nuisance, unless she intended to cause injury to East's chicken business.

D. not a nuisance, because her activities preceded East's decision to raise chickens.

81. East's chances of obtaining judicial relief in court with regard to the slush pit would be *least* aided by evidence that

A. West is wealthier than East.

B. others downstream also suffer hardships as a result of the stream pollution from West's slush pit.

C. West's well is an economically marginal operation.

D. West knew the waste material was percolating into the stream that ran through East's land.

82. Baker, the seller, authorized Smith in writing to sign a contract on her behalf for the sale and purchase of land. Arthur, the buyer, orally authorized Thomas to sign the contract for him. The contract adequately described the terms of the transaction. Smith and Thomas signed the contract: "Baker by Smith, her agent" and "Arthur by Thomas, his agent." Arthur refused to complete the purchase. Baker sued Arthur, who asserted that the contract is unenforceable by reason of the Statute of Frauds. Baker probably will

A. win, because the sales contract was signed by Thomas.

B. win, because her agency contract was in writing.

C. lose, because she did not sign the contract personally.

D. lose, because Arthur's agency contract was not in writing.

83. Jones, as seller, and Williams, as buyer, orally agreed to the purchase and sale of Jones's summer home. Without Jones's knowledge, Williams's wife moved into the house with a key given to Williams for inspection of the premises and spent substantial sums in renovating it. One month later, Jones refused to enter into a written agreement to convey the land or give a deed to Williams. Williams sued Jones for specific performance. Jones contended in rebuttal that evidence of the alleged oral agreement is inadmissible under the Statute of Frauds. The decision probably will be controlled by

A. the doctrine of part performance.

B. the fact that Williams has not tendered the agreed-upon purchase price to Jones.

C. Mrs. Williams's knowledge of the contract.

D. the fact that Mrs. Williams acted without Jones's knowledge.

Questions 84-85 are based on the following fact situation:

Sue owned a five-acre tract of land, one acre of which had previously been owned by Opal, but to which Sue believed she had acquired title by adverse possession. Sue contracted to convey the full five-acre tract to Peg, but the contract did not specify the quality of title Sue would convey.

84. Suppose that at the closing Peg paid the purchase price and accepted a deed. Subsequently, Sue's title to the one acre proves inadequate, and Opal ejects Peg from that acre. Peg sues Sue for damages. Which of the following statements is most accurate with respect to Peg's rights?

A. Sue's deed was fraudulent, and therefore Peg is entitled to rescission.

B. The terms of the deed control Sue's liability.

C. The only remedy available is damages because 80 percent of the transfer was valid.

D. Peg's rights are based on the implied covenant that title shall be marketable.

85. Suppose Sue's contract had called for the conveyance of "a good and marketable title." Pursuant to that contract, Peg paid the purchase price and accepted a quitclaim deed from Sue. Sue's title to the one acre subsequently proved defective and Peg was ejected by Opal. Peg sued Sue for the reasonable value of the one acre recovered by Opal. Which of the following results is most likely?

A. Peg will win, because Sue's deed was fraudulent.

B. Peg will win, because the terms of the deed control Sue's liability.

C. Sue will win, because the terms of the deed control her liability.

D. Sue will win, because a deed incorporates the terms of the contract.

86. Four years ago, Owen held Blackacre, a tract of land, in fee simple absolute. In that year, he executed and delivered a quitclaim deed to Price, which purported to release and quitclaim to Price all of the right, title, and interest of Owen in Blackacre. Price accepted the deed and placed it in his safe deposit box.

Owen was indebted to Crider in the amount of $35,000. Three months ago, Owen executed and delivered to Crider a warranty deed, purporting to convey Blackacre in fee simple to Crider in exchange for a full release of the debt he owed to her. Crider immediately recorded her deed.

One month ago, Price recorded her quitclaim deed to Blackacre and notified Crider that she (Price) claimed title. Crider contested Price's claim.

Assume that (1) there was no evidence of occupancy of Blackacre, and (2) the jurisdiction in which Blackacre is situated has a recording statute that requires good faith and value as elements of a subsequent grantee's priority. Which of the following is the best comment concerning the conflicting claims of Price and Crider?

A. Price cannot succeed because the quitclaim deed through which she claims title prevents her from being bona fide (in good faith).

B. The outcome will turn on whether Crider paid value within the meaning of the statute requiring this element.

C. The outcome will turn on whether Price paid value (a fact not given).

D. Price's failure to record until one month ago estops her from asserting title against Crider.

Questions 87-89 are based on the following fact situation:

Owen held Farmdale, a large tract of vacant land, in fee simple. The state in which Farmdale is situated has a statute that provides, in substance, that unless a conveyance is recorded, it is void as to a subsequent purchaser who pays value without notice of such conveyance. The following transactions occurred in the order given.

First: Owen conveyed Farmdale, for market value, to Allred by general warranty deed. Allred did not immediately record.

Second: Owen executed a mortgage on Farmdale to secure repayment of a loan concurrently made to Owen by Leon. Leon had no notice of the prior conveyance to Allred and duly recorded the mortgage promptly.

Third: Owen, by general warranty deed, gratuitously conveyed Farmdale to Niece, who duly recorded the deed promptly.

Fourth: Allred duly recorded her deed from Owen.

Fifth: Niece, by general warranty deed, conveyed Farmdale for value to Barrett. Barrett had no actual notice of any of the prior transactions and promptly recorded the deed.

87. Asserting that her title was held free of any claim by Barrett, Allred instituted suit against Barrett to quiet title to Farmdale. If Barrett prevails, it probably will be because

A. Allred's prior recorded deed is deemed to be outside Barrett's chain of title.

B. Barrett's grantor, Niece, recorded before Allred.

C. as between two warranty deeds, the latter one controls.

D. Barrett's grantor, Niece, had no notice of Allred's rights.

88. Asserting that her title was held free of any claim by Leon, Allred instituted suit against Leon to quiet title to Farmdale. Judgment should be for

A. Allred, because Leon is deemed not to have paid value.

B. Allred, because she gave value without notice of any competing interests to Farmdale.

C. Leon, because he recorded before Allred.

D. Leon, because he advanced money without notice of Allred's rights.

89. Assume for this question only that Niece had not conveyed to Barrett. After Allred recorded her deed from Owen, Allred asserted that her title was held free of any claim by Niece and instituted suit against Niece to recover title to Farmdale. Judgment should be for

A. Niece, because she had no notice of Allred's rights when she accepted the deed from Owen.

B. Niece, because she recorded her deed before Allred recorded hers.

C. Allred, because Niece was not a bona fide purchaser who paid value.

D. Allred, because she had paid value for Farmdale.

90. Vetter and Prue each signed a memorandum that stated that Vetter agreed to sell and Prue agreed to purchase a tract of land and that the contract should be closed and conveyance made and accepted "by tender of general warranty deed conveying a good and marketable title" on a specified date. The memorandum signed by the parties contains the elements deemed essential and necessary to satisfy the Statute of Frauds except that the purchase price to which they had agreed was omitted. Vetter has now refused to perform the contract, and in an action by Prue for specific performance, Vetter relies on the Statute of Frauds as a defense.

If, in support of his claim, Prue offers evidence, in addition to the written memorandum, that the parties had agreed on a purchase price of $35,000, Prue should

A. prevail, because Vetter is estopped to deny the existence of a contract.

B. prevail, because the law will imply a reasonable price where the contractual amount is not stated.

C. lose, because the price agreed on is an essential element of the contract and must be in writing.

D. lose, because the evidence does not show that the price agreed on is, in fact, the fair market value of the land.

Questions 91-92 are based on the following fact situation:

The owner of Newacre executed and delivered to Power Company a right-of-way deed for building and maintenance of an overhead power line across Newacre. The deed was properly recorded. Newacre then passed through several intermediate conveyances until it was conveyed to Sloan about 10 years after the date of the right-of-way deed. All intermediate deeds were properly recorded, but none of them mentioned the right of way.

Sloan entered into a written contract to sell Newacre to Jones. By the terms of the contract, Sloan promised to furnish an abstract of title to Jones. Sloan contracted directly with Abstract Company to prepare and deliver an abstract directly to Jones. Abstract Company did so. The abstract omitted the right-of-way deed. Jones delivered the abstract to his attorney and asked the attorney for an opinion as to title. The attorney signed and delivered to Jones a letter stating that, from the attorney's examination of the abstract, it was her "opinion that Sloan had a free and unencumbered marketable title to Newacre."

Sloan conveyed Newacre to Jones by a general warranty deed. Jones paid the full purchase price. After Jones had been in possession of Newacre for more than a year, he learned about the right-of-way deed. Sloan, Jones, Abstract Company, and Jones's attorney were all without actual knowledge that the right of way existed prior to the conveyance from Sloan to Jones.

91. If Jones sues Abstract Company for damages caused to Jones by the presence of the right of way, the most likely result will be a decision for

A. Jones, because he was a third-party beneficiary of the contract between Sloan and Abstract Company.

B. Jones, because the abstract prepared by Abstract Company constitutes a guarantee of Jones's title to Newacre.

C. Abstract Company, because it had no actual knowledge of the existence of the right of way.

D. Abstract Company, because Sloan, rather than Jones, retained its services.

92. If Jones sues Sloan because of the presence of the right of way, the most likely result will be a decision for

A. Jones, because Sloan is liable for her negligent misrepresentation.

B. Jones, because a covenant in Sloan's deed to Jones had been breached.

C. Sloan, because Jones relied on Abstract Company, not Sloan, for information concerning the title.

D. Sloan, because she was without knowledge of any defects in the title to Newacre.

93. Venner, the owner of Greenacre, entered into an enforceable written agreement with Brier, which provided that Venner would sell Greenacre to Brier for an agreed price. At the place and time designated for closing, Venner tendered an appropriate deed, but Brier responded that she had discovered a mortgage on Greenacre and would not complete the transaction because Venner's title was not marketable. Venner said that he would pay the mortgage from the proceeds of the sale, and offered to put the proceeds in escrow with any responsible escrowee, for that purpose. The balance due on the mortgage was substantially less than the contract purchase price. Brier refused Venner's proposal. Venner began an appropriate legal action against Brier for specific performance.

There is no applicable statute. Venner's best legal argument in support of his claim for relief is that

A. as the seller of real estate, he has an implied right to use the contract proceeds to clear the title being conveyed.

B. the lien of the mortgage shifts from Greenacre to the contract proceeds.

C. under the doctrine of equitable conversion, title has already passed to Brier.

D. no specific provision of the contract has been breached by Venner.

Questions 94-95 are based on the following fact situation:

Albert, the owner of a house and lot, leased the same to Barnes for a term of five years. In addition to the house, there was also an unattached, two-car brick garage located on the lot. Barnes earned her living working in a local grocery store, but her hobby was making small furniture. Barnes installed a work bench, electric lights, and a radiator in the garage. She also laid pipes connecting the radiator with the heating plant inside the house. Four years into the lease, Albert mortgaged the premises to Bank to secure a loan. Barnes was not given notice of the mortgage, but the mortgage was recorded. Six months later, Albert defaulted on his mortgage payments, and Bank began foreclosure proceedings. By this time, Barnes's lease was almost ended. Barnes began removing the equipment she had installed in the garage. Bank brought an action to enjoin the removal of the equipment mentioned above. Both Barnes and Albert were named as defendants.

94. If the court refuses the injunction, it will probably be because

A. Barnes was without notice of the mortgage.

B. the circumstances reveal that Barnes did not intend the items involved to become fixtures.

C. in the absence of a contrary agreement, a residential tenant is entitled to remove any personal property she voluntarily brings on the premises.

D. the Statute of Frauds precludes Bank from claiming any interest in the equipment.

95. If the equipment at issue had been installed by Albert, but the facts were otherwise unchanged, the effect on Bank's prayer for an injunction would be that the

A. likelihood of Bank's succeeding would be improved.

B. likelihood of Bank's succeeding would be lessened.

C. likelihood of Bank's succeeding would be unaffected.

D. outcome of the litigation would depend on whether the mortgage expressly mentioned personal property located on the premises.

96. Chase, as seller, and Smith, as buyer, enter into a written contract for the sale and purchase of land. The contract is complete in all respects except that no reference is made to the type of title to be conveyed. Which of the following will result?

A. The contract will be unenforceable.

B. Chase will be required to convey a marketable title.

C. Chase will be required to convey only what he owned on the date of the contract.

D. Chase will be required to convey only what he owned on the date of the contract plus whatever additional rights he might acquire in the land prior to the closing date.

97. Arthur owns a 500-acre farm on which his dwelling is situated. He enters into the following written agreement:

> I, Arthur, hereby agree to sell Walter my dwelling and a sufficient amount of land surrounding the same to accommodate a garden and lawn. Price: $20,000. Received: $1 on account.
>
> /s/ Arthur

Arthur now refuses to perform the agreement. Walter sues for specific performance. Judgment will likely be for

A. Arthur, because Walter did not sign the agreement.

B. Arthur, because $1 is too nominal to constitute consideration.

C. Arthur, because the agreement fails to satisfy the Statute of Frauds..

D. Walter, because valid contracts for the sale of land ordinarily are enforceable by specific performance.

98. Five years ago, Carla asked permission to drill some test wells on Baker's land to determine whether there were oil deposits beneath the land. After determining that there appeared to be substantial oil deposits, Carla asked Baker to lease the land to her for oil and gas production. At that point, Baker told Carla that he was not the true owner and so he could not give Carla permission to drill. Carla then approached Baker's neighbor, David, whose land also overlay the reservoir, with the same offer. The neighbor agreed to lease his land to Carla. Carla carefully drilled wells on David's land to produce the oil.

Baker sues to enjoin Carla's oil production. Who will most likely prevail?

A. Baker under the prior appropriation doctrine.

B. Baker, because Carla did not own the adjacent land.

C. Carla, as long as none of her wells encroached on the substrata of Baker's property.

D. Carla, because she was the first to extract the oil.

99. Tommy loves to dress up as a pirate and reenact scenes from his favorite private movies. Tommy often sneaks onto his neighbor's vacant land to stage his reenactments. One day, while playing "pirate," Tommy found a tin can full of gold coins buried under a tree stump. The tin was in such a condition to suggest that it had been buried there for quite a while.

If Larry, the neighboring landowner, sues Tommy for return of the coins, who will most likely prevail?

A. Tommy, because he found the gold coins.

B. Tommy, because the coins would be considered treasure trove.

C. Larry, but he must pay Tommy a finder's fee.

D. Larry, because Tommy was trespassing at the time he found the coins.

Questions 100-101 are based on the following fact situation:

Able owns Corneracre, a four-acre tract of land. Fifteen years ago Able vanished without a trace. Twelve years ago, Baker paid for and received a deed to Corneracre from Swindler, who, unbeknownst to Baker, did not own Corneracre. Baker immediately moved onto Corneracre, built a home, and resided there exclusively, continuously, and quite openly for the last 12 years. One month ago, Able returned.

The following statute is in force: "Except as provided below, any action to recover title to, or possession of, real property must be brought within 20 years after the cause thereof accrued. Where there has been an actual continued occupation of the premises by someone acting under color of title, the limitation period will be 10 years."

100. If Able sues to eject Baker, who will most likely prevail?

A. Able, because Baker has been in possession fewer than 20 years.

B. Able, because Baker never had Able's permission to be on the land.

C. Baker, because he has been in possession for more than 10 years.

D. Baker, because Able abandoned the property.

101. For the purposes of this question, assume that, while Corneracre consists of four acres of land, Baker only occupied (and built on) one acre (the acre on which the house was located).

If Able's ejectment action is not successful, Baker could claim ownership to

A. none of Corneracre.

B. the one acre of Corneracre Baker occupied.

C. all of Corneracre.

D. the house only, but Baker would have an easement of ingress and egress to reach the house.

102. Susan and Eddie own neighboring properties. For years each complained to the other about the narrowness of each of their respective driveways. Ten years ago, Eddie suggested, and Susan agreed, that they should take out the wood-slat fence that then separated their two properties and combine the two driveways to create an extra-wide common driveway. The common driveway extended five feet onto each property. Both contributed money and labor to the effort. For the last ten years both regularly have used the common driveway. Six months ago Susan sold her property to Peter. Peter commissioned a survey of the land and discovered that the common driveway encroached five feet onto his property.

If Peter places a chain-link fence down the middle of the common driveway, but on Peter's side of the boundary line, and Eddie sues to have it removed, who will most likely prevail? (Assume that the statutory period for adverse possession and prescriptive easement is five years.)

A. Peter, because he has every right to erect a fence on his own property.

B. Peter, because by erecting the fence he effectively revoked Eddie's permission to use the driveway.

C. Eddie, because he probably has an easement by estoppel, with which the fence interferes.

D. Eddie, because he probably has an easement by prescription, with which the fence interferes.

103. Belinda entered into a valid sales contract to buy a house from Sally for $300,000. Belinda paid $30,000 down as a deposit. The seller, Sally, executed a general warranty deed in favor of Belinda and gave the deed to her attorney, Albert, to hold in escrow until Belinda paid the balance of the purchase price. One month before the deal with Belinda was due to close, Patricia, who knew about the Belinda-Sally agreement, offered Sally $325,000 for the house. Patricia paid Sally

$325,000 in cash and Sally executed a quitclaim deed in her favor. Patricia immediately recorded her deed. At the closing Belinda sent a check for $270,000, the balance of the purchase price, to Attorney Albert. Albert immediately released the deed from escrow and delivered it to Belinda who immediately recorded it.

Assuming this all takes place in a race-notice jurisdiction, in a subsequent title dispute between Belinda and Patricia, who will most likely prevail?

A. Belinda, because the $30,000 down payment constituted payment of value.

B. Belinda, because Patricia knew about contract between Belinda and Sally.

C. Patricia, because she recorded before Belinda recorded.

D. Patricia, because deposit of the deed with an escrow agent does not transfer legal title.

104. Amy owned a one-acre parcel of land on a bluff overlooking the ocean. Amy decided to subdivide the parcel into two half-acre lots, one on the bluff and the other behind the first, away from the bluff. Amy sold the lot away from the bluff to Baxter, and retained the lot on the edge of the bluff for herself. Baxter constructed a large, two-story residence on his lot, including a second-story deck outside of a glass-walled entertainment room, facing the ocean and providing a panoramic view. Six months after Baxter's house was completed, Amy commenced construction of a house on her retained half-acre lot. A three-story structure, Amy's house will substantially obstruct the view of the ocean from the entertainment room of Baxter's residence. If Baxter brings an action against Amy to enjoin Amy from constructing her three-story residence, who would win according to most courts?

A. Amy, because she is acting within her rights.

B. Amy, as long as she informed Baxter at the time of the sale of the lot that she intended to construct a multistory residence on the retained lot.

C. Baxter, because Amy's residence will block Baxter's view from his second-story deck and entertainment room.

D. Baxter, because Amy did not object when Baxter constructed his house with the deck and entertainment room.

105. All of the landowners in Easyacre development agreed to mutually restrict their land to single-family residences to ensure they all benefit from a peaceful community. The agreement, which was in writing, was properly recorded against each property within the development. Since making that agreement, the land outside Easyacre has changed dramatically. Several commercial developments have been built on either side of Easyacre. The city recently rezoned Easyacre to permit multiple-family dwellings. Vince, the owner of one of the lots, has decided to convert his home into a four-unit apartment building.

If Ernestine, Vince's neighbor, sues to enjoin the conversion, who will most likely prevail?

A. Vince, because he is engaged in a socially useful activity.

B. Vince, as long as he conforms to the new zoning ordinance.

C. Ernestine, because the zoning change is unconstitutional.

D. Ernestine, because Vince's plan to build an apartment building violates the neighborhood restrictions.

106. For years Farmer has been appropriating 100,000 cubic feet of water per day from the river to irrigate crops on his large commercial farm. Many years later, as City's population increased, new housing developments popped up along the river, downstream from Baker's farm. Two years ago there was a drought that severely reduced the river's water level. Baker built an earthen dam to create a pool from which to irrigate his crops. This dam reduced the flow of water to downstream owners, who relied on it for drinking water.

If the downstream owners sue to force Baker to remove the dam, who will most likely prevail?

A. Baker, because he began withdrawing water from the river first.

B. Baker, because irrigation is a socially valuable use.

C. Downstream owners, because Baker interfered with the natural flow of the water.

D. Downstream owners, because their use takes priority over Baker's use in most states.

107. Jerry and Tess owned Parkacre as joint tenants with a right of survivorship. Without telling Jerry, Tess secretly conveyed her interest in Parkacre to Bob. Bob did not record the deed. Instead, he kept the deed from Tess in a shoebox under his bed. Three months ago, Jerry was hit and killed by a runaway bus while crossing the street. In his will, Jerry left all of his property, "to my sister Sofie for life, then to my nieces and nephews." Jerry was survived by his parents and his only sister, Sofie, who had one child, Charlie. Tess, Bob, Sofie, and Charlie have all claimed an interest in Parkacre.

Who owns what interest in Parkacre?

A. Tess owns the entire property because she survived Jerry.

B. Bob is a co-owner with Sofie, who has a life estate. Her life estate is followed by a reversion in Jerry's heirs.

C. Bob is a co-owner with Sofie, who has a life estate. Her life estate is followed by a vested remainder subject to open in Charlie.

D. Bob owns the entire property because he survived Jerry.

108. Tiffany owned approximately 100 acres of undeveloped land. In 2000, Tiffany sold 95 of the 100 acres to Developer via quitclaim deed; she retained a 5-acre parcel, which contained Tiffany's house. Developer then subdivided the 95 acres he purchased and began constructing homes. Contemporaneously with the 2000 transaction, Tiffany provided Developer with a separate agreement providing that, if Tiffany or her heirs or assigns ever attempted to sell the 5-acre parcel, then Developer could purchase it for the market value at the time of the sale or match any offer. Developer immediately placed the deed in her office wall-safe.

Tiffany died last year and left all her property to her niece, Jennifer. Jennifer has no desire to live on her aunt's ranch and would prefer to sell the property and buy a condo in the city. Neighbor, an owner of neighboring land who wants to prevent Developer from building more houses, offers Jennifer $300,000 for the property. Developer offers to match the offer, but Jennifer decides to accept Neighbor's offer because Neighbor has agreed to keep the land in its natural, undeveloped state. Developer sues to void the sale. If Jennifer is successful, the most likely reason is:

A. because Developer's cause of action must be based on the deed and not the contract.

B. because the right of first refusal could be exercised too far into the future.

C. because Developer failed to record.

D. because Developer was not an intended third party beneficiary of the agreement between Jennifer and Neighbor.

109. Octavio conveyed his 10-acre farm "to Adisa for life, then to Belinda's first child." Adisa died. At the time of Adisa's death, Belinda was single and childless. One year later, Belinda gave birth to a son, Timmy. When he turned 18, Timmy sold the property to CropDust, a large farming operation. In a jurisdiction that follows the traditional common law doctrine of destructibility of contingent remainders, who is entitled to possession of the property?

A. Adisa's heirs

B. Octavio

C. CropDust

D. Belinda

Questions 110 and 111 are based on the following facts:

John owned a home in an older area of City. The homes in John's community were built in the 1940s, long before housing developments with their "conditions, covenants, and restrictions" became the standard. Over the last 20 years, developers have purchased acres of surrounding land and built several modern housing developments in the surrounding communities. While the values in the homes within the developments have increased in value, homes outside the development have decreased in value. John convinces all except two of his neighbors that they need to create their own restricted community. The neighbors hire an attorney to draw up the necessary paperwork. The attorney drafts a master document of "Conditions, Covenants, and Restrictions," which is promptly recorded. The attorney then instructs each of the homeowners to convey their deeds in escrow to the attorney, who then conveyed the deeds back to the owners, including a reference to the CC&Rs. The updated deeds were duly recorded with the county. The CC&Rs limit each property to residential use only. The document also called for the creation of a Homeowners' Association (the "Association") with the power to enforce the provisions of the CC&Rs.

110. John sold his home to Zachary. Zachary proceeded to operate a tax preparation business from his home. Based on the foregoing it is most likely that

A. the Association may enjoin Zachary and recover damages since there is both horizontal and vertical privity, and Zachary took with notice.

B. the Association may enjoin Zachary but not recover damages because there was no horizontal privity between Zachary and the Association.

C. the Association may not enforce the covenant against Zachary because John failed to tell him of the restrictions.

D. the Association may not enforce the covenant against Zachary because the Association lacks standing to sue Zachary.

111. Assume Calvin, one of the two neighbors who did not agree to the restrictions, sells his home to Audra. Although Calvin did not originally agree to restrict his lot, Calvin came to appreciate the benefits of living in a restricted community. Calvin insisted that Audra agree that she would abide by the restrictions. Audra gave Calvin "her word" that she would comply with the restrictions. Two years after the sale, Audra decides to operate a daycare center from her home.

Based on the foregoing, it is most likely that

A. the Association may enforce the covenant because Audra's promise to Calvin was intended to benefit the other owners in the community.

B. the Association may enforce the covenant against Audra because operating a day care center in a residential neighborhood would constitute a nuisance per se.

C. the Association may not enforce the covenant against Audra, because there was no privity between Audra and the Association.

D. the Association may not enforce the covenant against Audra because Calvin never agreed to the restrictions.

112. Jason, who is currently unemployed and homeless, found an empty house that caught his attention. (According to the county property records, Olivia holds title to the land.) Jason then loaded all of his possessions in a truck and moved into the empty home. Jason repaired the broken windows, replaced a missing mailbox, and turned on the power to the home. He lived in the home as a normal owner would until ten years later when he took ill and was placed in the hospital for several months. While Jason was in the hospital, Ted moved into the house without Jason's permission or knowledge. Olivia arrives to find Ted living in her house. Olivia files suit two days after Ted moved into the home to remove Ted from the land. The decision should be for (assume the statute of limitation for recovery of possession of property is five years)

A. Ted, because Olivia has been absent from the property for more than five years.

B. Olivia, because Ted has not satisfied the requirements for adverse possession.

C. Ted, because Olivia abandoned the property.

D. Ted, because Olivia should not be able to interfere in Ted's peaceful enjoyment of the land.

113. Against his father's wishes, after completing college, Xavier left home to pursue an acting career. Omar issued an ultimatum: either Xavier complete law school or he would leave the cottage to Yolanda. Omar had his attorney type up a deed and deliver it to Xavier. In the deed Omar conveyed his lake cottage "to Xavier if he completes law school, otherwise to Yolanda." Two years later Xavier gave up acting and applied and was accepted to law school. After his first year of law school, Xavier drove to the lake cottage and discovered Yolanda had taken up residence. If Xavier sues to eject Yolanda, the decision should be for

A. Xavier because the conveyance created a fee simple subject to executory limitation in Xavier.

B. Xavier because it does not appear that Yolanda signed a formal lease agreement.

C. Yolanda because the conveyance to Xavier violates the rule against perpetuities.

D. Yolanda because Omar has taken no steps to terminate Yolanda's possession.

114. Osvaldo owns a large tract of largely barren land. At one time the land produced barrel after barrel of oil, but the reservoirs have long since been depleted. Osvaldo wants the land to stay intact for his children and grandchildren. While Osvaldo's son Benito never expressed any interest in the land, Osvaldo's other son Alonzo worked the land alongside his father. Osvaldo conveyed to "Alonzo, his heirs and assigns, but if Alonzo dies and is not survived by children, then to Benito and his heirs and assigns." Shortly after taking possession, Alonzo learned of a new technique for extracting oil and gas embedded deep within the shale rock underneath the land. Without Benito's knowledge or approval, Alonzo entered into a long-term lease agreement with Oil Company. Oil Company began removing large quantities of oil and gas. In an action by Benito for an accounting of the value of the oil and gas removed and for an injunction against further removal, the decision should be for

A. Alonzo, because the rule of capture grants ownership to the first possessor.

B. Alonzo, because the right to take oil and gas is an incident of his ownership.

C. Benito, because A committed waste.

D. Benito, because A acted in bad faith.

115. Ottavia conveyed to Anna for life "and five years after Anna's death, to Beatriz, her heirs and assigns." Subsequently Beatriz died, devising all of her estate to Xochitl. Beatriz is survived by Yara, her sole heir at law. Shortly thereafter Anna died, survived by Ottavia, Xochitl, and Yara, who all sue for possession. The decision should be for

A. Ottavia, because the condition precedent to Beatriz's possession has not been satisfied.

B. Xochitl, because Xochitl is the named devisee under Beatricz's will.

C. Yara, because she is Beatriz's heir.

D. Either Ottavia or Yara, depending upon whether the destructibility of contingent remainders is recognized in this jurisdiction.

116. In the bottom of the ninth inning of the seventh game of the World Series between the hometown Buzz and the visiting Starz, Billy Boyd, the homerun slugger for the visiting Starz, hit a long home run to win the game and the series. The ball landed in row ten of the bleachers where Charley, a Buzz fan, caught it. At the urging of the crowd and to show his own disgust with the outcome of the game, Charley attempted to throw the ball back onto the field. Unfortunately, because of Charley's lack of arm strength, the ball landed in row three, a mere seven rows in front of Charley and well short of the field. The ball was then picked up by Ollie Opportunist. The owners of the Starz have offered several thousand dollars for the ball.

If Charley files suit against Ollie to demand a share of the proceeds from the sale of the ball, the decision should be for

A. Charley if other fans at the game testify that Charley closed his mitt securely around the ball.

B. Charley if he can show Ollie went to the game without a valid ticket.

C. Ollie because "to the victor belongs the spoils."

D. Ollie because he has the ball.

117. Growers, Inc. and Cattle Company are neighboring landowners in an agricultural part of the state. Each owns several acres of land. Growers, Inc. is a large farming operation. A recent nationwide Escherichia coli or E. coli (a bacteria that can cause infection) outbreak is traced to

Growers' grand of triple-washed, prepackaged lettuce. Specifically, samples of cattle feces on Growers' farm tested positive for the same stain of E. coli that sickened 100 people. Growers suspects that the source of contamination is cattle from Cattle Company's feedlot wandering onto Growers' land. In any subsequent lawsuit by Grower against Cattle Company for trespass, which fact, if true, would help Cattle Company?

A. The feedlot had been in continuous operation before Growers opened the farm.

B. Growers had "no trespassing" signs posted.

C. Cattle Company used the best and most sanitary fee lot procedures.

D. The cattle feces that were the source of the E. Coli were tracked onto Growers' land by wild pigs.

118. Ten years ago, Bertha rescued a wounded alligator. Bertha nursed the alligator back to health. Bertha and the rescued alligator have developed what Bertha calls a "friendship." The alligator is so comfortable with Bertha, he will eat right out of Bertha's hand. While she allows the alligator to come and go as it pleases, Bertha did place a collar around its neck that says, "If found, please return to owner" and lists her name and address. Everyone in town is aware of the special bond between Bertha and her "pet" alligator.

Last week, Allan, a famous alligator hunter, waded into the swampy waters near Bertha's home. While in public waters he captured an alligator and was surprised to find a collar around the animal's neck. Allan removed the animal's collar and removed the animal to his gator farm, where he is planning to use him in a new alligator wrestling show he hopes to sell to a local television station.

If Bertha sues to get the alligator back, who will most likely prevail?

A. Bertha, because she found the alligator first

B. Bertha, because based on these facts, the alligator would be classified as a domesticated, rather than a wild animal.

C. Alan, because he captured the alligator in public waters.

D. Alan, because his proposed use—televising an animal wrestling show—is more socially beneficial than Bertha's proposed use.

119. Five years ago, Omer gave a deed to Blankacre to his favorite niece, Agatha. Subsequently, Omer became unhappy with Agatha because he heard she was running around with "a bad crowd." This information was erroneous, but Omer nevertheless notified Agatha in writing that he had revoked the deed to Blankacre intended to leave the property to her brother, Barney. Agatha did not respond to O's letter. Two months ago, Omer, Agatha, and Barney were killed in a 12-car pileup on the interstate while on their way to a family reunion. In his will Omer left Blankacre "to my beloved nephew Barney for life, remainder to his children then living." In her will, Agatha left all of her property to her daughter, Dahlia. Barney is survived by his son Salim. Based on the foregoing, it is most likely that

A. Dahlia is the rightful owner of Blackacre.

B. Salim is the rightful owner of Blackacre.

C. Omer's heirs are the rightful owners of Blackacre.

D. Since Omer died intestate (without a will), Omer's property escheats back to the state.

Multiple-Choice Answers

1. **D** The bracelet is lost rather than mislaid property because it is unlikely that someone would intentionally leave a valuable bracelet on the floor of a coffeehouse. The ***finder*** of a lost article acquires ***rights superior to those of everyone except the true owner***. When lost property is found on someone's premises, even by one invited to the premises, courts are divided. Some courts hold the owner of the premises has rights superior to the finder's, others grant possession to the finder. (*See* ELO ch.2-I(C)(5).) Choice **D** is the best answer. Anna found the bracelet *after entering* the coffeehouse, so in some courts Anna's rights would be inferior to the owner of the premises. Choice **A** is incorrect because the finder of lost property does not have rights superior to the true owner's. Choice **B** is incorrect for the same reason as choice **A**, and it is also wrong in those jurisdictions that prefer the finder to the owner of the premises. Choice **C** is wrong because shopkeeper's wife's claim is based on the shopkeeper's claim.

2. **B** In contrast with the facts in question 1, here, Anna found the bracelet outside the coffeehouse. In this case, Anna's rights are inferior to the true owner's, but superior to the rights of the coffeehouse. When ***property*** is ***acquired by means other than theft***, such as by a finder or by voluntary delivery of possession, the possessor generally is held to have a ***voidable title***. One having a voidable title may deliver good title to a purchaser who pays valuable consideration and who takes without notice of another person's interest. It is likely that Anna cannot recover the bracelet from the customer, who was a ***bona fide*** purchaser for value. (*See* ELO ch.2-III(A).) As between Anna and the manager, however, because he converted Anna's property to his own use, he is liable to her for its fair market value. (*See* ELO ch.2-I(C)(3).) The correct answer is choice **B**. Choice **A** is incorrect. The shopkeeper had a voidable title that he delivered to the customer. Choice **C** is incorrect because Anna can recover the full value of the bracelet. Choice **D** is incorrect in that the shopkeeper is liable to Anna for the full value of the bracelet.

3. **B** The arrangement between Cory and the repair shop created a bailment for mutual benefit. A ***bailment*** is the ***rightful possession*** of goods by ***one who is not their owner***. Generally, a bailee (the repair shop, in this case) in a bailment for mutual benefit must use ordinary care to protect the bailed item while it is in his possession. The issue raised is whether the duty is modified by a blanket waiver of liability. Most courts do not allow bailees for mutual benefit to exempt themselves from liability for ordinary negligence, although they may allow

reasonable limits on the extent of liability. (*See* ELO ch.2-IV(C)(1)(a).) Here, the repair shop attempted to remove all liability would not succeed. Choice **A** is incorrect because the bailment is not gratuitous; it is for the mutual benefit of the bailor and bailee. Choice **C** is incorrect in that bailees are not absolute insurers of the goods delivered to them; ordinarily, they must exercise only ordinary care to protect the goods from damage. Finally, choice **D** is incorrect because the language of the waiver is too broad. It attempts to relieve the repair shop of all liability. The correct answer is choice **B**.

4. B A gift is the voluntary transfer of property from the donor to the donee without consideration. In order for a ***gift*** to be complete, there must be (1) ***delivery*** of the item or a writing that embodies the terms of the gift, (2) an ***intent*** to make a gift, and (3) ***acceptance*** by the donee. (*See* ELO ch.2-V(A)(3).) Delivery of a gift through a third party will constitute valid delivery only if the third party is acting as an ***independent*** agent, or as the agent of the ***donee***. (*See* ELO ch.2-V(B)(2).) Here, the donor (Anna) delivered the jewelry to Gina with instructions to deliver it at her death to Kate, a person who was then unavailable. Gina was acting as an independent person or as Kate's agent and was not acting as the agent for Anna alone. Therefore the surrender of the jewelry to Gina constituted delivery, and the gift was complete. The correct answer is choice **B**. There is nothing in the facts to indicate that Anna made the gift in contemplation of death, so the gift is not a gift ***causa mortis***. Choice **C** is therefore incorrect. Choice **A** is incorrect because there was a completed gift to Kate. Choice **D** is incorrect because intent alone, however clear, is not sufficient to create a valid gift. There must also be delivery and acceptance.

5. C The facts describe a bank account commonly referred to as a "Totten trust." (The name derives from the case of *In re Totten*.) A ***"Totten trust"*** is created where the ***trustor deposits funds*** in an account ***in trust for another*** person. Even though the arrangement does not meet the requirements of a formal trust (because the depositor retains full rights to the funds on deposit during his lifetime), it has been sustained as a trust so long as the donor had a donative intent. Here, Edward expressed such a donative intent. He wanted the funds to go to John at his death. (*See* ELO ch.2-V(E)(1).) Choice **A** is incorrect. Totten trusts are recognized everywhere, though they do not meet the requirements of a formal trust. They are considered a poor man's substitute for a formal will or trust document. Choice **B** is incorrect. Even though Edward manifested his intent to dispose of the account to John, he did not intend to give John control of the funds until he died. The gift was not completed until Edward died. Finally, choice **D** is incorrect. Totten trusts are valid even though the donor retains control over the account until he dies. The correct answer is choice **C.**

6. A Because record title to the disputed property is in Ann, Maryellen must prove ownership by adverse possession. ***Adverse possession*** requires possession that is (1) ***actual,*** (2) ***open and notorious,*** (3) ***exclusive,*** (4) ***continuous,*** and (5) ***"hostile"*** (i.e., without the owner's consent), and that satisfies the requirements of the ***statutory period*** in that jurisdiction. (*See* ELO ch.3-IV(A).) In this case, the statutory period is ten years. Although Maryellen's possession likely satisfies the other requirements, it appears doubtful that she has been in continuous possession. Her visits were sporadic and there were relatively large gaps in time when she was not in possession. Although the facts state that this was a vacation house, Maryellen's visits would seem too infrequent to satisfy the test of continuous possession. Choice **A** is the best answer. Choice **B** is incorrect on the facts. Maryellen was apparently in exclusive possession of the property on which her house sat. Choice **C** is incorrect in that compliance with the statutory time requirement is not enough to create title through adverse possession. The other elements must also be met. Finally, choice **D** is incorrect in that good faith is ***not*** generally a requirement of adverse possession. Even if this jurisdiction had a good faith requirement, good faith alone is not enough to establish title through adverse possession. Maryellen must prove all of the elements for the requisite statutory period.

7. D ***Adverse possession*** can ultimately confer good title even when it begins under a ***mistake as to a property boundary line.*** Under the majority view, a person who occupies his neighbor's land under the mistaken belief that he has only possessed up to the boundary of his own land meets the requirements of ***hostile*** possession. (*See* ELO ch.3-III(C).) Here, the land mistakenly occupied by Todd did not belong to his grantor but belonged to a stranger to his title. Nevertheless, by building and occupying the house and by landscaping and gardening Chad's land, Todd's possession of Chad's half acre was open, hostile, and continuous. Choice **D** is the correct answer because Todd's possession for more than 10 years extinguished all other titles. Choice **A** is incorrect because it was not necessary for the house itself to encroach on Chad's land. Todd occupied Chad's land by landscaping and gardening on it. Choice **B** is incorrect because the majority view is that land occupied by mistake can be the subject of adverse possession. Finally, choice **C** is incorrect in that Todd did not occupy Chad's land under "color of title." Chad did not convey any land to Todd; and Barbara did not have the power to convey Chad's land. Todd's possession is the result of a mistake between two parties unrelated to Chad's title.

8. D A's interest is a ***life estate***, pure and simple. There are no words of inheritance, A's interest lasts for his life, and provision is made for a remainder following A's death. (*See* ELO ch.4-IV(B).) Choice **A** is incorrect because the gift to A is a life estate, not a gift in fee simple. A's interest is limited by the phrase "for life." Choice **B** is incorrect; if there is no fee simple, there is no fee simple determinable. Finally, choice **C** is incorrect in that no condition is attached to the life estate in A.

9. C B most likely has a ***vested remainder subject to divestment*** (sometimes described as a vested remainder in fee simple subject to executor limitation). B has a remainder following A's life estate. The remainder is vested because B is born and ascertainable, and there is no condition precedent to B's interest becoming possessory except the close of A's life estate. It is a remainder in fee simple because the conveyance contained words of inheritance ("and his heirs"). However, the gift to B is subject to divestment because B's interest is limited by the restriction that B and his heirs continue to use the property for residential purposes. It is subject to divestment by an executory interest, because if B fails to use the property for residential purposes, B's interest will be cut off and the property will vest in a third party, C, rather than in the grantor. (*See* ELO ch.5-IV(G)(4)(b).) The correct answer is choice **C**, which correctly states that this is a fee simple subject to an executory limitation. Choice **A** is incorrect. Restrictions of this kind create one of three categories of fees simple: a fee simple determinable, a fee simple subject to a condition subsequent, and a fee simple subject to an executory limitation. A fee simple determinable simply lapses on the failure of the restriction. Because the gift here provided for a gift over to C and his heirs, this is not a fee simple determinable. A fee simple subject to a condition subsequent occurs when the grantor reserves the right to terminate the estate and reenter the property on failure of the condition. That is not the case here, and choice **B** is therefore wrong. Finally, choice **D** is incorrect because the restriction providing for termination of B's interest is not unlawful. B's interest will continue so long as he observes the restriction.

10. C C most likely has a ***shifting executory interest in fee simple absolute.*** C's interest will come into being only if B fails to observe the restriction imposed by the grantor upon B's remainder. It is not a remainder because it will not come into effect, if it comes into effect at all, by virtue of the natural expiration of the prior estate, but only because the prior estate has been disrupted by the failure of B to observe the restriction. (*See* ELO ch.5-IV(G)(4)(b).) Choices **A** and **B** are, therefore, both wrong. As we have seen, B's interest is a fee simple subject to an executory limitation. (See Answer 9.) C's interest is therefore a shifting executory interest in fee simple absolute. The correct answer is choice **C**. Choice **D** is incorrect because a springing executory interest springs from the grantor and divests the grantor of his interest upon an event occurring in the future. (Example: A conveys "to B and her heirs when B marries.") A shifting executory interest (as in this question), on the other hand, divests another grantee, not the grantor.

11. A The conveyance to Bill is a ***life estate*** because it contains the words "for life." (*See* ELO ch.4-IV(B).) The interest of Bill's oldest child who survives Bill is a ***contingent remainder*** because it takes effect following Bill's life estate and the taker (Bill's eldest child who survives Bill) is neither born nor identified at the time of the conveyance. (*See* ELO ch.5-IV(H).) The contingent remainder is subject to the ***Rule Against Perpetuities*** but does not violate the rule. The rule states "no interest is good unless it must vest, if at all, not later than 21 years after some life in being at the creation of the interest." Here, Bill is a life in being at the creation of the interest. Since the identity of "Bill's eldest child who survives Bill" will be known at Bill's death, there is no possibility that the contingent remainder will vest outside the perpetuities period. Gene's interest is a reversion since it was not certain at the time of conveyance that the contingent remainder would ever vest. (*See* ELO ch.5-III(A).) Choice **B** is incorrect in that the remainder cannot be vested because Bill has no children and a remainder cannot be vested if the person who may take it is unborn. If it were vested, Gene would have no reversion. Choice **C** is incorrect in that the remainder in Bill's oldest child who survives Bill is a valid contingent remainder; this choice ignores the interest of a child of Bill who may be born and survive Bill. Finally, choice **D** is incorrect in that the interest of Bill's oldest child who survives Bill will vest at Bill's death, and is thus a remainder. Because it is a present contingent remainder, Gene's interest is a reversion, not a springing executory interest. A springing executory interest is a future interest in a grantee that springs out of the grantor at a date subsequent to the conveyance.

12. B The conveyance is a ***fee simple determinable*** because the words "so long as" are used to define the condition subsequent. When the grantor conveys all his interest, subject to a condition that may or may not happen, he gives a fee simple determinable. If the condition does occur, possession automatically reverts to the grantor, who then has an immediate right to possession and may immediately bring an action to evict the grantee, who is now a trespasser. (*See* ELO ch.4-(II)(B)(1).) The correct answer is choice **B**. Choice **A** is incorrect in that title automatically reverts to Toni upon occurrence of the condition subsequent. Toni may have to sue to evict the District, but not to recover title. Choice **C** is incorrect in that title automatically reverts to Toni. She may recover the land in an action to evict. She is not limited to a suit for damages. Finally, choice **D** is incorrect in that Toni's interest is a possibility of reverter, not a reversion. If the fee simple determinable comes to an end, possession reversed to the grantor; since it is not certain that this will ever occur, the word "possibility" is used. (*See* ELO ch.5-II(B).

13. D Ann's interest is a ***life estate***; this is established by the use of the words "for life" in the grant to her. (*See* ELO ch.4-IV(B).) The remainder in Ann's eldest child is a ***contingent remainder*** that is invalid under the Rule Against Perpetuities. (*See* ELO ch.5-IX(C)(1).) The Rule states "no interest is good unless it must vest, if at all, not later than 21 years after some life in being at the creation of the interest." In these facts, because Ann had no children at the time of the conveyance, there is no certainty that a child born to Ann will have reached the age of 25 within a period of 21 years following the deaths of both Ann and Sherri. For example, suppose that Ann had a child, and then Sherri and Ann both die. The child, who was not a life in being at the time the interest were created, could gain title more than 21 years after Ann and Sherri's deaths (the two lives in being at the time the interest was created). Choice **A** is incorrect because the contingent remainder to Ann's eldest child is void under the Rule. Choice **B** is incorrect because the remainder is void under the Rule and because it cannot be deemed vested in any case because no child of Ann is ascertainable. Following the life estate, there is a reversion to Sherri. Finally, choice **C** is incorrect in that the grant to Ann was limited by the phrase "for life" and is thus a life estate. Choice **D** is the right answer because it correctly reflects the fact that the conveyance to Ann's eldest daughter is void, resulting in a reversion to Sherri following Ann's life estate.

14. C Arthur's conveyance "to my son, Roger, for life; remainder to my grandchildren when they reach 21" created a ***life estate*** in Roger and appears to create a ***vested remainder subject to open*** in Arthur's grandchildren when they reach 21, but the conveyance to the grandchildren is void because it violates the ***Rule Against Perpetuities.*** Even though two grandchildren were alive at the time of the conveyance, neither of them has reached the age of 21, and it is possible that neither of them will. The remainder is invalid under the Rule Against Perpetuities. Remember that under the common law, the perpetuities period starts to run when the contingent future interest is created. At the time of Arthur's conveyance it was not certain that the remainder in his grandchildren would vest within 21 years after lives then in being. It was possible for Arthur to have another child whose children might not become 21 within the requisite period. The interest of Arthur's grandchildren is therefore void. Because the interest of the grandchildren is void, the reversion in Arthur's heirs will take effect following Roger's life estate. (*See* ELO ch.5-IX(C)(1).) The correct answer is choice **C**. Choice **A** is incorrect. The remainder in Arthur's grandchildren is void under the Rule Against Perpetuities. Choices **B** and **D** are incorrect because the contingent remainder in the grandchildren is void.

15. B There is nothing in the conveyance to indicate that Oliver intended a right of survivorship in Anna or Staci. The modern view is that any ambiguity in a conveyance as between a joint tenancy and a tenancy in common will be resolved in favor of the latter. (*See* ELO ch.7-II(C).) The conveyance to Anna and Staci will therefore be construed as creating a tenancy in common. A ***tenancy in common*** is an estate ***shared by two or more people in the same property at the same time.*** However, there is ***no right of survivorship*** in a tenancy in common. Any of the tenants is able to convey his undivided interest in the property to another, and Anna's gift to John transferred all her interest as tenant in common to John. (*See* ELO ch.7-II(B).) The correct answer is therefore choice **B**. After Anna's death, the property was owned as tenants in common by Staci and John. Choice **A** is incorrect because as one of two tenants in common, Staci does not have a right of survivorship. Choice **C** is incorrect. John takes Anna's share as a result of the conveyance from her during her life.

Following the conveyance, Anna had no interest to bequeath or convey. Finally, choice **D** is incorrect. Anna had the power to (and did) convey her one-half interest to John. John owns an undivided one-half interest, and Staci continues to own only her original undivided one-half interest. At her death, Anna had no property to bequeath to her heirs.

16. C The conveyance to Jeanne, Joan, and Jonni created a ***joint tenancy with right of survivorship***. Because they took their interests at the same time and from the same instrument, they have equal ownership interests and equal rights of possession. (*See* ELO ch.7-I(A).) When Jeanne conveyed her interest to Ted, the joint tenancy was ***severed*** as to her interest, and Ted became a tenant in common with Joan and Jonni, who remained joint tenants as to each other. (*See* ELO Ch.7-I(E)(1).) When Joan died, her interest passed to Jonni by right of survivorship. Thus, Jonni and Ted became tenants in common. However, Ted's interest was as to one-third of the property and Jonni's as to two-thirds. Tenants in common may have unequal shares. The correct answer is choice **C**. Choice **A** is incorrect in that Bill acquired no interest. Joan's interest was extinguished at her death and taken by Jonni by right of survivorship. Choice **B** is incorrect because Ted's interest was not as joint tenant but as tenant in common and Bill took no interest at all. Finally, choice **D** is incorrect because Jeanne could not convey her right of survivorship to Ted. Because Ted did not acquire his interests at the same time or by the same instrument as Joan and Jonni, he cannot be their joint tenant.

17. D As ***joint tenants***, Moira and Colin have ***equal rights to occupy*** the premises, subject to the equal rights of the other. (*See* ELO ch.7-I(A).) Here, the two have reached a reasonable accommodation. Colin is farming the land, and Moira is in possession of the two houses. Normally, a co-tenant who has not excluded the other co-tenant has no duty to account to his co-tenant for his use of the property. (*See* ELO ch.7-IV(B)(2).) Colin does not have to account to Moira for the income from his farming, nor does Moira have to account to him for the rental value of the house she occupies. However, when one co-tenant leases all or part of the property to a third person, a different rule applies. The co-tenant now has a duty to account for the rents received. (*See* ELO ch.7-IV(C).) Thus, Moira has a duty to account to Colin for the rents she receives from Ian. The correct answer is choice **D**. Choices **A** and **B** are incorrect in that each co-tenant has a right to possession of the premises and has ***no***

duty to account for profits produced from occupation of the land or for the fair rental value of his or her occupancy. Choice **C** is incorrect for the same reason.

18. B ***Each co-tenant*** has a ***duty to pay her share*** of taxes and payments due on mortgages. A tenant who pays a mortgage or taxes is entitled to reimbursement from his co-tenant(s) and can compel contribution from the other cotenants (although if the tenant is in sole possession of the property, he will receive reimbursement only for the amount that exceeds the rental value of the property). (*See* ELO ch.7-IV(D)(1).) John can seek contribution from Rita for the taxes and mortgage. Rita probably cannot seek immediate contribution from John for the cost of necessary repairs. Although courts are split on whether the co-tenant who makes necessary repairs can compel contribution, the majority view is that she can, provided she has notified the other co-tenant of the need for repairs. It does not appear, however, that Rita has notified John of the need for repairs. The correct answer is choice **B**. Choice **A** is incorrect because while John likely has a right to seek contribution, in most states Rita must provide notice before she can seek contribution from John. Choice **C** is incorrect in that John can seek immediate contribution for the mortgage payments and taxes. Finally, choice D is incorrect because John is entitled to seek immediate contribution.

19. D Since the lease in these facts has a ***fixed beginning and*** a fixed end covering a period of three years, it is a ***tenancy for a term of years.*** It is the usual practice, even in a long-term lease, to state the rent as an annual obligation payable in monthly installments. (*See* ELO ch.8-II(B).) A term of years cannot be terminated by either party during the term. Tenant's notice of her intent to terminate has no legal effect. She is liable for the entire three-year term. The correct answer is choice **D**. Choice **A** is incorrect; this is not a month-to-month tenancy. Choices **B** and **C** are incorrect. This is not a year-to-year tenancy; the lease has a fixed beginning and end.

20. A When a ***tenant wrongfully holds over*** following termination of the tenancy, the tenant becomes a ***tenant at sufferance***, and landlord ordinarily has an election of remedies. The landlord may (1) evict the tenant and hold him responsible for the reasonable rental value of the premises during the period of holding over, or (2) hold the tenant to a new term under the original lease terms. Once the landlord makes an election, he may not subsequently choose another remedy. (*See* ELO ch.8-III(E)(1).) In this case, Landlord has elected not to accept the rent and to evict Tenant. He is entitled to recover possession of the premises and the reasonable rental value for the period of the holdover. The correct answer is choice **A**. Choice **B** is incorrect in that the recovery is not the rent stipulated in the lease, but the reasonable rental value of the premises, which may or not be the stipulated rent. Choice **C** is incorrect on these facts, which show that Landlord has already elected to evict Tenant; he may not repudiate that election. Finally, choice **D** is incorrect for the same reason, and for stating that the lease rent may be recovered in the eviction action, instead of the reasonable value of the premises for the holdover period.

21. C Statutes in many states follow the so-called English rule. Under the ***English rule***, the landlord has a duty to deliver ***actual possession*** to Tenant. If the landlord fails to deliver possession, as in this case, tenant may ***terminate the lease*** and ***recover damages*** for the landlord's breach. Or, he may continue the lease and recover damages until either he or the landlord can evict the holdover tenant. (*See* ELO ch.8-III(A).) Because Tenant has a superior legal right to the premises, Tenant may evict the holdover tenant. Choice **C** is the correct answer because it correctly states Tenant's remedies in a jurisdiction that observes the English rule. Choice **A** is incorrect because it misstates the English rule. Choice **B** is incorrect because it misstates the American rule. Under the American rule, the landlord has the duty only to deliver the legal right to possession (which Landlord has done), not actual possession. Landlord has no obligation to evict the holdover; it falls to the Tenant to evict him. Finally, choice **D** is incorrect because Tenant cannot sue Landlord for breach or for damages under the American rule; his remedy is to evict the holdover.

22. B In recent decades, the courts have expanded the tenant's right to rely on the landlord's ***implied warranty of habitability***, especially with respect to residential leases. (*See* ELO ch.8-IV(E).) On these facts, there would seem to be little question that the landlord has breached the warranty. Few courts would require that a tenant suffer a lack of toilets and hot water, or an infestation of roaches. (*See* ELO ch.8-IV(F).) Most courts now look unfavorably on a waiver of the warranty by the tenant, especially when the waiver is part of "boilerplate" language in the lease. On these facts, few courts would find a waiver by the tenant, not even in the light of landlord's statement that there were "some problems with the place." Even in those jurisdictions that follow the Uniform Residential Landlord and

Tenant Act (URLTA) in allowing a tenant to waive the warranty, the waiver must be set forth in a separate writing, signed by the parties, and supported by adequate consideration. (*See* ELO ch.8-IV(H).) On these facts, choice **B** is the correct answer. Choice **A** is incorrect in that the majority of states now do permit a tenant to waive the implied warranty of habitability, but only if the necessary formalities are observed. Choice **C** is incorrect in that Tenant did not effectively accept the premises in "as is" condition; in most jurisdictions, the "as is" clause will not be construed as a waiver; some jurisdictions reject it altogether; and the majority require compliance with the URLTA, which requires a separate writing supported by consideration to effectuate a waiver. Finally, choice **D** is incorrect in that the waiver, if any, was not in a separate writing nor for a separate, clearly described consideration.

23. C Upon breach by the landlord of the ***implied warranty of habitability***, Tenant has several options: He may simply terminate the lease and move out; he may also recover damages for the landlord's breach; or he may remain in the premises and withhold part or all of the rent until the premises are repaired and made habitable. In some jurisdictions, he may even make the necessary repairs himself and deduct the cost from the rent. (*See* ELO ch.8-IV(I).) Choice **C** correctly describes the tenant's remedies. Choice **A** is incorrect in that omits the tenant's right to remain in possession and withhold all or part of the rent. Choice **B** is incorrect. It omits Tenant's remedy of suing for consequential damages or of setting them off against any rent still owed. Finally, choice **D** is incorrect. If Tenant remains in possession, he is not unconditionally relieved of all further liability for rent; his credit against the rent will be calculated by the court in accordance with one of several alternative methods.

24. B When Landlord leased the premises to Tenant, Landlord and Tenant were in privity of contract and privity of estate. The transaction described in these facts is a ***sublease*** by Tenant, not an assignment of his interests. An assignment is the transfer by the lessee of his entire interest in the leased premises. (*See* ELO ch.8-VIII(B).) Here, Tenant put his subtenant in possession only for a period of two years and reserved the balance of his term. Because Tenant did not transfer his entire interest, Tenant remains liable for the payment of rent unless and until released by Landlord. A ***sublessee*** has ***no privity of estate or contract with the Landlord***. For this reason, Ben is not liable to Landlord for the payment of rent. Choice **B** correctly identifies the obligations of the parties. Choice **A** is incorrect in that Ben is not in privity of estate or contract with Landlord and is not liable for the payment of rent. Choice **C** reverses Landlord's remedies against Tenant and Ben, and therefore is incorrect. Choice **D** is incorrect. Landlord may hold Tenant for the entire lease; he may not look to Ben at all.

25. C Unless the parties to a lease agree otherwise, either may transfer his interest. Although the parties may include a ***prohibition against assignment and subletting***, such a provision is ***construed strictly*** against the landlord. (*See* ELO ch.8-VIII(A).) Here, the lease agreement provided that tenant may not "assign the lease" but did not specifically prohibit subletting. Because no such prohibition on subletting is contained here, the provision will be construed as only prohibiting assignment. Because the prohibition in this case is only against assignment, Jill can sublease the apartment to a subtenant for less than her remaining term. Choice **C** is the correct answer. Choices **A** and **B** are incorrect. The agreement is generally enforceable as written, but only to prevent assignments, not subleases. The agreement will not be enforced to prevent Jill from subleasing the premises. Finally, choice **D** is incorrect because a growing majority of jurisdictions now requires the landlord to act reasonably even when there is a blanket prohibition against assignment.

26. D An ***easement*** is an interest in the land of another and generally must be ***created in a writing*** that satisfies the Statute of Frauds. If the easement is one that must satisfy the ***Statute of Frauds*** and the parties fail to do so, a license will generally result. (*See* ELO ch.9-II(B)(1).) In this case, the right of Albert to cross Brad's land was created orally and did not comply with the Statute of Frauds. Because no easement was created, Brad may interfere with access by Albert at any time. The correct answer is choice **D**. Choice **A** is incorrect. Because the easement is not in writing, as required by the Statute of Frauds, at most, Albert had a license that was revocable by Brad at any time. Albert does not have an easement by estoppel, which generally requires a showing that the licensee relied on the licensor's oral representation by expending money or labor or made improvement on or with reference to the easement. Choice **B** is incorrect in that Albert never legally acquired an easement. If he had, Brad could not now block Albert's access across Whiteacre. An express easement created by a writing that satisfies the Statute of Frauds is enforceable as an interest in land. Finally, choice **C** is incorrect because the facts do not indicate that Albert had no other access to his land. Also, there are no facts to suggest that Blackacre and Whiteacre were once commonly owned, a requirement for an easement by necessity.

27. A An easement by necessity is created where two parcels that were once under ***common ownership*** are separated and an easement over one is ***strictly necessary*** to the enjoyment of the other. (*See* ELO ch.9-II(D).) Here, both halves of Blackacre were originally owned by Okie and were divided by sale of the back half to Purchaser, Purchaser has an easement by necessity because otherwise his property is landlocked. The easement arises even though the deed is silent. But an easement by necessity exists only so long as the necessity exists, and the owner of the servient estate may locate the easement so long as he acts reasonably. The correct answer is choice **A**. Choice **B** is incorrect. An easement by necessity does not exist in perpetuity. It is limited in duration to the period of necessity. Choice **C** is incorrect in that there are no facts that indicate that the front half was previously used for access to the back half; further, an easement by necessity does not need a showing of prior use. Finally, choice **D** is incorrect in that Purchaser has an easement by necessity because he is otherwise landlocked. There's nothing in the facts to indicate that Purchaser agreed to renounce the easement because he had found some other means of egress from his property.

28. B When an easement is created, the ***land that benefits from the easement*** becomes the ***dominant tenement***, and the ***parcel that is burdened by the easement*** is called the ***servient tenement.*** (*See* ELO ch.9-I(B)(1).) Here, Tract A is the dominant tenement, and Tract B is the servient tenement. When Jim acquired Tract C, it represented additional property that is not part of the dominant tenement. It is therefore not entitled to the benefit of the easement. This is true whether or not the burden on the servient tenement is increased. (*See* ELO ch.9-III(C).) The best answer is choice **B**. Although Jim probably may continue his access across Tract B from Tract A, he may not do so from Tract C. (Jim may also have lost his easement through Tract B if building a repair shop on Tract A unreasonably increased the burden on Tract B.) Choice **A** is incorrect because Tract C cannot use the easement owned by Tract A. Choices **C** and **D** are incorrect in that Jim probably may continue to use the easement for ingress and egress to Tract A. It is still the dominant estate and the beneficiary of the easement.

29. D April's entire one-acre tract is the dominant estate. Generally, when a dominant estate is subdivided, the ***benefit of an appurtenant easement*** attaches to each subdivided lot. However, if the burden on the servient estate is substantially greater than at the creation of the easement, the easement will not available to the subdivided lots. (*See* ELO ch.9-IV(B).) Here, April divided her tract into two half-acre lots. It does not appear that the subdivision creates a substantially greater burden since only one lot was added. Chris and Colleen may both use the easement, making choice **D** the correct answer. (Note: Consider what the result would be if Barbara had sold her parcel to a bona fide purchaser who had no notice of the easement.) Choice **A** is incorrect. Following the sales by April, the easement became appurtenant to both parcels of land, which were carved out of April's one-acre tract. Choice **B** is incorrect. Both Chris and Colleen now own portions of the dominant estate, and a dominant estate may be subdivided so long as the burden on the servient estate is not increased unreasonably. Finally, choice **C** is incorrect because the easement is appurtenant to the land, not a personal right of April. Ownership of the easement passes to succeeding owners of the land.

30. B On these facts, Staci and Shelly have entered into an ***agreement*** that creates reciprocal burdens and benefits. Each is burdened by her promise not to build anything but a residence, and each has the benefit of the other's promise not to build. However, because there is ***no horizontal privity*** between them (i.e., neither transferred an interest in land to the other), most jurisdictions would agree that the covenants are not enforceable at law as between Staci and Bill. (*See* ELO ch.9-VIII(D)(1).) However, in the case of equitable servitudes, horizontal privity is not required, and two adjoining landlords who are strangers to each other's title can enforce the covenant against subsequent possessors with notice of the restriction. (*See* ELO ch.9-IX(G).) The correct answer is choice **B**. It does not matter that neither Staci nor Shelley recorded the agreement because Bill had actual notice of the covenant. Choice **A** is incorrect. Because Bill had actual notice of its terms, the agreement may be enforced against him in equity as an equitable servitude. Choice **C** is incorrect. Staci cannot sue Bill for damages because the covenant does not bind Shelly's grantees at law because of the lack of horizontal privity between Staci and Shelly. It may, however, be enforced in equity by injunction as an equitable servitude. Finally, choice **D** is incorrect because the covenant can be enforced in equity by injunction.

31. **A** The ***agreement*** between Shelley and Staci is an enforceable contract based on mutual promises. It is enforceable at law in an action for damages, and, as between Staci and Shelly, by injunction, provided Staci can show she will suffer irreparable harm. A covenant running with the land is no different from any other contract, except with respect to the rights and duties of assignees from the original parties. Because there is ***no horizontal privity*** between Staci and Shelley, this contract is not a covenant running with the land, but an ordinary, enforceable contract between the contracting parties. (*See* ELO ch.9-VIII(A).) The correct choice is choice **A.** Choice **B** is incorrect. Staci may enforce her claim by an action for damages since Shelley is a party to the contract. Choice **C** is incorrect. Staci may enforce the contract by an injunction, provided she proves that irreparable harm will result from the construction. Finally, choice **D** is incorrect. Horizontal privity is relevant only when enforcement is being sought at law against a grantee from one of the parties. That is not the case here.

32. **D** The transfer from Lon to Sarah was a ***sublease*** rather than an assignment because the interest conveyed was less than Lon's entire interest. (*See* ELO ch.8-VIII(B).) A sublease by a tenant ***does not establish privity of estate between the sublessee and the lessor.*** Consequently Rod, the lessor, may not sue Sarah, the sublessee, for damages for the breach of any covenant running with land. (*See* ELO ch.8-VIII(A)(2).) The covenant may be enforced by Rod as an equitable servitude as privity is not required in an action for an injunction. While privity is not required, Rod must nevertheless show that Sarah had notice of the restriction. (*See* ELO ch.9-IX(C).) Here, Sarah took with constructive notice of the covenant in the lease between Rod and Lon because the lease was recorded. Choice **A** is incorrect in that Rod may not sue Sarah for damages. The covenant does not run at law since there was no privity between Rod and Sarah. Choice **B** is incorrect for the same reason as choice **A.** Finally, choice **C** is incorrect in that Rod may sue for an injunction without regard to whether there was horizontal or vertical privity since Sarah took with notice of the covenant contained in the lease.

33. **A** The best answer is choice **A.** The ***Statute of Frauds*** requires that contracts for the sale of land be in writing. A written memorandum is enough to satisfy the statute if it ***recites the basic terms and is signed by the party against whom enforcement is sought.*** (*See* ELO ch.11-I(B).) Here, the buyer, Lynn, seeks to back out of the

agreement offering the Statute of Frauds as a defense. For the seller, Chad, to prevail he must show an exception to the Statute of Frauds applies.

One major exception to the statute's requirements is part performance, which recognizes that a party is entitled to enforce an oral contract if he has relied on it to this detriment. However, this exception usually requires acts that are unequivocally referable to the contract (such as taking possession and paying part of the purchase price, or taking possession and making valuable improvements to the property). Payment of a deposit is not usually enough without more. (*See* ELO ch.11-I(B)(3).) Choice **B** is incorrect because it begs the issue; on these facts, there was no enforceable contract. Choice **C** is incorrect because payment of a portion of the purchase price alone is not ordinarily sufficient to avoid the requirement of a writing. Finally, choice **D** is incorrect in that, because the contract is not enforceable, Lynn can recover her entire deposit.

34. C ***Marketable title*** is one that is ***"free from reasonable doubt."*** Privately negotiated use restrictions constitute defects in title, without regard to whether they benefit the property. (*See* ELO ch.11-I(D).) Here, the residential restrictions constitute title defects. Thus, Kyla has not delivered "marketable title," and John is justified in rejecting the title. Choice **C** is the correct answer. Choice **A** is incorrect in that the use restrictions are title defects without regard to whether they benefit the property. Choice **B** is incorrect in that Kyla, without regard to whether the restrictions benefit the property, cannot successfully sue for damages or compel specific performance (since the title is not marketable). Finally, choice **D** is incorrect in that Kyla may not sue for damages since her title is not marketable. To constitute marketable title, the property may not be affected by private use restrictions even if they benefit the property.

35. D The violation of the setback requirement constitutes a zoning violation. Most courts treat ***violations of zoning ordinances*** as ***encumbrances*** that make title unmarketable. (*See* ELO ch.11-I(D)(5)(b)(vii).) On these facts, most courts would find Bob's title unmarketable. Bob cannot successfully seek specific performance or damages from Carol because his title is unmarketable. The best answer is choice **D**. Choice **A** is incorrect. Bob's title is unmarketable because there is an existing violation of a municipal zoning ordinance. Choice **B** is incorrect. The term "restrictions of record" usually refers to impairments in the record title, not to ordinances, which are ***not*** part of the title record. Choice **C** is incorrect. The mere existence of the ordinance does not make title unmarketable. Title is unmarketable because the structure violates the ordinance, not because the ordinance exists.

36. B In a majority of jurisdictions, the ***risk of loss*** in the "gap" period between execution of the contract and the closing of title is on the purchaser, whether or not the purchaser has taken possession. The ***doctrine of equitable conversion*** treats the buyer as owning the property from the date the contract is signed. (*See* ELO ch.11-I(H)(3).) The correct answer is choice **B**. Choice **A** represents the minority view or "Massachusetts rule," which places the risk of loss on the seller until the passing of title, even though the buyer is in possession. Choice **C** is incorrect. The change of possession is not the basis for allocating the risk of loss in a majority of jurisdictions. The risk is on the buyer not because she is in possession but because she is the buyer. Finally, choice **D** is incorrect because no court would attempt to allocate the loss on these facts.

37. C In a majority of jurisdictions, the ***risk of loss*** is on the purchaser. However, if a vendor has insured the premises, most courts give the purchaser the benefit of the vendor's insurance in order to prevent a windfall to the vendor, who would otherwise get both the insurance proceeds and the purchase price, leaving the purchaser with the full burden of the loss. The purchaser is given an abatement of the purchase price equal to the insurance proceeds. (*See* ELO ch.11-I(H)(4).) Choice **A** is incorrect. In the majority view, the risk of loss is not allocated to the vendor, whether or not she has secured insured. Choice **B** represents the minority or English rule, which allows the vendor to keep the proceeds on the theory that the insurance policy is a personal contract. However, there are exceptions to this rule, which are not applicable on these facts. Finally, choice **D** is incorrect in that the vendor has no duty to rebuild under either rule; her obligation under the majority rule is only to credit the insurance proceeds against the purchase price.

38. D In the usual transaction between seller and buyer in which the seller provides the ***mortgage financing***, the ***buyer executes a promissory note*** as well as a ***purchase-money mortgage***. The mortgage acts as security for the payment of the purchase price balance and is therefore recorded. The promissory note is the buyer's personal promise to pay the balance of the purchase price and subjects him to personal liability. The note is not usually recorded. When the buyer sells the property, if his buyer takes subject to the mortgage but does not assume it, as is the case here, there is no personal liability by the new buyer. (*See* ELO ch.11-II(B)(3).) Mary promised to satisfy the mortgage but did not assume personal liability for the note. The correct answer is therefore choice **D**. Olivia may hold Ted personally responsible for any deficiency since Ted signed the promissory note. Choice **A** is incorrect because Mary took "subject to" the indebtedness and did not assume it. Her statement to Ted that she would satisfy the mortgage is not enforceable because it was not in writing and is negated by the language in the conveyance. Choice **B** is incorrect because Olivia may hold Ted personally liable for payment of the deficiency. Finally, choice **C** is incorrect in that Mary is not personally liable. She took subject to the indebtedness, but did not assume it.

39. D ***To convey title*** to a parcel of real estate, it is necessary to ***execute and deliver a deed.*** It is not ordinarily necessary to acknowledge or record the deed. (*See* ELO ch.11-III(C)(5).) When the deed was executed and delivered to Ben, title passed to him. Ben's title may not be divested, except by a formal conveyance from him. Ben's return of Ron's deed is ineffective to return title to Ron. Ben must execute a new deed with the usual formalities to return title to Ron. The correct answer is choice **D**. Choice **A** is incorrect in that consideration is not required for an effective conveyance; property may be gifted by deed. Choice **B** is incorrect in that an acknowledgment by the grantor is not a necessary requisite to the validity of the deed. In some states, it is merely a prerequisite to recordation. Finally, choice **C** is incorrect in that Ben's return of Ron's deed is ineffective to return title to Ron. Ben must execute a new deed with the usual formalities.

40. A It is not unusual for a ***deed*** to be ***delivered to an escrow agent*** with instructions to surrender the deed only upon performance of specified conditions. Under these circumstances, title remains in the grantor until the conditions are satisfied. (*See* ELO ch.11-III(D)(5)(d).) Here, Norma never intended to have the deed delivered until the payment of the balance on closing. Therefore, delivery of the deed was ineffective to pass title to Nikki. The correct answer is choice **A**. Choice **B** is incorrect because title did not pass to Nikki. Choice **C** is incorrect for the same reason. Choice **D** is also incorrect. Title has not passed to Nikki, and Norma's remedy is to have the deed and recording nullified and set aside. She is not limited to an action in negligence.

41. **B** Angela appears to be a ***bona fide purchaser for value*** since she paid $80,000 for the property and had no notice of Norma's interest. That she paid less than Nikki does not necessarily defeat her claim. In most jurisdictions, payment of something more than mere nominal consideration suffices to meet the "purchaser for value" standard. On the other hand, since Nikki and Angela are sisters and the amount of Angela's payment matches exactly the amount Nikki owes may suggest some collusion between them, which could defeat Angela's claim. Assuming that Angela is a bona fide purchaser for value, Angela would be granted title, free of any interest in the property by Norma. While there is a conflict among the courts about the rights of a bona fide purchaser to receive good title from a grantee who has recorded a deed mistakenly delivered to her by an escrow agent, all the courts agree that a bona fide purchaser from a grantee ***who has taken possession*** after mistakenly obtaining delivery of the deed and recording it does have priority over the original grantor. (*See* ELO ch.11-III(D)(5)(d).) Here, the deed was mistakenly delivered to Nikki, who, in turn, sold the land to Angela, a bona fide purchaser. The correct answer is choice **B**. Title is in Angela. However, Norma does have an action against the escrow agent and against Nikki. Choice **A** is incorrect. Because Angela was a bona fide purchaser without notice, Norma does not have title. Choice **C** is incorrect. Norma has no further interest in the property. Choice **D** is incorrect. Nikki transferred any interest she may have had in the property—if, indeed, she had any title interest at all—to Angela, a bona fide purchaser.

42. **B** The covenant ***against encumbrances*** is a representation by the grantor that there are no mortgages, liens, easements, or covenants affecting the property. (*See* ELO 11-III(F)(2).) The mortgage on Whiteacre is such an encumbrance. Shelley has breached this covenant by not disclosing the existence of the outstanding mortgage, and the correct answer is choice **B**. Choice **A** is incorrect. The covenant of seisin is breached where the grantor does not have the quality or quantity of title he purports to convey. Here, the facts indicate that Shelley did own a fee simple absolute, but the mortgage operated as a lien against title (in most jurisdictions). Choice **C** is incorrect because Shelley did not breach the covenant of seisin. Finally, choice **D** is incorrect in that a covenant against encumbrances is

breached when made if there is in fact an encumbrance, whether or not the terms of the encumbrance are being performed.

43. C A ***general warranty deed*** is said to contain six covenants, among which is a covenant ***against encumbrances***. The covenant against encumbrances is a present covenant, which is breached, if at all, at delivery of the deed. (*See* ELO ch.11-III(F)(5).) The general warranty deed from Gary to Randy violated the covenant against encumbrances because the mortgage on Whiteacre was not disclosed to Randy. While Randy may sue Gary for the breach of the covenant against encumbrances, Randy may not sue Shelley. Even though the mortgage likely breached the covenant against encumbrances contained in the Shelley-Gary deed, Randy is not a proper party to enforce. In most jurisdictions, present covenants do not run with the land and are not enforceable by a future grantee. The correct answer is choice **C**. Choices **A** and **B** are incorrect in that, under the majority view, Randy may not sue Shelley because the covenant in Shelley's deed does not run with the land. Finally, choice **D** is incorrect because Randy may sue Gary for breach of the covenant against encumbrances in the warranty deed given to Randy by Gary.

44. D The usual ***measure of damages*** for breach of the covenant ***against encumbrances*** is the cost of removing the encumbrance (presumably the unpaid balance of the debt), including accrued, but unpaid, interest. This puts the grantee in the same position he would have enjoyed if the breach had not occurred. The best answer is choice **D**. Choice **A** is incorrect since this may give Randy a windfall equal to his equity in the property.. Choice **B** is incorrect. Restitution of the purchase price does not measure Randy's damage; Randy is out the amount of the mortgage plus interest and the cost of removing it. Finally, choice **C** is incorrect because the value at trial is not what the parties bargained for.

45. B Louis has breached only the covenant of ***seisin*** because he has misrepresented his capacity to convey free of Tim's interest. Louis has not breached the covenant of quiet enjoyment. The covenant of seisin is breached if legal title is in someone other than the grantor. (*See* ELO ch.11-III(F)(2)(a).). Here, legal title was in Tim at the time Louis purported to convey title to Marsha. Marsha cannot, however, enforce the covenant of quiet enjoyment because Tim has not attempted to disturb her possession. The covenant of quiet enjoyment is breached if the grantee's possession is disturbed by another party with superior rights. However, the covenant of quiet enjoyment is deemed a future covenant, which is not breached until the grantee is evicted or finds his possession disturbed. (*See* ELO ch.11-III(F)(3)(b).) The correct answer is choice **B**. Choice **A** is incorrect in that Louis will not have breached the covenant of quiet enjoyment until Tim attempts to evict Marsha. Choice **C** reverses the correct and incorrect answers. Finally, choice **D** is incorrect in that Louis has breached the covenant of seisin but not the covenant of quiet enjoyment.

46. D Refer to Answer 45 above. Assuming Tim is asserting his right to take possession of the property (the facts are not clear on this point), the covenant of ***quiet enjoyment*** has now been breached. Laura may sue Amy for breach of both the covenant of seisin and the covenant of quiet enjoyment because Amy, Laura's grantor, did not hold legal title at the time of the conveyance (breach of covenant of seisin) and Tim has disturbed Amy's possession (breach of covenant of quiet enjoyment) . However, Laura cannot sue Louis for breach of the covenant of seisin based on the general warranty deed Louis conveyed to Marsha because the covenant of seisin is a present covenant, and most courts hold that present covenants do not run with the land to future grantees like Laura. (*See* ELO ch.11-III(F)(5).) Laura may sue Louis, however, for breach of the covenant of quiet enjoyment since that covenant does run to future grantees (despite the intervening quitclaim deed). Choice **A** is incorrect in that Laura may not sue Louis for breach of the covenant of seisin for the reasons explained above, and she may not sue Marsha because Marsha's quitclaim deed contained no covenants. Choice **B** is incorrect in that Laura may not sue Louis for breach of the covenant of seisin for the reasons explained above. Finally, choice **C** is incorrect in that Laura may sue Louis for breach of the covenant of quiet enjoyment, despite the intervening quitclaim deed, because the covenant contained in the warranty deed continues to run with the land to later grantees.

47. B A document that is not entitled to be recorded does not give ***constructive notice*** (sometimes call "record" notice), even if the document is mistakenly accepted for recording. Here, the lack of an acknowledgment should have compelled the clerk to reject the deed. The clerk's failure to do so acted to prevent record notice to subsequent purchasers. (*See* ELO ch.12-II(K)(1).) The correct answer is choice **B**. Choice **A** is incorrect in that the deed from Seller to Purchaser did not constitute notice to Buyer because it was ***not*** entitled to be recorded. Choice **C** is incorrect in most jurisdictions. Buyer was not put on "inquiry" notice because the facts tell us that Buyer did not examine the record. Even if he had, in most jurisdictions, he would not be required to inquire after a defective deed. In some jurisdictions, however, he would be considered on "inquiry" notice; if further inquiry showed the deed between Seller and Purchaser was effective, Buyer's title would be inferior to Purchaser's. Choice **D** is incorrect because we do have to consider whether Buyer was put on "inquiry" notice in those jurisdictions that consider it relevant.

48. B In jurisdictions that have ***"race-notice"*** recording statutes, the superior title goes to the ***first person to record*** an effective deed, provided he takes ***without notice*** of the prior conveyance. (*See* ELO ch.12-II(B)(3).) The facts do not indicate that Cliff had notice of the deed to Bill. Therefore, Cliff is a subsequent purchaser without notice and since Cliff was the first to record, Cliff is protected by the recording act and has priority to Greenacre. The correct answer is choice **B**. Choice **A** is incorrect in that Abbott owned the interest he conveyed to Bill. Thus, he did not breach the covenant of seisin. Finally, choices **C** and **D** are incorrect in that Bill's interest is ***not*** superior to Cliff's. Because this is so, Abbott is not liable to Cliff for breach of any covenant.

49. A In jurisdictions that have ***"race-notice"*** recording statutes, the superior title goes to the ***first person to record*** an effective deed, provided he takes ***without notice*** of the prior conveyance. (*See* ELO ch.12-II(B)(3).) However, a subsequent purchaser can claim the protection of the recording act only if all instruments in her chain of title are recorded. (*See* ELO ch.12-II(K)(3)(a)(ii).) Here, Marlo's deed to Connie was not recorded. Since the deed from Marlo to Connie was ***not*** recorded, Debbie cannot claim priority under the applicable recording act. Debbie can sue Connie for breach of the covenant of seisin because the interest that Connie purported to convey to Debbie was actually owned by Amy. (*See* ELO ch.11-II(F)(a).) The correct answer is choice **A**. Choice **B** is incorrect in that the covenant that was breached was the covenant of seisin, not the covenant against encumbrances. The covenant of seisin covers problems in title. The covenant of encumbrances provides against existing mortgages and liens. Finally, choice **C** is incorrect. Though Debbie recorded first, the conveyance to her from Connie was not in the chain of title because Connie failed to record. Choice **D** is incorrect for the same reason. Also, Marlo is not liable to Amy because Amy's title is protected by the recording system.

50. D In states that have ***"notice"*** statutes, a subsequent ***bona fide purchaser*** who takes ***without notice*** prevails over a prior grantee who fails to record. (*See* ELO ch.12-II(B)(2).) Here, Carl is not protected of his own right but is sheltered by Baker's status. An instrument issued by a grantor whose own source of title is not recorded is referred to as a "wild" deed. Here, the facts do not state that Baker recorded his deed from Ed, the Ed-Baker deed would be considered "wild." For Carl to seek protection of the recording statute in his own right, he must see that his entire chain of title is recorded. Carl needed to record the Ed-Baker deed in addition to his deed. But Carl is protected under the "shelter doctrine." Under the "shelter doctrine" one who purchases from a bona fide purchaser is also protected even if he buys with actual notice of the prior conveyance. When Ed conveyed Blackacre to Baker, Baker took without notice of Adam's interest. Under the applicable "notice" statute, Baker's interest was superior to that held by Adam. Under the "shelter" concept, Carl, a subsequent purchaser from Baker, is treated as a bona fide purchaser, even though Adam's deed was recorded before Carl's. (*See* ELO ch.12-II(N)(1).) The correct answer is choice **D**. Choice **A** is incorrect. Even if Carl had actual knowledge of Adam's claim, he is protected by the superior title of his grantor, Baker, who was a bona fide purchaser without notice and was protected under the applicable recording act. Choice **B** is incorrect in that, under the applicable notice statute, Carl prevails. Constructive notice is no better than actual notice. Finally, choice **C** is incorrect in that Adam's interest is not superior to Carl's for the reasons explained above.

51. C Title companies insure only against matters disclosed in the record title. They do not go outside the record or make an inspection of the property. (*See* ELO ch.12-IV(D).) Most ***title policies contain a number of exceptions*** such as the rights of parties in possession not shown by the public record. Thus title policies do not generally protect against ***adverse possession*** claims. (*See* ELO ch.12-IV(D)(3)(b).) Here, the policy expressly excludes such claims. Unless Joan had filed a *lis pendens*—a document announcing that a suit affecting land has been started—the record would not disclose Joan's claim of adverse possession. Therefore, the title company is not liable to Elise since Joan's claim is based on adverse possession (which is ***not*** a matter of record). (Note, however, that in most states, Joan's attorneys would have filed a *lis pendens.)* The title company is not liable, but Steve has violated the covenant of seisin because Joan's claim does affect his title. The covenant of seisin is breached if legal title is in someone other than the grantor. Here, if Joan is successful, she, not, Steve, would have legal title to the 15 acres. On these facts, the correct answer is choice **C**. Choice **A** is incorrect in that, even though Steve may not have title to the 15 acres, Joan's claim is based on adverse possession (which is not a matter of record in the absence of the filing of a *lis pendens*). Choice **B** is incorrect because title companies do not inspect properties, and, as a consequence of the policy exclusion, the title company had no duty to determine the rights of parties in possession that were ***not*** a matter of public record. Finally, choice **D** is incorrect in that Steve may be liable to Elise for breach of the covenant of seisin (if Joan prevails in her suit) since Steve may not actually have owned the disputed 15 acres at the time he conveyed the tract to Elise.

52. D If an owner commits a ***nuisance*** in the use of his land by ***interfering*** with his neighbors' ***use and enjoyment*** of their land, he becomes subject to a suit for damages or an injunction. A nuisance occurs when the owner commits an intentional act that is unreasonable. Violation of a zoning ordinance is strong proof that the conduct is unreasonable. (*See* ELO ch.13-I(C)(2)(b).) Here, Peter is conducting a noisy business in a residential district at night in violation of a zoning ordinance. The correct answer is choice **D**. Choice **A** is incorrect. The fact that Peter did not create the noise for the purpose of disturbing his neighbors is irrelevant; he knew that auto repair was a noisy business and acted with unreasonable disregard for the sleep of his neighbors. Choice **B** is incorrect in that Peter's actions are unreasonable; they constitute a commercial use in a residential zone and interfered with the neighbors' use of their property, both of which he knew or should have known. Finally, choice **C** is incorrect in that there is no general rule of strict liability for nuisance. Plaintiffs must show that defendant's use of his property is a substantial and unreasonable interference with the use and enjoyment of their own property.

53. A An owner of land has an absolute right to ***lateral support*** from his neighbor's land. However the absolute right to lateral support exists only with respect to land in its natural state. (*See* ELO ch.13-II(B).) Because the facts suggest that Rick's land was still in its natural state, Lita is liable to Rick, even if she acted with reasonable care in the excavation. The correct answer is choice **A**. Choice **B** is incorrect in that Rick does not have to prove negligence. Lita is strictly liable for failure to provide lateral support when she undertook to excavate her lot to build her house. Choice **C** is incorrect. The basis for liability in lateral support cases is strict liability, not negligence. Negligence per se is a torts doctrine that is applied to impose liability when a defendant violates a statute that proscribes some act or conduct. Finally, choice **D** is incorrect in that, even if Lita was making reasonable use of her land, she is strictly liable because she undertook the excavation.

54. A However unsympathetic they may be to the concept of forfeiture, most courts will enforce an ***installment contract*** for the purchase of land unless the buyer has paid a substantial portion of the purchase price. (*See* ELO ch.11-II(C)(2).) Here, Buyer paid only 5 percent of the purchase price, an insubstantial amount. Thus the contract will be enforced as written, and Seller may retain all the money as liquidated damages. The correct answer is choice **A**. Choice **B** is incorrect in that most jurisdictions do not require judicial foreclosure, unless the buyer has paid a substantial portion of the purchase price. Finally, choices **C** and **D** are incorrect in that most jurisdictions do ***not*** require a seller to give the buyer a reasonable period of time to cure arrears or to pay the entire balance prior to forfeiture, but will adhere to the terms of the installment contract.

55. C Although the City Council has the right to pass ***zoning ordinances*** that restrict the uses of property, an existing nonconforming user must at least be given a substantial amount of time in which to continue the nonconforming use in order to protect her investment. Otherwise, a Fifth Amendment "taking" occurs, and the affected landowner must be compensated. (*See* ELO ch.10-IV(J)(1).)Choice **A** is incorrect in that the City Council's action is not, without more, a per se taking; the Council can provide Erin with a substantial time in which to protect her investment. Choice **B** is incorrect in that the City Council is not required to continue Erin's nonconforming use indefinitely, but only to give her a reasonably significant time in which to continue her use. Choice **D** is incorrect in that Erin has no constitutional right to continue her use indefinitely. Her rights are satisfied if the City Council gives her a reasonable extension in which to continue her use.

56. B Alice appears to have intended to create a ***fee simple subject to executory limitation*** in Barbara and an ***executory interest*** in Charles. Barbara's fee interest is subject to a condition subsequent (premises must be "used for residential and farm purposes"). Because Alice intends the future interest to vest in Charles, a third party, if the condition is violated, Alice purports to create an executory interest in Charles. (*See* ELO ch.5-VII(G)(2).) However, an executory interest is subject to the ***Rule Against Perpetuities*** and is invalid unless it will vest, if at all, within 21 years after the death of an ascertainable life that was in being at the time such executory interest was created. (*See* ELO ch.5-IX(C)(4).) The grant to Charles is ***void*** under the Rule Against Perpetuities since it is an executory interest that might vest outside of the 21-year period (i.e., the condition could be violated more than 21 years after the death of Alice, Barbara, or Charles). Thus, the purported grant to Charles would be stricken from the conveyancing document and the interest re-classified. Since language normally associated with a fee simple determinable ("so long as") has been used, the interest held by Alice would be a possibility of reverter. Choice **A** is incorrect because Alice, by law, has retained a possibility of reverter. Choice **C** is incorrect because language normally associated with a fee simple subject to a condition subsequent was not used in the conveyancing document. Finally, choice **D** is incorrect because Alice did not retain a reversion since a fee simple interest (a fee simple determinable) was granted to Barbara.

57. C Based on the language in the deed, Owen purported to create a ***fee simple subject to executory limitation*** in Alpha and an ***executory interest*** in the American Red Cross since if the condition on Alpha's interest is violated, the property is intended to revert to the American Red Cross and not the grantor (Owen). An executory interest is subject to the ***Rule Against Perpetuities*** and is invalid unless it will vest, if at all, within 21 years after the death of an ascertainable life that was in being at the time such executory interest was created. (*See* ELO ch.5-IX(C)(4).) The grant to the American Red Cross violates the rule since the land might be used for other than residential purposes more than 21 years after Alpha's demise. Therefore the interest to the American Red Cross would be stricken and the grant re-classified as a fee simple determinable in Alpha and a possibility of reverter in Owen. At Owen's death he devised his property to Bill. Since a possibility of reverter is devisable by will, Owen's will properly devised Owen's possibility of reverter to Bill. (*See* ELO ch.5-II(B)(2).) Thus, Joan was justified in asserting that a fee simple was not being offered to her because Bill was not conveying his possibility of reverter in Blackacre. Choice **A** is incorrect because Alpha owns only a fee simple determinable, and Sam owns no interest whatsoever. Choice **B** is incorrect because Alpha owns a fee simple determinable (rather than a fee simple absolute). Finally, choice **D** is incorrect because the interest held by the American Red Cross is void under the Rule Against Perpetuities.

58. B Based on the language in the deed, Owen purported to create a ***fee simple subject to executory limitation*** in Alpha and an ***executory interest*** in the American Red Cross since if the condition on Alpha's interest is violated, the property is intended to revert to the American Red Cross and not the grantor (Owen). An executory interest is subject to the ***Rule Against Perpetuities*** and is invalid unless it will vest, if at all, within 21 years after the death of an ascertainable life that was in being at the time such executory interest was created. (*See* ELO ch.5-IX(C)(4).) The grant to the American Red Cross violates the rule since the land might be used for other than residential purposes more than 21 years after Alpha's demise. Therefore the interest to the American Red Cross is void. Choice **A** is incorrect because a remainder interest cannot follow a fee simple interest (in this instance, a fee simple determinable). Choice **C** is incorrect because the interest held by the American Red Cross is invalid as a consequence of the Rule Against Perpetuities. Finally, choice **D** is incorrect for the same reason that choice **A** is incorrect.

59. A Since the grant to the American Red Cross was ***void*** under the ***Rule Against Perpetuities*** (see answer to question 59), Alpha had received a fee simple determinable (i.e., the grant to Alpha was characterized by the words "so long as," which are ordinarily associated with a fee simple determinable), and Owen, by law, retained a possibility of reverter. At Owen's death the possibility of reverter was then transferred to Bill. (*See* ELO ch.5-II(B)(2).) Choices **B** and **C** are incorrect because an executory interest vests the land in someone other than the grantor when the event that terminates the preceding fee simple interest occurs. Here, the interest created was a possibility of reverter in the grantor that the grantor then devised in his will. Finally, choice **D** is incorrect because Owen transferred his possibility of reverter to Bill.

60. A With respect to Whiteacre, based on the language in the deed, Owen created in Beta a ***determinable fee subject to an executory interest*** in the Salvation Army. The Salvation Army's executory interest is subject to the ***Rule Against Perpetuities*** and is invalid unless it will vest, if at all, within 21 years after the death of an ascertainable life that was in being at the time such executory interest was created. (*See* ELO ch.5-IX(C)(4).) The grant to the Salvation Army does not violate the Rule Against Perpetuities. By the terms of the conveyance, the interest must vest, if at all, within 20 years. However, if Beta were to use the land for other than residential purposes beyond the 20-year period, the land would revert to Owen by reason of his possibility of reverter. (*See* Rest. Prop. §44.) Thus, Beta and the Salvation Army could not convey a fee simple absolute (i.e., an estate without qualification or condition) to Yates unless Owen relinquished his possibility of reverter. Choice **B** is incorrect because Beta and the Salvation Army did not own a fee simple absolute interest in Whiteacre. Choice **C** is incorrect because the Rule Against Perpetuities does not apply to a possibility of reverter. Finally, choice **D** is incorrect because there is ordinarily no strong public policy precluding a grantor from requiring land to be used for residential purposes.

61. B Carla has a ***vested remainder*** because she is an identifiable person and her interest is not subject to a condition precedent (rather, her interest is subject to a condition subsequent—enrolling in law school). (*See* ELO ch.5-IV(G).) However, Carla's interest is ***subject to complete divestment*** if she were to enroll in law school. (*See* ELO ch.5-IV(G)(4)(b).) Choice **A** is incorrect because Carla's interest is not absolutely vested (i.e., it is divested if she enrolls in law school). Choice **C** is incorrect because Carla's interest does not divest Bea of her possessory interest prior to its natural termination (i.e., Carla would not have a right to possession until Bea dies). Finally, choice **D** is incorrect because Carla is an identifiable person and her interest is not subject to a condition precedent.

62. C Assuming Carla's interest becomes possessory, she would then have a ***fee simple subject to an executory limitation***. The Legal Aid Society would have an ***executory interest*** because its right to possession would become effective upon termination of Carla's fee simple interest. (*See* ELO ch.5-IV(G)(4)(b).) Choices **A** and **D** are incorrect because a remainder cannot follow any type of fee simple interest. Finally, choice **B** is incorrect because the Legal Aid Society does not have a fee simple interest in Redacre. Rather, it has a future interest (not one that is present or possessory), which will become effective only if Carla undertakes specified conduct.

63. D The time during which the land must be ***occupied by the adverse possessor*** includes the period during which another occupies the land under or through the possessor's permission. (*See* ELO ch.3-IV(E).) Alex probably acquired title to Flatacre by adverse possession since the continuous occupation of Flatacre by Alex and/or Bill exceeded five years. Choice **A** is incorrect because even though Alex has not been in possession of Flatacre for five consecutive years, Bill's possession of Flatacre could be tacked onto her own. Choice **B** is incorrect because the rightful owner's actual knowledge that his land is being occupied is irrelevant for purposes of determining whether an adverse possession has occurred. Finally, choice **C** is incorrect because the adverse possession period must be continuous. While Alex has been in possession of the land for more than five years total, the two-and-a-half-year hiatus would prevent her from claiming title to the land by adverse possession (unless she were to benefit, as she does here, from the tacking on of another's possession).

64. A Where real property is taken by ***eminent domain***, the value of the land paid by the governmental entity is distributed amongst all of the parties with an interest (present or future) therein. (*See* ELO ch.8-III(E)(4).) Here, Bill's lease agreement contained an option to purchase and Bill notified Alex of his intent to exercise the option prior to the condemnation. Where the option has been exercised prior to condemnation, the optionee is usually entitled to compensation on the condemnation of the property. (*See* C.J.S. (Eminent Domain), §247). If an appraisal of the land by the governmental entity exceeded the purchase price determined by the appraiser chosen mutually by Bill and Alex, Bill would be entitled to the excess. Choice **B** is incorrect because Bill could not rightfully obtain possession to Flatacre without having previously paid the price set by the appraiser. Choice **C** is incorrect because Bill has an interest in Flatacre (a right to purchase) that could be exercised during Alex's life. Finally, choice **D** is incorrect because, as discussed in the preceding answer, Owen has no interest in Flatacre.

65. C Where an ***adverse possessor*** enters the land under ***color of title*** (i.e., pursuant to a defective conveyancing document), he acquires ownership to all of the real property described in the applicable documents. (*See* ELO ch.3-VI(C)(2).) Since Alex entered Flatacre pursuant to a deed that she believed was valid, Alex would acquire all of Owen's land that was described in the deed. Choice **A** is incorrect because, under these circumstances, Alex acquired an ownership interest in all of Flatacre by adverse possession. Choices **B** and **D** are incorrect because, having entered Flatacre under color of title, Alex is entitled to the entire property.

66. D One who occupies another's land without permission is liable to the latter for *mesne* profits (i.e., the reasonable rental value of the land). (*See* ELO ch.3-VI(A)(2).) If Owen were successful in his ejectment action against Alex (i.e., if Alex did not acquire title to the land under adverse possession), Bill's occupancy of Flatacre was wrongful. He therefore would be liable to Owen, the rightful owner, for the reasonable rental value of the land. Choice **A** is incorrect because Owen's lack of awareness of Bill's occupancy would not prevent Owen from successfully suing Bill for the reasonable rental value of the land. Choice **B** is incorrect because Steve never acquired any interest in Flatacre. Finally, choice **C** is incorrect because Alex, not having acquired title to Flatacre by adverse possession, would have had no legal right to rent the land to Bill.

67. C A purchaser of an interest in land is charged with ***constructive notice*** of all documents within the grantor's chain of title. (*See* ELO ch.12-II(K).) Since the Water District's easement has been recorded, it is binding upon Peterson (even though the deed from Owens to Peterson did not refer to the easement). Since the easement expressly included the right to "repair, maintain, and replace" the pipes, the proposed excavation is proper. (*See* ELO ch.9-III(A)(1).) Choice **A** is incorrect because Peterson is charged with constructive notice of any interest against the land within the chain of title. Choice **B** is incorrect because once an easement is acquired, it is not lost by nonuse alone. An easement may be lost by abandonment, but this does not occur unless the holder of the easement fails to use it ***and*** has the intention of abandoning it. Finally, choice **D** is incorrect because the fact that the Water District's plan may be "fair and equitable" is irrelevant. It is permissible for the Water District to make any use of Peterson's land that is within the scope of its express easement. There is no indication that the Water District ever intended to relinquish its easement.

68. D An ***easement holder not liable for damages*** he causes to the servient estate owner as long as his ***use of the easement is reasonable.*** (*See* Ely & Bruce, The Law of Easements and Licenses in Land §8.3.) Since the Water District acted within the parameters of its express easement, it would have no liability to Peterson for disrupting her easement, it would have no liability to Peterson for disrupting her garden. Further, since Peterson is charged with constructive notice of the Water District's easement, she assumed the risk of interference with her garden if replacing the pipes became necessary. (*See* ELO ch.12-II(K).) Choice **A** is incorrect because one is charged with constructive notice of all interests within the chain of title. Choice **B** is incorrect because an easement holder is not required to maintain the servient estate in exactly the condition it was in prior to exercising the applicable use. The easement holder's obligation is only to refrain from using the easement in an excessive or an unreasonable manner. Finally, choice **C** is incorrect because the Water District would have to condemn the land and reimburse Peterson if the public had a strong interest in maintaining a continuous water supply.

69. A An ***easement*** is ***extinguished*** when a ***merger of the dominant and servient estates*** occurs. (*See* ELO ch.9-V(C).) When Jane became the owner of Redacre through adverse possession, her easement across that parcel of land ceased to exist because a merger of Blackacre and Redacre had occurred. Choice **B** is incorrect because the mere nonuse of the easement does not extinguish it. An easement may be lost by abandonment. However, there is no indication that Jane intended to abandon the express easement granted to her by Bill. Choice **C** is incorrect because the fact that Jane had no reason to use the easement would not, in itself, extinguish it. Choice **D** is incorrect because the easement was extinguished by reason of the merger of the dominant and servient estates.

70. D A ***tenancy by the entirety*** can exist only between a ***husband and wife.*** Since common law marriage is not recognized in this jurisdiction, Wade and Mary cannot hold the property as tenants by the entirety. (*See* ELO ch.7-III(A).) Where property is held concurrently and there is uncertainty as to how the estate should be characterized, there is a judicial preference for viewing concurrent ownership as a tenancy in common. (*See* ELO ch.7-II(C).) Therefore, Wade and Mary probably would be deemed to be holding the land as tenants in common. Thus, Mary's prayer for partition probably would be granted because a co-tenant may successfully commence an action for partition at any time. Choice **A** is incorrect because, while legally true (i.e., a tenant by the entirety has no right of partition), Wade and Mary probably assumed title to the land as tenants in common; they had not wed, and common law marriages are not recognized in the state in question. Choice **B** is incorrect because the deed named both Wade and Mary as grantees. Choice **C** is incorrect because no tenancy by the entirety was ever created (despite the language in the deed given to Wade and Mary) because Wade and Mary were ***not*** married.

71. C In the absence of an express agreement to the contrary, a co-tenant ordinarily may assign a fractional part of his leasehold interest. (*See* ELO ch.7-II(B)(1).) Since there was no express agreement to the contrary between Talbot and Rogers, Talbot cannot restrain Rogers from assigning a portion of her interest in the lease. In this case, however, the provision in question declaring any assignment to be null and void was intended to benefit Lane, not Talbot. Thus, Talbot is not a proper party to pursue this action. (*See* ELO ch.8-VIII(F).) Choice **A** is incorrect because a co-tenant ordinarily has the right to assign a part of his leasehold interest. Choice **B** is incorrect because the provision prohibiting assignment is assertable only by Lane. Finally, choice **D** is incorrect because even though clauses restricting the alienability of leasehold interests are strictly construed, they ordinarily have been sustained.

72. A A ***periodic tenancy*** is a tenancy which ***continues from one period to the next automatically, unless either party terminates*** it at the end of a period with notice. Here, Lin leased to Ted on a ***year-to year*** basis. Although Ted provided valid legal notice terminating his tenancy at the end of the year, Ted remained in possession after the termination date. When a tenant remains in possession of leased premises after termination of her tenancy, the landlord can elect to hold the tenant to another term. (*See* ELO ch.8-II(E)(1).) Since Ted did not vacate the premises on or before December 31, Lin could elect to hold him liable for another term. Although the original lease calculated rentals on an annual basis, most courts interpret the new term as a year-to-year lease. (*See* ELO ch.8-II(E)(4).) Ted would be liable for the entire annual rental of $3,600. In some jurisdictions, the landlord cannot elect to hold a tenant liable for the full term when the tenant holds over due to circumstances beyond his control. However, the desire to avoid an unpleasant odor probably would ***not*** constitute a sufficient justification for failing to vacate the leased premises. Choice **B** is incorrect because even if Ted had informed Lin that he would be holding over for a few days, Lin would still have been legally entitled to elect to renew the initial term of the lease. Choices **C** and **D** are incorrect because a landlord may elect to hold a tenant to another full term if that person remains in possession of the premises after his tenancy has concluded.

73. C Where a ***landlord*** assigns her entire interest in a leasehold estate to another, her ***assignee*** is in ***privity of estate with the tenant.*** (*See* ELO ch.8-VIII(E)(1).) Here, Landlord conveyed the store and lease to Owner. Owner, therefore, succeeds to the benefits of covenants that run with the land, including the covenant to pay rent. Where a tenant assigns his entire interest in a leasehold and is liable for the performance of any promises whose borden runs with the land estate to another, his assignee is in privity of estate with the landlord and is liable for the performance of any promises whose burden runs with the land, so long as that person occupies the premises. (*See* ELO ch.8-VIII(D)(4).) Since Tenant had assigned his entire interest in the lease to Assignee, Assignee stood in privity of estate with Owner Choice **A** is incorrect because one can occupy land without paying the rightful owner, such as occurs when one acquires title to real property by adverse possession. Choice **B** is incorrect because Assignee owed rent pursuant to the lease to whoever occupied the position of lessor under the lease. Because Assignee did not make any rental payments, his lack of notice of the conveyance by Landlord to Owner is irrelevant. Finally, choice **D** is incorrect because even though transfers of interests in land must ordinarily be in writing, the Statute of Frauds can be asserted only by a party to the agreement (i.e., Assignee could assert the Statute of Frauds against Tenant, or Tenant could assert the Statute of Frauds against Assignee). Since Owner was not a party to the Tenant-Assignee agreement, she cannot successfully assert the Statute of Frauds.

74. B In the absence of a statutory or contractual restriction to the contrary, ***leasehold interests*** are ***alienable.*** (*See* ELO ch.8-VIII(A).) Since the lease did not prohibit an assignment, Tenant's transfer of his leasehold interest to Assignee would be effective, assuming the above elements were met. Choice **A** is incorrect because the assignment of a lease that still has a term in excess of one year must comply with the Statute of Frauds to be enforceable between the parties thereto. (Thus, without a writing, Tenant could ***not*** successfully sue Assignee for failing to meet his rental obligations to Owner.) Choice **C** is incorrect because leasehold interests are ordinarily assignable. Finally, choice **D** is incorrect because there is no legal requirement that the assignor of a lessee's interest give notice of the assignment to the landlord.

75. C ***A sublease*** is a ***transfer by lessee of less than his entire estate.*** A leasehold estate is ordinarily alienable, inheritable, and devisable.

(*See* Stoebuck & Whitman, The Law of Property (3d ed.) §6.11). Since Assignee died testate, his interest in the lease would pass to whomever he had devised such property to in his will. The devisee, however, would also be liable for any obligations of Assignee under the lease. Choice **A** is incorrect because a leasehold interest ordinarily survives the death of a lessee. Choice **B** is also incorrect because even if the distinction between freehold (fees, fee tails, and life estates) and nonfreehold estates was abolished, such action would have no effect on Assignee's interest in the lease because leasehold interests are ordinarily devisable. Finally, choice **D** is incorrect because a leasehold interest does ***not*** automatically revert to an assignor upon the assignee's death.

76. B A ***leasehold*** estate is ordinarily ***alienable, inheritable, and devisable.*** Since the lease did not prohibit a transfer by Tenant, Tenant was free to sublease it. (*See* ELO ch.8-VIII(A).) Choice **A** is incorrect because, absent a contractual or statutory provision to the contrary, a leasehold interest ordinarily may be subleased. Choice **C** is incorrect because a sublessee (as opposed to an assignee) does not stand in privity of estate with the landlord. In addition, for one to be an assignee, the assignor must have parted with his entire estate under the lease. Finally, choice **D** is incorrect because a sublessee does ***not*** stand in privity of estate with the landlord. (A sublessee, however, may be liable to the landlord if the landlord is deemed to be a third-party beneficiary of the sublease between the lessee and sublessee.)

77. D A ***trespass*** occurs when the defendant has ***intentionally intruded*** upon, beneath, or above the surface of the plaintiff's land. (*See* Restatement (Second) of Torts §159.) If a trespass has occurred, the defendant is liable for at least nominal damages. The overhanging eaves would constitute a trespass. Restatement (Second) of Torts §159(f), illus. 1. Choice **A** is incorrect because a trespasser is liable to the plaintiff for at least nominal damages (whether or not the plaintiff has suffered any actual harm). Restatement (Second) of Torts §158. Choice **B** is incorrect because Allen's intent to build the structure whose eaves now overhang Bates's land would constitute sufficient "intent" to intrude upon Bates's land. Choice **C** is incorrect because it is not necessary for Bates to prove that Allen's action actually interfered with her use of the land to recover in trespass.

78. C A ***landowner*** is ***strictly liable*** for the ***removal or alteration*** of his ***property in a manner*** that ***causes*** an ***adjacent owner's land in its natural state to subside.*** However, where an improvement is damaged because of a lack of lateral support, the defendant is strictly liable for damages only if the plaintiff can show that his land would have subsided even had the improvement not existed. (*See* ELO ch.13-II(B)(1).) Since Allen is unable to show that there would have been any settling or falling of his land if it had been in its natural condition, under the majority view, Bates would not be strictly liable to Allen as a result of the obligation to provide lateral support (although Allen could still bring a negligence action against Bates). Choice **A** is incorrect because Bates is only strictly liable to support Allen's land in its natural state. Choice **B** is incorrect because the mere fact that Bates failed to give Allen notice of the excavation is not a basis for recovery by Allen. Finally, choice **D** is incorrect because, in addition to the obligation to perform an excavation in a careful manner (i.e., in a nonnegligent manner), a landowner also has the obligation to provide lateral support so that a neighbor's adjoining land in its natural state will not subside.

79. A A ***landowner*** is ***strictly liable*** for the ***removal or alteration of*** his ***property in a manner*** which ***causes*** an ***adjacent owner's land in its natural state to subside.*** However, where an improvement is damaged because of a lack of lateral support, the defendant is strictly liable for damages only if the plaintiff can show that his land would have subsided even had the improvement not existed. (*See* ELO ch.13-II(B)(1).) Since Allen's land, even in its natural condition, would have subsided as a result of Bates' excavation, Bates is absolutely liable for the damages sustained by Allen. Choice **B** is incorrect because a landowner is ordinarily ***not*** entitled to support for her land in an improved condition (i.e., one is ordinarily entitled to support for her land only in its natural state). Choice **C** is incorrect because liability for failure to provide lateral support when required is absolute (i.e., foreseeability of harm to the adjoining landowner is irrelevant). Finally, Choice **D** is incorrect because liability for failure to provide lateral support is not predicated upon the malice or ill will of the party undertaking the excavation.

80. B A ***nuisance*** occurs when the defendant has, in a nontrespassory manner, caused an ***unreasonable and substantial interference*** with, or impairment of, the plaintiff's use of his land. (*See* ELO ch.13-I(A).) In determining whether there has been an unreasonable interference with the plaintiff's use and enjoyment of his land, the court ordinarily will weigh (1) the social value or utility of the defendant's conduct or activity to the area, (2) the suitability of the defendant's activity to the character of the locality, and (3) the impracticability of precluding or avoiding the defendant's conduct. Restatement (Second) of Torts §828. Polluting a stream used by an adjacent landowner and interfering with his ability to sleep together probably constitute an unreasonable interference, by West, with East's use of his property. Choice **A** is incorrect because the fact that one has interfered with another's commercial enterprise does not automatically require a finding that the former's activity is a nuisance (i.e., the interference must be unreasonable, and the utility to the community of both enterprises must be weighed). Choice **C** is incorrect because one may have liability for nuisance even though she did not intend to injure the plaintiff. It is only necessary that the defendant have intentionally or consciously engaged in the activity that unreasonably interfered with the plaintiff's use of his land. Finally, choice **D** is incorrect because the fact that West had been dumping waste into the slush pit prior to the time East commenced his chicken-raising business does not, *per se*, relieve West from liability under a nuisance theory.

81. A The relative wealth of West and East is irrelevant in determining whether West's activities have unreasonably interfered with East's use of his land. (*See* ELO ch.13-I(C)(2).) Choice **B** is pertinent in that it would show numerous persons were injured as a consequence of West's activities, which would weigh against permitting those activities to continue. Choice **C** would aid East because if West's oil well operation was only marginally profitable, then requiring its cessation would not impact severely upon her. Finally, choice **D** would aid East because a realization by West that she was polluting her neighbor's land would certainly weigh against West.

82. A The ***Statute of Frauds*** requires the ***signature of the party to be charged*** (i.e., the party against whom enforcement is sought). (*See* ELO ch.11-I(B)(1).) Even though only Thomas, Arthur's agent, signed the contract, the Statute of Frauds is satisfied because Thomas was authorized to execute the agreement on Arthur's behalf. While a few states require that an agency agreement involving the transfer of real property be in writing, the majority rule is contrary to this position. Choice **B** is incorrect because the fact that Baker's agency agreement was in writing would ***not*** withstand a Statute of Frauds defense by Arthur if the contract was not signed by him (or his agent). Choice **C** is incorrect because it is not necessary that Baker (or her agent) have signed the contract. The agreement must merely be signed by the party (or his agent) against whom enforcement is sought (i.e., Arthur). Finally, choice **D** is incorrect because in most states it is not necessary that Arthur's agency agreement be in writing. It is necessary only for Arthur to authorize Thomas to sign the contract for him and for Thomas to sign the contract, which he did. (Conceivably, Arthur might deny that Thomas was authorized to sign the agreement on his behalf; if the jury believes otherwise, Baker's lawsuit would be successful.)

83. A Under the ***Statute of Frauds***, for a contract for the purchase and sale of an interest in land to be enforceable, it must be embodied in a ***writing*** that contains the ***essential terms and is signed by the party against whom enforcement is sought***. (*See* ELO ch.11-I(B)(1).) However, under the doctrine of part performance, where the party attempting to compel performance has done acts that are unequivocally referable to the existence of a contract for the sale and purchase of land, many courts will permit evidence of the purported agreement to be admissible. (*See* ELO ch.11-I(B)(3).) Since Mrs. Williams moved into the dwelling and spent a substantial sum of money in renovating it, it is likely that a court would permit evidence of the oral agreement for the sale of Jones's summer home to be admissible. It would have been illogical for Mrs. Williams to have spent a significant amount of money to improve the summer home unless a contract for its sale to the Williamses existed. Choice **B** is incorrect because Mr. Williams was relieved of his obligation to tender the purchase price when Jones unequivocally advised Williams that he would not complete the transaction (i.e., when an anticipatory repudiation occurs, the aggrieved party is relieved of his prospective obligations under the agreement). Choice **C** is incorrect because the mere fact that Mrs. Williams was aware of the contract would not have any impact on whether the oral agreement is admissible under the Statute of Frauds. Finally, choice **D** is incorrect because the fact that Mrs. Williams renovated the summer home without Jones's actual knowledge would not be dispositive. Since she was acting under the good faith belief that Jones would consummate the transaction with her husband, her possession of the dwelling prior to the time a contract had been prepared and signed would (at most) permit Jones to recover only the reasonable rental value of the summer home prior to the time the transaction would otherwise have been consummated.

84. B Under the ***merger doctrine, all promises and warranties*** (express or implied) contained ***in an agreement for the sale and purchase of real property*** are ***deemed*** to be ***merged into the deed.*** (*See* ELO ch.11-III(A)(1).) Thus, the terms of the deed that Peg accepted will control Sue's liability. If Peg accepted a quitclaim deed, no remedy against Sue may be available. On the other hand, if a full warranty deed was tendered to Peg, she might have a right to recover damages. Choice **A** is incorrect because Sue's deed was not fraudulent. The facts indicate she believed that she had acquired title to the acre in question by adverse possession. This belief, albeit erroneous, precludes a finding of the intent to deceive that is necessary for one's actions to be deemed fraudulent. Choice **C** is incorrect because depending on the type of deed Peg received, she might well have an action for rescission of the entire transaction. (*See* 20 Am. Jur. 2d Covenants §113). Finally, choice **D** is incorrect because, even though there is an implied covenant that title shall be marketable in all contracts for the sale and purchase of real property, an objection to the seller's title must be made ***prior*** to acceptance of the deed by the grantee. Once the deed is accepted, the implied covenant of marketable title is merged into the deed.

85. C Under the ***merger doctrine, all promises and warranties*** (express or implied) contained ***in an agreement for the sale and purchase of real property*** are ***deemed*** to be ***merged into the deed.*** (*See* ELO ch.11-III(A)(1).) Since Sue tendered, and Peg accepted, a quitclaim deed, Peg would have no action against Sue. Choice **A** is incorrect because Sue's deed was not fraudulent (i.e., there was no intent on her part to deceive Peg). Choice **B** is incorrect because the terms of the quitclaim deed control and Peg will lose her action against Sue. Finally, choice **D** is incorrect because a deed does ***not*** ordinarily incorporate the terms of a contract to purchase and sell real property.

86. B To be protected by the ***recording statute,*** Crider must show that he took the property in ***good faith*** (i.e., without notice of the prior interest) and ***paid value.*** Here, Crider did not have notice of Price's prior interest. Price did not record the deed (i.e., no constructive notice). The facts do not indicate that Crider was told of Price's interest (i.e., no actual notice), nor was there evidence that Blackacre was occupied (i.e., no inquiry notice). Thus, Crider's claim turns on whether Crider paid value. In most jurisdictions, receipt of a deed in exchange for a release of an outstanding obligation constitutes giving value by the grantee. In a few states, however, the grantee must part with contemporaneous consideration to have given value. (*See* ELO ch.12-II(E)(5).) Thus, whether Crider has priority will depend on this jurisdiction's view as to whether the release of a preexisting obligation constitutes giving value. Choice **A** is incorrect because, in most jurisdictions, receipt of a quitclaim deed does not automatically prevent one from having taken land in good faith. Although, in a few jurisdictions, receipt of a quitclaim deed is deemed to put the grantee on inquiry notice with respect to the land being transferred. Choice **C** is incorrect because, under the applicable statute, whether an earlier grantee paid value is irrelevant for purposes of determining whether a subsequent transferee will have priority. Finally, choice **D** is incorrect because Crider, not having parted with new consideration, probably could not contend that she relied on the apparent state of Owen's title in agreeing to accept Owen's deed.

87. A Barrett as a purchaser of an interest in land is charged with ***constructive notice*** of all documents within his ***chain of title***. Since Allred recorded her deed from Owen after Niece recorded her deed from Owen, Barrett's review of the grantor/grantee index would not have revealed the deed that Owen had given to Allred. (Barrett would have checked for any transfers by Niece since her deed from Owen was recorded, as well as for any recorded deeds made by Owen prior to the time his deed to Niece was recorded). (*See* ELO ch.12-II(K)(3).) Choice **B** is incorrect because the fact that Niece recorded her deed before Allred's filing would not give Niece priority over Allred since Niece received her conveyance gratuitously (i.e., without parting with value). Choice **C** is incorrect because the applicable statute does not attach any importance to the type of deed received. Finally, choice **D** is incorrect because the fact that Niece had no notice of Allred's right would ***not*** give Niece priority over Allred since she had not given consideration for her deed.

88. D Generally under the ***recording acts***, a subsequent grantee can prevail over a prior grantee if the subsequent grantee is a ***bona fide purchaser for value*** and takes ***without notice***. Here, Leon prevails because even though he purchased after Allred, Allred had ***not*** recorded her deed at the time Owen executed a mortgage in favor of Leon. Therefore, Leon did not have notice of Allred's interest and Leon's mortgage would have priority under the recording statute. (*See* ELO ch.12-II(K)(3).) Choice **A** is incorrect because Leon did give value to Owen (the loan was made to Owen at the time Leon received the mortgage). Choice **B** is incorrect because, while factually true, it offers no justification why a subsequent grantee who falls within the requisites of the priority statute should not have priority over Allred. Finally, choice **C** is incorrect because the fact that Leon recorded before Allred would not be the reason Leon obtains priority over Allred. The applicable statute assigns priority to a subsequent grantee if he or she has given value without notice of the prior grantee's interest, ***not*** on the basis of early recordation.

89. C Since Niece has not paid value (i.e., she received the deed to Farmdale gratuitously), she is not protected by the applicable ***recording act***, which ***protects "a subsequent purchaser who pays value,"*** not a gratuitous donee. (*See* ELO ch.12-II(E)(1).) Therefore, Niece would not have priority to the land. Choice **A** is incorrect because, in addition to having no notice of Allred's rights when she accepted the deed from Owen, Niece would also have to have paid value to attain priority to Farmdale. Choice **B** is incorrect because recordation is not the focus of the applicable priority statute. Finally, choice **D** is incorrect because the fact that Allred paid value for Farmdale is irrelevant in this instance. Even if Allred had received the land as a gift, she would still have priority over Niece because Niece does not come within the statute that gives a subsequent grantee priority over an earlier one.

90. C Under the ***Statute of Frauds***, for a contract for the sale of real property to be enforceable, it must be embodied in a ***writing*** that contains the ***essential terms and*** must be ***signed by the party against whom enforcement is sought.*** The price of a parcel of land, in virtually all instances, will constitute an essential term of the agreement. (*See* ELO ch.11-I(B)(1).) Therefore, Vetter cannot be forced to perform the contract. Choice **A** is incorrect because the circumstances underlying the doctrine of estoppel (i.e., the plaintiff has foreseeably relied on the contract to his substantial detriment) do not appear to be present. There is no indication from the facts that Prue will suffer in some significant way if the agreement is unenforceable. Choice **B** is incorrect because the law will ***not*** imply a reasonable price into a contract for the purpose of avoiding a problem with the Statute of Frauds. Finally, choice **D** is incorrect because there is no rule of law that a sale may be avoided simply because the seller agreed to accept a price that is less than the fair market value of the land.

91. A When an ***abstract of title*** is obtained by the owner of land for the purpose of delivering it to a prospective purchaser, the prospective purchaser probably will be deemed to be a ***third-party beneficiary*** of the agreement. (*See* ELO ch.12-IV(C)(2)(a).) Since Sloan contracted to have the abstract delivered directly to Jones, Abstract Company was on notice that Jones would be a beneficiary of its contract with Sloan. Since Abstract Company breached its contract by failing to include the deed to Power Company, Jones would have a cause of action against Abstract Company. Choice **B** is incorrect because an abstract does not guarantee title. An abstract only purports to include copies of all properly recorded instruments affecting title to the land. Guarantees are ordinarily purchased from a title insurance company. Choice **C** is incorrect because Abstract Company was obliged to include in its abstract all properly recorded documents affecting the land, not simply those of which it had actual knowledge. Finally, choice **D** is incorrect because Abstract Company was aware that its work product was to be delivered to Jones and that Jones would probably rely on it.

92. B Since Sloan delivered a ***general warranty deed*** to Jones, Sloan warranted to Jones, among other things, that Newacre would be free from any encumbrances (i.e., impediments to title that diminish the value of the land). (*See* ELO ch.11-III(F)(2)(c).) Here Power Company's right of way for the building and maintenance of a power line across Newacre is an encumbrance. Sloan's warranty was breached. Choice **A** is incorrect because Sloan acted reasonably under the circumstances in retaining Abstract Company to prepare the abstract (presumably, Abstract Company was a reputable entity). Choice **C** is incorrect because Jones presumably relied on ***both*** the abstract and the general warranty deed he received from Sloan in taking title to Newacre. Finally, choice **D** is incorrect because the fact that Sloan did not have actual knowledge of Power Company's right of way would not preclude her liability to Jones as a result of the general warranty deed she delivered to Jones.

93. A ***Marketable title*** is that which is ***reasonably free from doubt*** (i.e., it would be acceptable to a reasonably prudent purchaser). (*See* ELO ch.11-I(D).) Generally, an outstanding lien would render title unmarketable. However, if a seller of real property is willing and able to fully discharge a lien from the proceeds of the sale of land at the time of closing, an outstanding mortgage does not make the title unmarketable. A seller of land has the implied right to use proceeds to be derived from the purchaser to satisfy any outstanding monetary encumbrances. (*See* ELO ch.11-I(D)(5)(b)(i).) Since

Venner is willing to apply the proceeds (placed in escrow) to satisfy the mortgage, Brier cannot legally withdraw from the contract. Choice **B** is legally incorrect, in that the mortgage would not shift to the contract proceeds. The mortgage would remain against the land until the obligation it secures is paid in full. Choice **C** is incorrect because, even though equitable title has passed to Brier, she would nevertheless be entitled to withdraw from the transaction if Venner could not furnish marketable title at the closing. Finally, choice **D** is incorrect because it is ordinarily implied into contracts for the sale of land that the seller will convey marketable title at the closing. Venner, however, is entitled to satisfy the mortgage with proceeds to be received from Brier upon the sale of Greenacre.

94. B Whether a ***chattel*** is deemed a ***fixture***, and therefore the property of the owner of the land, depends on the intention of the party who affixed the item to the real property, as determined from all of the circumstances. (*See* ELO ch.8-VI(C)(2).) Since Barnes presumably desired to continue her hobby after the lease had expired and the chattels can (apparently) be removed without significant damage to the premises, a court probably would conclude that she did not intend the items to become fixtures. Choice **A** is incorrect because notice of a mortgage is irrelevant in determining whether a tenant intended her attached chattels to become fixtures. Choice **C** is incorrect because there is no rule of law that a residential tenant is automatically entitled to remove personalty that has been affixed to the premises. Finally, choice **D** is incorrect because even if Bank's mortgage did not ***expressly*** extend to fixtures, a mortgagee of real property automatically has a claim to fixtures that exist on the land at the inception of the mortgage.

95. A Whether a ***chattel*** is deemed to be a ***fixture***, and therefore the property of the owner of the land, depends on the intention of the party who affixed the item to the real property, as determined from all of the surrounding circumstances. (*See* ELO ch.8-VI(C)(2).) Because the items in question had been installed by Albert, Bank's chances of succeeding would improve. Albert (as the owner of the land) probably would have intended the chattels to become a permanent part of the real property. Choices **B** and **C** are incorrect because, as explained above, Bank's chances of succeeding would be improved if Albert were the party who affixed the chattels to the real property. Finally, choice **D** is incorrect because it is not necessary for a mortgage to explicitly refer to fixtures. Those fixtures that exist on the land at the inception of a mortgage are automatically covered by the mortgage.

96. B If the contract does not designate the kind of title to be conveyed by the vendor at closing, an obligation to convey marketable title will be implied. (*See* ELO ch.11-I(D)(1).) Since the contract between Chase and Smith makes no reference to the type of title to be conveyed, Chase will be obliged to convey marketable title. Choice **A** is incorrect because, as just stated, even though no reference was made to the type of deed to be conveyed, the court probably will imply whatever type (full warranty, special warrant, or quitclaim) is ordinarily given in this kind of transaction in this area. Choice **C** is incorrect because a vendor is required to convey marketable title at the closing, regardless of the status of his title on the date the contract was made. Similarly, choice **D** is incorrect because Chase is obliged to convey marketable title to Smith at the closing, regardless of whatever title he had when the contract was made or thereafter.

97. C As a general rule, an ***agreement for the sale of land*** must be in a ***writing sufficient to satisfy the Statute of Frauds.*** The writing must contain the essential terms and must be signed by the party against whom enforcement is sought. The essential terms of the agreement must be sufficiently definite. (*See* ELO ch.11-I(B)(1)(a).) Here, the amount of land adequate to "accommodate a garden and lawn" cannot be determined with reasonable certainty. Therefore, the agreement is probably unenforceable. (It is also possible that the language "my dwelling" could be ambiguous if Arthur owns more than one piece of property with a dwelling on it, a fact not indicated by the fact pattern.) Choice **A** is incorrect because the Statute of Frauds is satisfied as long as the party against whom enforcement is sought (in this instance, Arthur) signed the agreement. Choice **B** is incorrect because the consideration in this instance is $20,000. The "$1" referred to in Arthur's writing alluded only to the deposit Arthur had received from Walter. Presumably, the balance would have been due at the closing. Finally, choice **D** is incorrect because, even though contracts for the sale of land are ordinarily enforceable by specific performance, this rule does not apply when an enforceable contract has ***not*** been formed.

98. C The majority view is that a landowner has a right to extract oil that is underneath the surface of her property as long as she does not trespass onto neighboring land. Here, Carla did not trespass on Baker's land; the wells from which Carla extracted the oil were completely on neighboring property. Choice **A** is incorrect. The prior appropriation doctrine is generally used to determine water rights. Carla's status as an invitee or trespasser on David's land is not relevant to determine her rights vis-à-vis Baker. Choice B is incorrect. Baker's permission is not required. Carla only needed David's permission because David was the owner upon whose lands the wells were drilled. Choice **D** is not the best answer. While some states view oil in its underground state as unowned property, similar to a wild animal, with ownership going to the first to capture it, even in these jurisdictions a different outcome is likely where the extractor was trespassing at the time she captured the oil.

99. D The gold coins would likely be viewed as ***mislaid*** property, custody of which should be given to the landowner. (*See* ELO ch.2-I(C)(6).) Choice **A** is wrong. Where the finder is a trespasser, courts generally award the property to the landowner of the real estate where the object is found. Choice **B** is wrong. While English courts have established a separate category of "treasure trove" for valuables that have been intentionally buried beneath the surface and never reclaimed by their owner, most American courts have declined to establish a separate category. Under English law, such property belongs to the state. American courts generally treat such items as mislaid property. Choice **C** is wrong. There was no legal obligation at common law to pay a "finder's fee." Quite the opposite, in some jurisdictions, under certain circumstances, a finder can be awarded the found property.

100. C In this jurisdiction a 20-year ***statute of limitations*** applies to ***adverse possession*** and a 10-year statute applies to adverse possession under color title. While it is true that the 20-year statute has not run, in this case, the 10-year statute is the applicable time because Baker entered Corneracre under color of title and Baker has been in adverse possession for more than 10 years. (*See* ELO ch.3-III(A)(4).) Choice **A** is wrong. Since Baker entered under color of title, the 10-year statute applies to his possession. Choice **B** is wrong because Baker does not need (indeed, cannot have) Able's permission to gain title through adverse possession. Choice **D** is wrong. Mere non-use of property is not enough to establish abandonment.

101. C While, in general, the ***adverse possessor*** only gains title to the land actually occupied, when the adverse possessor enters under ***color of title*** and occupies a portion of the property, he gains title to the entire parcel described in the defective deed. (*See* ELO ch.3-VI(C)(2).) Choice **A** is not the correct answer. Baker has occupied the land long enough to gain title through adverse possession under color of title. Choice **B** is wrong. An adverse possessor under color of title gains title to the entire parcel described in the defective deed as long as he occupied a portion of the land. Choice **D** is wrong. Baker's right to the house based on adverse possession.

102. B Although the agreement between Eddie and Susan is not in writing and therefore does not satisfy the requirements for creating an express easement, an ***easement by estoppel*** was likely created. Eddie's reliance on the access (he has used the common driveway for seven years) and expenditures in reliance on access (he contributed money and labor to the erection of the common driveway) likely satisfies the requirements for the creation of an easement by estoppel. (*See* ELO ch.9-II(G).) The burden of that easement likely runs to Peter. Generally the burden of the easement transfers when title to the property is transferred as long as new purchaser is on notice. (*See* ELO ch.12-II(D)(1)(b).) Here, Peter was likely on inquiry notice from the visible evidence of the common driveway. Choice **A** is not the best answer. Although an owner of land general has a right to use her property as she wishes, she cannot interfere with another's owner's rights. In this case, Eddie probably has an easement across Susan's property; an easement with which Peter cannot interfere. Choice **C** is wrong because Eddie used the driveway with Susan's permission. Choice **D** is wrong. The general rule is that licenses are generally revocable. An exception to this rule is where the licensee (Eddie) has relied on continued access by expending money and making improvements with the licensor's knowledge.

103. B Here, Sally delivered the deed to Belinda through escrow. At the close of escrow, when the stated conditions are satisfied (i.e., the balance of the sale price is paid), the custodian delivers the deed to the grantee. (*See* ELO ch.11-III(D)(5).) The delivery ***"relates back"*** to the date the deed was handed to the custodian. Two requirements must be met for the doctrine of relation back to operate. First, there must be an ***enforceable contract of sale*** between the grantor and grantee (i.e., sales contract between Belinda and Sally). Second, the grantor must have reserved ***no legal power to recall*** the ***deed*** from the custodian. Sally delivered the deed to her lawyer to hold in escrow and retained no power to recall the deed. Therefore, the deed is considered delivered on the date Sally handed the deed to her attorney. While the relation back doctrine does not apply where the grantor conveys to a bona fide purchaser, here Patricia would not qualify as a bona fide purchaser because she knew about the Belinda-Sally agreement. Choice **A** is wrong. It is Patricia, the subsequent purchaser, rather than Belinda, who must demonstrate that she is a bona fide purchaser for value under the recording statute. Choice **C** is wrong because to be protected as a bona fide purchaser, Patricia must take without notice of the earlier conveyance and record first. Here, Patricia knew about the Belinda-Sally agreement. Choice **D** is wrong. While it is true that deposit of deed with escrow agent usually does not act to transfer legal title, the relation back doctrine is an exception to that rule.

104. A B is claiming a ***negative easement*** over A's property. Generally courts hold that negative easements for light, air and view cannot arise by implication. They can only be created by express grant. (*See* ELO ch.9-II(C)(6).) Here, the parties did not expressly agree to such a right, so Baxter is unable to stop Amy from blocking his view. Choice **B** is wrong. Amy was under no legal obligation to inform Baxter of her intentions for her own property. Choice **C** is wrong. Baxter does not have a right to a view absent an express grant from Amy. Choice **D** is wrong. Amy was under no obligation to object to Baxter's construction.

105. D Here, the commercial development occurred outside of the restricted development. Generally courts will not relieve owners of a restriction based on changes occurring outside the restricted area unless the changes outside the tract affect the entire tract in such a way that the benefits of the restrictions are no longer generally available. (*See* ELO ch.9-IX(O)(4).) The only change that has occurred inside the development is a zoning change. A change in zoning alone is not sufficient evidence of changed conditions to warrant lifting a residential restriction. Choice **D** is the best answer. The restrictions probably have ***not*** terminated because of changed conditions, and Vince's plans to build an apartment building violate the restrictions. Choice **A** is wrong. While the social utility of Vince's actions might be relevant in a nuisance analysis, it is irrelevant to determine whether the restriction should terminate based on changes in the neighborhood. Choice **B** is wrong. Since a change in zoning alone is not sufficient evidence of changed conditions to warrant lifting a residential restriction, Vince's ultimate compliance with the ordinance is irrelevant. Choice **C** is wrong, as a zoning change is not necessarily unconstitutional. As long as procedural requirements are met, the ordinance is not adopted for an improper purpose (e.g., such as for a racially discriminatory purpose) and does not so drastically interfere with the property owner's use or value of his property, then such ordinances generally pass constitutional muster.

106. D Most courts follow the ***reasonable use*** approach to ***riparian rights.*** Under this approach, a riparian owner is entitled to only so much of the water as he can put to beneficial use on his land. Each riparian owner has an absolute right to all or any part of the water for natural uses, without regard to the effect this use has on other owners. But, with respect to artificial uses, a riparian owner may not take any water for such use, until the natural needs of all other riparian owners has been satisfied. (*See* ELO ch.13-III(B)(2)(c).) Here, the downstream owners' natural use (as a source of drinking water) would have priority over farmer's artificial use (to irrigate a large scale commercial operation). Choice **A** is wrong. The prior appropriation rule (the first to use has priority over subsequent uses) is a minority rule. Choice **B** is wrong. While the social utility of farmer's use is relevant in a nuisance analysis, here the applicable standard is one of reasonable use. Choice **C** is wrong. The natural flow theory is followed in a minority of jurisdictions.

107. B Tess's conveyance to Bob ***severed*** the ***joint tenancy*** between Jerry and Tess, resulting in a tenancy in common between Bob and Jerry. (*See* ELO ch. 7-I(E)(1).) At Jerry's death his property would be distributed according to his will. In his will Jerry purports to create a life estate in Sofie and a remainder in his "nieces and nephews." The gift to his nieces and nephews, however, runs afoul of the ***Rule Against Perpetuities***, which applies to class gifts. When a gift is made to all members of a class, the entire class gift fails unless the interest of each member of the class must vest or fail within the perpetuities period. (*See* ELO ch.5-IX(E)(6).) Since Jerry's parents are still alive at the time of Jerry's death, the law presumes that they, regardless of age or physical condition, are capable of having more children. (*See* ELO ch.5-IX(E)(1).) If they have another child, that child, who is not a life in being at the time of grant, could have a child (a future niece or nephew of Jerry) more than 21 years after the death of the lives in being at the creation of the grant (i.e., Jerry's parents, his sister (Sofie) and nephew (Charlie).)

Because of this theoretical possibility the entire class gift is invalid and would be stricken, leaving a life estate in Sofie, followed by a reversion in Jerry's heirs. Choice **A** is wrong. Tess's conveyance to Bob severed the joint tenancy and destroyed the right of survivorship. Choice **C** is wrong. The gift to the class of nieces and nephews violates the RAP, and the entire gift would be stricken. Under modern modifications to the RAP, a court could separate the Charlie's vested interest, from the contingent interest in the unborn nieces and nephews and construe the grant as a vested remainder in Charlie. Choice **D** is wrong. Tess's conveyance to Bob severed the joint tenancy, making Bob a tenant in common with Jerry.

108. B The right of first refusal violates the rule against perpetuities. The rule states that an interest must vest, if at all, not later than 21 years following a life in being at the date of the conveyance. Here, the right of first refusal violates the rule because it purports to bind Tiffany's heirs and assigns without limitation; therefore, Developer's interest could vest too far into the future. Choice **A** is incorrect. Developer's action would be based on the agreement, not the deed. Choice **C** is incorrect. Failure to record does not invalidate the right. Choice **D** is incorrect. Developer's action is based on the agreement between Developer and Tiffany, not the agreement between Jennifer and Neighbor.

109. B Under the doctrine of destructibility of contingent remainders, a contingent remainder is destroyed if it has not vested before the preceding life estate ends. Here, Octavio conveyed a life estate in Adisa followed by a remainder in Belinda's first child and a reversion in the grantor, Octavio. The remainder is contingent since Belinda was childless at the time of the conveyance. Since the contingent remainder had not vested (i.e., Belinda had no children) at Adisa's death, the contingent remainder was destroyed and Octavio's reversion became possessory. Choice **A** is incorrect because a life estate terminates at the death of the life tenant, which means Adisa owned no property for her heirs to inherit. Choice **C** is incorrect. Timmy's interest was destroyed at Adisa's death so Timmy had nothing to sell to CropDust. Choice **D** is incorret. Belinda never had any interest in the property.

110. A To enforce a restrictive covenant the plaintiff must prove an enforceable between the original parties; the original parties intended the burden to run, the promise touched and concerned the land and notice. Traditionally, privity of estate was also required to enforce a restrictive covenant. By conveying the property to the attorney and having the attorney re-convey the deeds with the restrictions (a "straw person" transaction), the homeowners have satisfied the privity requirements. The conveyance of the deed from John to the attorney created a horizontal privity relationship between the John and the attorney. The sale from John to Zachary satisfied the vertical privity requirements. Further, the Association, as an agent of the homeowners, has standing to enforce the restriction. Choice **B** is incorrect because the Association can recover both damages and injunction because the privity requirements are met. Choice **C** is incorrect because Zachary would be considered on constructive notice as the deed was recorded. Choice **D** is incorrect because the Association, as an agent of the property owners, has standing to enforce those restrictions as long as the declaration gives the Association that power.

111. A Since Audra knew of the restriction and orally promised to comply with it, the promise is likely enforceable. Here, a court would likely hold that Audra would be estopped from denying the promise as it would be unjust to allow Audra to violate the common plan of the neighborhood despite the lack of restriction in her chain of title. Choice **B** is incorrect. Nuisance per se generally refers to abnormally dangerous activities. Choice **C** is incorrect. Although the Association does not own property in the community, as an agent of the property owners, the Association has standing to enforce the restrictions as long as the declaration gives the Association that power. Choice **D** is incorrect. The other homeowners within the restricted community would be considered intended third party beneficiary of Audra's promise to Calvin.

112. D Neither Olivia nor Ted has a claim to ***title*** to the property. While Olivia is the record titleholder, Jason's title by adverse possession supplants Olivia's title, and Ted has not been in possession long enough to claim title from Jason by adverse possession. Nevertheless, Ted has a superior claim to ***possession*** than Olivia. Generally, the prior peaceable possessor (Ted) prevails over a subsequent possessor (Olivia). Choice **A** is incorrect. Ted has not been in possession long enough to gain title. Ted also cannot tack onto Jason's claim since there is no privity between Jason and Ted. Choice **B** is incorrect. Although Ted did not satisfy the requirements for adverse possession, he has a superior claim based on possession. Choice **C** is incorrect because the owner must show an intent to abandon the property. There are no facts to support this conclusion.

113. D Omar conveyed a springing executory interest to Xavier, while retaining a fee simple subject to executory limitation for himself. Omar, the holder of the present possessory estate, has the right to lease his interest to Yolanda. Xavier, the future interest holder, has no right to interfere. Choice **A** is incorrect. Omar conveyed a future interest (a springing executory interest), not a present interest to Xavier. Choice **B** is incorrect. If Omar had conveyed his fee simple interest to Xavier, then Xavier would have the power to terminate Yolanda's tenancy. In this case, however, Omar conveyed a future interest to Xavier. Choice **C** is incorrect. The executory limitation is subject to the rule against perpetuities but does not violate it because the interest will vest or fail (i.e., Xavier will complete law school) within 21 years of the death of the lives in being on the effective date of the grant.

114. B As a result of the conveyance Alonzo has a fee simple subject to executory limitation, and Benito has an executory interest. The rule against perpetuities applies but is not violated. As the owner in fee, Alonzo has right to make full use of the property, including the right to extract oil and gas. Choice **A** is incorrect. While a true statement of law, the rule of capture does not apply to these facts. Choice **C** is incorrect. While a life tenant has a duty not to commit waste, such is not true for the owner of the fee estate. Choice **D** is incorrect. Alonzo's state of mind is irrelevant.

115. A Anna has a life estate. Ottavia has a reversion in fee simple subject to executory limitation. Bezatriz has a springing executory interest. At Beatriz's death, Beatriz's future interest would pass to Xochitl, the devisee under Beatriz's will. At Anna's death the property would revert to Ottavia for the gap period between Anna's death and Xochitl's right to possession. Choice **B** is incorrect. Xoxhitl, the holder of the future interest, does not have an immediate right of possession. Choice **C** is incorrect. Yara has no interest in the property since Beatriz disposed of her property through her will. Choice **D** is incorrect. The doctrine of destructibility of contingent remainders applies contingent remainders. It would not apply here where the future interest created is a reversion in fee simple subject to executory limitation in Ottavia followed by an executory interest in **B**.

116. D The custom in baseball is that any ball hit into the stands goes to the first person to gain possession of the ball. In this case, Charley gained first possession when he closed his mitt securely around the ball. However, by attempting to throw the ball back onto the field, Charley abandoned the ball. The rule is the first to gain possession of abandoned property becomes the owner. Here, Ollie is the owner of the property. **A** is incorrect. Although Charley took sufficient steps to gain ownership of the ball, he later abandoned his ownership by throwing the ball away. **B** is incorrect. Ollie's status would make no difference in the outcome of the dispute. **C** is incorrect. The phrase does not express an enforceable legal doctrine.

117. D A trespass is an unprivileged intentional intrusion on property possessed by another. The intrusion may occur by person or by object. Here, the intrusion is by wild pigs. Because wild pigs have no owner, Cattle Company cannot be held liable for the acts of animals it did not own. Choice **A** is incorrect. The length of Cattle Company's operation is irrelevant to whether a trespass occurred. Choice **B** is incorrect. The "no trespassing" sign shows that Growers did not consent to the trespass. Choice **D** is incorrect. Cattle Company's procedures are irrelevant to whether a trespass occurred.

118. C is the correct answer because although the general rule is that the right to possession belongs to the earliest known possessor, ownership of wild animals goes to the first to capture. Wild animals who regain their liberty generally become fair game, though such is not the case. if, by a band or brand, the previous possessor can be reliably identified. The usual first-in-time-first-in-right rule should apply.

119. A Omer's attempt to revoke the gift was likely ineffectual. Once property has been validly transferred, any subsequent transfer must conform to the same requirements. Here, Omer's demand that Agatha return the property has no legal effect. Therefore, at Agatha's death, the property would pass to Dahlia, her devisee under her will. Choice **B** is incorrect. Omer validly conveyed the property to Agatha, therefore no property passed from Omer to Barney or from Barney to Salim. Choice **C** is incorrect. The property was not part of Omer's estate when Omer died. There was nothing for Omer's heirs to inherit. Choice **D** is incorrect. Omer previously disposed of the property; therefore, the property was not part of Omer's estate when Omer died.

Index

References are to the numbers of the questions raising the issue. "E" indicates an Essay Question; "M" indicates a Multiple-Choice Question.